BACK TO A SHADOW IN THE NIGHT

MUSIC WRITINGS AND INTERVIEWS
1968 - 2001

JONATHAN COTT

John Lennon, art gallery owner Robert Fraser, Jonathan Cott (from left)
London: September 17, 1968, Lennon's basement flat
Photograph by Ethan Russell. ©1968-2002 by Ethan A. Russell

BACK TO A SHADOW IN THE NIGHT

MUSIC WRITINGS AND INTERVIEWS 1968-2001

Jonathan Cott

Some of the interviews and writings in this book first appeared in *The Ballad of John and Yoko, Conversions with Glenn Gould, Elle, The Los Angeles Times, The New York Arts Journal, The New York Review of Books, The New York Times, Rolling Stone*, and as liner notes for Steve Reich's *The Desert Music* and John Adams' *Harmonielehne* (Nonesuch Records).

Jacket painting, *La musique* by Henri Matisse © 2002 Succession H. Matisse Paris/ Artists Rights Society (ARS), New York. Used by permission of the Matisse estate.

Published by Hal Leonard Corporation
7777 West Bluemound Road
P.O. Box 13819
Milwaukee, WI 53213, USA

Trade Book Division Editorial Offices
151 West 46th Street, 8th Floor
New York, NY 10036
Visit us online at **www.halleonard.com**

Library of Congress Cataloging-in-Publication Data

Back to a shadow in the night : music writings and interviews, 1968-2001
/ [edited] by Jonathan Cott. -- 1st ed.
          p. cm.
Includes index.
   ISBN 0-634-03596-7
 1. Musicans -- interviews. 2. Composers--Interviews. 2.
Music--History and criticism. I. Cott, Jonathan.
   M1385 .B12 2002
780'.92'2--dc21

Printed in Canada
First edition

10 9 8 7 6 5 4 3 2 1

CONTENTS

3: REFLECTIONS

INDEX

PREFACE

This book is an attempt to suggest two notions: one, that in order to meet and converse with musicians such as Bob Dylan and John Lennon, Pierre Boulez and Steve Reich, one needs to have the luck of being in the right place at the right time; and two, that in order to discover inspiring works, both old and new, one should remain open to composers as different and disparate as Hildegard of Bingen and Charles Ives, Don Carlo Gesualdo and Edgard Varèse, as well as to the beauty, depths, and riches of non-western musical traditions such as the Balinese gamelan, the Japanese gagaku, the Portuguese Fado, and the Pakistani qawwali. To those who prefer only one kind of musical fare—Renaissance masses, punk rock, European serial music—this book will probably provide an unappetizing menu. Others, however, might agree with the brilliant young American composer Steven Mackey, who, talking about the music of Stravinsky, declared that "the completely unselfconscious blend of vernacular and learned, exotic and domestic music of intelligence that 'rocks' is a welcome prophecy to a generation who grew up in the global village of rock 'n' roll."

During the past thirty years or so, a number of independent college and community radio stations in the United States have been programming an eclectic blend of, for example, medieval, jazz, avant-garde, and world music. The foremost practitioner of this kind of programming has been John Schaefer, whose *New Sounds* is an hour-long nightly program on National Public Radio. Also on NPR has been the innovative series called *Schickele Mix*. Peter Schickele (aka P.D.Q. Bach)—whose motto for his show is Duke Ellington's remark "If it sounds good, it is good"—has organized his programs around a specific "theme" (variation, fugue, dynamics) in which he brings together a gallimaufry of pieces such as a movement of an early Mozart symphony, an Islamic chant, an African Pygmy song, a Gerry Mulligan solo, the Beach Boys' "Good Vibrations," and, in a program dedicated to "melisma" (a grouping of few notes performed on a single syllable), will conclude his program with a short passage of Gregorian chant and, finally, with Conway Twitty singing, "I'm lying here with Lin-Lin-Linda on my mind!"

And let us not forget Studs Terkel. For forty-five years, five times a week on Chicago's WFMT radio, Terkel interspersed his extraordinary on-the-air interviews with the music of Enrico Caruso, Woody Guthrie, Mahalia Jackson, and, as he says, "those other of the God possessed."

Undoubtedly, the apogee of man's expression of universal diversity can be heard on the recording titled *Murmurs of Earth: The Voyager Interstellar Record*. Launched by NASA in 1977, *Voyager One* and *Two*—two identical spacecraft—contain thirty-two examples of the world's music—as well as, among other things, spoken greetings in fifty-five languages and the sounds of Earth: of whales and crickets; of wind, rain, and surf; of ship, horse, bus, automobile; of volcanoes, earthquakes, thunder; and of heartbeats, footsteps, and laughter. No longer bounded by the sun's gravity, the robot ships are now billions of miles from the earth, passing through the cold, dark near vacuum that constitutes interstellar space. Meanwhile, the energy, strength, grace, and healing powers of the human imagination are contained in a musical offering including works from India, China, Peru, Bulgaria, Java, and Senegal; excerpts from pieces by J. S. Bach, Mozart, Beethoven, and Stravinsky; and, in the spirit of sublime largesse, Chuck Berry's "Johnny B. Goode" and Blind Willie Johnson's incomparable "Dark Was the Night." (A *Saturday Night Live* skit had a newscaster conveying a message from outer space: "Send more Chuck Berry!") Lucky are the one or ones who come across this small gift from all of us.

It is interesting to note that many of today's leading music critics are equally conversant in different kinds of music, and not, as in years past, interested in writing just about one culture, genre, or tradition. For my own part, *Back to a Shadow in the Night* is an attempt to, hopefully, illuminate this multifaceted era in interviews, articles, profiles, and reflections from the past thirty years.

ALSO BY JONATHAN COTT:

Stockhausen: Conversations with the Composer

Conversations with Glenn Gould

Dylan

Forever Young

Visions and Voices

Pipers at the Gates of Dawn

Isis and Osiris

The Search for Omm Sety

Wandering Ghost: The Odyssey of Lafcadio Hearn

Homelands (poems)

Thanks to John Cerullo, Sarah Lazin, Barbara Ritola, Ben Schafer, Cathy Trentalancia, Gregory Villepique, and Jann Wenner for making this book possible.

INTERVIEWS

JOHN LENNON
The First *Rolling Stone* Interview

UNLIKE ALMOST ANY OTHER ARTIST, John Lennon allowed himself to be interviewed at crucial points in his life in order to reveal and, perhaps, define for himself where he was in his world. In this first of four major *Rolling Stone* interviews, John hesitatingly began to define himself as John Lennon and not just Beatle John Lennon.

The interview took place at John Lennon and Yoko Ono's temporary basement flat in London—a flat where Jimi Hendrix, Ringo Starr, and William Burroughs, among others, have stayed. But the flat seemed as much John and Yoko's as the Indian incense that took over the living room. The walls were covered with photos of John, of Yoko, a giant Sgt. Pepper ensign, Richard Chamberlain's poster collage of news clippings of the Rolling Stones drug bust, the Time magazine cover of the Beatles.

We arrived at five on the afternoon of September 17, 1968, said hello to gallery owner Robert Fraser, who had arranged the interview, and to John and Yoko, sitting together. We sat down around a simple wooden table covered with magazines, newspapers, sketch paper, boxes, drawings, a beaded necklace shaped in the form of a pentangle.

John said he had to be at a recording session in half an hour, so we talked for a while about John's show at the Fraser Gallery.

When we arrived the next afternoon, September 18, John was walking around the room, humming what sounded like "Hold Me Tight"—just singing the song to the air. Old fifties 45s were scattered about the floor, and John played Rosie and the Originals' version of "Give Me Love." We talked about the lyrics of Gene Vincent's "Woman Love." In spite of having slept only two hours, John asked us to sit down on the floor and begin the interview.

Any suspicions that John would be ornery, mean, cruel, or brutish—feelings attributed to him or imagined by press reports— never arose. As John said simply about the interview: "There's nothing more fun than talking about your own songs and your own records. I mean, you can't help it, it's your bit, really. We talk about them together. Remember that."

I've listed a group of songs that I associate with you, in terms of what you are or what you were, songs that struck me as embodying you a little bit: "You've Got to Hide Your Love Away," "Strawberry Fields," "It's Only Love," "She Said She Said," "Lucy in the Sky," "I'm Only Sleeping," "Run for Your Life," "I Am the Walrus," "All You Need Is Love," "Rain," "Girl."

The ones that really meant something to me—look, I don't know about "Hide Your Love Away," that's so long ago—probably "Strawberry Fields," "She Said," "Walrus," "Rain," "Girl," there are just one or two others, "Day Tripper," "Paperback Writer," even. "Ticket to Ride" was one more, I remember that. It was a definite sort of change. "Norwegian Wood"—that was the sitar bit. Definitely, I consider them moods or moments.

There have been a lot of analyses written about your songs, "Strawberry Fields" in particular . . .

Well, they *can* take them apart. They can take anything apart. I mean, I hit it on all levels, you know. We write lyrics, and I write lyrics that you don't realize what they mean till after. Especially some of the better songs or some of the more flowing ones, like "Walrus." The whole first verse was written without any knowledge. And "Tomorrow Never Knows"—I didn't know what I was saying, and you just find out later. I know that when there are some lyrics I dig, I know that somewhere people will be looking at them. And I dig the people that notice that I have a sort of strange rhythm scene, because I've never been able to keep rhythm on the stage. I always used to get lost. It's me double offbeats.

What is Strawberry Fields?

It's a name, it's a nice name. When I was writing "In My Life"— I was trying "Penny Lane" at that time—we were trying to write about Liverpool, and I just listed all the nice-sounding names, just arbitrarily. Strawberry Fields was a place near us that happened to be a Salvation Army home. But Strawberry Fields—I mean, I have visions of *strawberry fields*. And there was Penny Lane, and the Cast Iron Shore, which I've just got in some song now, and they were just good names—just groovy names. Just good sounding. Because Strawberry Fields is anywhere you want to go.

Some rock critics often try to read something into your songs that isn't there.

It is there. It's like abstract art really. It's just the same really. It's just that when you have to think about it to write it, it just means that you labored at it. But when you just *say* it, man, you know you're saying it, it's a continuous flow. The same as when you're recording or just playing. You come out of a thing and you *know* "I've been there," and it was nothing, it was just pure, and that's what we're looking for all the time, really. I mean, we got a bit pretentious. Like everybody, we had our phase and now it's a little change over to trying to be more natural, less "newspaper taxis," say. I mean, we're just changing. I don't know what we're doing at all, I just write them. Really, I just like rock 'n' roll. I mean, these [*pointing to a pile of fifties records*] are the records I dug then; I dig them now and I'm still trying to reproduce "Some Other Guy" sometimes or "Be-Bop-A-Lula." Whatever it is, it's the same bit for me. It's really just the sound.

The Beatles seem to be one of the only groups who ever made a distinction between friends and lovers. For instance, there's the "baby" who can drive your car. But when it comes to "We Can Work It Out," you talk about "my friend." In most other groups' songs, calling someone "baby" is a bit demeaning compared to your distinction.

Yeah, I don't know why. It's Paul's bit that—"Buy you a diamond ring, my friend"—it's an alternative to *baby*. You can take it logically, the way you took it. See, I don't know really. Yours is as true a way of looking at it as any other way. In "Baby, You're a Rich Man" the point was, stop moaning. You're a rich man and we're all rich men, heh, heh, baby!

I've felt your other mood recently: "Here I stand, head in hand" in "Hide Your Love Away" and "When I was a boy, everything was right" in "She Said She Said."

Yeah, right. That was pure. That was what I meant all right. You see, when I wrote that, I had the "She said she said," but it was just meaning nothing. It was just vaguely to do with someone who had said something like he knew what it was like to be dead, and then it was just a sound. And then I wanted a middle eight. The beginning had been around for days and days and so I wrote the first thing that came into my head and it was "When I was a boy," in a different beat, but it was real because it just happened.

It's funny, because while we're recording we're all aware and listening to our old records and we say, we'll do one like "The Word"—make it like that. It never does turn out like that, but we're always comparing and talking about the old albums—just checking up, what is it? Like swatting up for the exam—just listening to everything.

I'd like to make a record like "Some Other Guy." I haven't done one that satisfies me as much as that satisfied me. Or "Be-Bop-A-Lula" or "Heartbreak Hotel" or "Good Golly, Miss Molly" or "Whole Lot of Shakin'." I'm not being modest. I mean, we're still trying it. We sit there in the studio and we say, "How did it go, how did it go? Come on, let's do *that*." Like what Fats Domino has done with "Lady Madonna"—"See how they ruhhnnn."

Wasn't it about the time of Rubber Soul *that you moved away from the old records to something quite different?*

Yes, yes, we got involved completely in ourselves then. I think it was *Rubber Soul* when we did all our own numbers. Something just happened. We controlled it a bit. Whatever it was we were putting over, we just tried to control it a bit.

Are there any other versions of your songs you like?

Well, Ray Charles's version of "Yesterday"—that's beautiful. And "Eleanor Rigby" is a groove. I just dig the strings on that. Like thirties strings. Jose Feliciano does great things to "Help!" and "Day Tripper." "Got to Get You into My Life"—sure, we were doing our Tamla Motown bit. You see, we're influenced by whatever's going. Even if we're not influenced, we're all going that way at a certain time. If we played a Stones record now, and a Beatles record—and we've been way apart—you'd find a lot of similarities. We're all heavy. Just heavy. How did we ever do anything light?

What we're trying to do is rock 'n' roll, with less of your philosorock, is what we're saying to ourselves. And get on with rocking because rockers is what we really are. You can give me a guitar, stand me up in front of a few people. Even in the studio, if I'm getting into it, I'm just doing my old bit—not quite doing Elvis Legs but doing my equivalent. It's just natural. Everybody says we must do this and that but our thing is just rocking—you know, the usual gig. That's what this new record is about [the White Album]. Definitely rocking. What we were doing on *Pepper* was rocking—and not rocking.

"A Day in the Life"—that was something. I dug it. It was a good piece of work between Paul and me. I had the "I read the news today" bit, and it turned Paul on. Now and then we really turn each other on with a bit of song, and he just said "yeah"—bang bang, like that. It just sort of happened beautifully, and we arranged it and rehearsed it, which we don't often do, the afternoon before. So we all knew what we were playing, we all got into it. It was a real groove, the whole scene on that one. Paul sang half of it and I sang half. I needed a middle eight for it, but that would have been forcing it. All the rest had come out smooth, flowing, no trouble, and to write a middle eight would have been to write a middle eight, but instead Paul already had one there. It's a bit of a *2001*, you know.

Songs like "Good Morning, Good Morning" and "Penny Lane" convey a child's feeling of the world.

We write about our past. "Good Morning, Good Morning," I was never proud of it. I just knocked it off to do a song. But it was writing about my past, so it does get the kids because it was me at school, my whole bit. The same with "Penny Lane." We really got into the groove of imagining Penny Lane—the bank was there, and that was where the tram sheds were and people waiting and the inspector stood there, the fire engines were down there. It was just reliving childhood.

You really had a place where you grew up.

Oh, yeah. Didn't you?

Well, Manhattan isn't Liverpool.

Well, you could write about your local bus station.

In Manhattan?

Sure, why not? Everywhere is somewhere.

In the Magical Mystery Tour *theme song you say, "The Magical Mystery Tour is waiting to take you away." In* Sgt. Pepper *you sing, "We'd like to take you home with us." How do you relate this embracing, come-sit-on-my-lawn feeling in the songs with your need for everyday privacy?*

I take a narrower concept of it, like whoever was around at the time wanting to talk to me talked to me, but of course it does have that wider aspect to it. The concept is very good and I went through it and said, "Well, okay. Let them sit on my lawn." But of course it doesn't work. People climbed in the house and smashed things up, and then you think, "That's no good, that doesn't work." So actually you're saying, "Don't talk to me," really.

We're all trying to say nice things but most of the time we can't make it—90 percent of the time—and the odd time we do make it, we do it together as people. You can say it in a song: "Well, whatever I did say to you that day about getting out of the garden, part of me said that but, really, in my heart of hearts, I'd like to have it right and talk to you and communicate." Unfortunately we're human, you know—it doesn't seem to work.

Do you feel free to put anything in a song?

Yes. In the early days I'd—well, we all did—we'd take things out for being banal, clichés, even chords we wouldn't use because we thought they were clichés. And even just this year there's been a great release for all of us, going right back to the basics. On "Revolution" I'm playing the guitar and I haven't improved since I was last playing, but I dug it. It sounds the way I wanted it to sound.

It's a pity I can't do better—the fingering, you know—but I couldn't have done that last year. I'd have been too paranoiac. I couldn't play *ddddddddddd*. George must play, or somebody better. My playing has probably improved a little bit on this session because I've been playing a little. I was always the rhythm guy anyway, but I always just fiddled about in the background. I didn't actually want to play rhythm. We all sort of wanted to be lead—as in most groups— but it's a groove now, and so are the clichés. We've gone past those days when we wouldn't have used words because they didn't make sense, or what we thought was sense. But of course Dylan taught us a lot in this respect.

Another thing is, I used to write a book or stories on one hand and write songs on the other. And I'd be writing completely free form in a book or just on a bit of paper, but when I'd start to write a song I'd be thinking *dee duh dee duh do doo do de do de doo*. And it took Dylan and all that was going on then to say, oh, come on now, that's the same bit, I'm just singing the words.

With "I Am the Walrus," I had "I am he as you are he as we are all together." I had just these two lines on the typewriter, and then about two weeks later I ran through and wrote another two lines and then, when I saw something, after about four lines, I just knocked the rest of it off. Then I had the whole verse or verse and a half and then sang it. I had this idea of doing a song that was a police siren, but it didn't work in the end [*sings like a siren*]: "I-am-he-as-you-are-he-as . . . " You couldn't really sing the police siren.

Do you write your music with instruments or in your head?

On piano or guitar. Most of this session has been written on guitar 'cause we were in India and only had our guitars there. They have a different feel about them. I missed the piano a bit because you just write differently. My piano playing is even worse than me guitar. I hardly know what the chords are, so it's good to have a slightly limited palette, heh heh.

What did you think of Dylan's "version" of "Norwegian Wood" ("Fourth Time Around")?

I was very paranoid about that. I remember he played it to me when he was in London. He said, "What do you think?" I said, "I don't like it." I didn't like it. I was very paranoid. I just didn't like what I felt I was feeling—I thought it was an out-and-out skit, you know, but it wasn't. It was great. I mean, he wasn't playing any tricks on me. I was just going through the bit.

Is there anybody besides Dylan you've gotten something from musically?

Oh, millions. All those I mentioned before—Little Richard, Presley.

Anyone contemporary?

Are they dead? Well, nobody sustains it. I've been buzzed by the Stones and other groups, but none of them can sustain the buzz for me continually through a whole album or through three singles even.

You and Dylan are often thought of together in some way.

Yeah? Yeah, well we were for a bit, but I couldn't make it. Too paranoiac. I always saw him when he was in London. He first turned us on in New York actually. He thought "I Want to Hold Your Hand"—when it goes "I can't hide"—he thought we were singing "I get high." So he turns up with Al Aronowitz and turns us on, and we had the biggest laugh all night—forever. Fantastic. We've got a lot to thank him for.

Do you ever see him anymore?

No, 'cause he's living his cozy little life, doing that bit. If I was in New York, he'd be the person I'd most like to see. I've grown up enough to communicate with him. Both of us were always uptight, you know, and of course I wouldn't know whether he was uptight, because I was so uptight. And then, when he wasn't uptight, I was—all that bit. But we just sat it out because we just liked being together.

What about the new desire to return to a more natural environment? Dylan's return to country music?

Dylan broke his neck and we went to India. Everybody did their bit. And now we're all just coming out, coming out of a shell, in a new way, kind of saying, remember what it was like to play.

Do you feel better now?

Yes . . . and worse.

What do you feel about India now?

I've got no regrets at all, 'cause it was a groove and I had some great experiences meditating eight hours a day—some amazing things, some amazing trips—it was great. And I still meditate off and on. George is doing it regularly. And I believe implicitly in the whole bit. It's just that it's difficult to continue it. I lost the rosy glasses. And I'm like that. I'm very idealistic. So I can't really manage my exercises when I've lost that. I mean, I don't want to be a boxer so much. It's just that a few things happened, or didn't happen. I don't know, but *something* happened. It was sort of like a [*click*] and we just left and I don't know what went on. It's too near—I don't really know what happened.

You just showed me what might be the front and back album photos for the record you're putting out of the music you and Yoko composed for your film Two Virgins. *The photos have the simplicity of a daguerreotype . . . .*

Well, that's because I took it. I'm a ham photographer, you know. It's me Nikon what I was given by a commercially-minded Japanese when we were in Japan, along with me Pentax, me Canon, me boom-boom, and all the others. So I just set it up and did it.

For the cover, there's a photo of you and Yoko standing naked facing the camera. And on the backside are your backsides. What do you think people are going to think of the cover?

Well, we've got that to come. The thing is, I started it with a pure . . . it was the truth, and it was only after I'd got into it and done it and looked at it that I'd realized what kind of scene I was going to create. And then suddenly, there it was, and then suddenly you show it to people and then you know what the world's going to do to you, or try to do. But you have no knowledge of it when you conceive it or make it.

Originally, I was going to record Yoko, and I thought the best picture of her for an album would be her naked. I was just going to record her as an artist. We were only on those kind of terms then. So after that, when we got together, it just seemed natural for us, if we made an album together, for both of us to be naked.

Of course, I've never seen me prick on an album or on a photo before: "Whatnearth, there's a fellow with his prick out." And that was the first time I realized me prick was out, you know. I mean, you can see it on the photo itself—we're naked in front of a camera—that comes over in the eyes, just for a minute you go!! I mean, you're not used to it, being naked, but it's got to come out.

How do you face the fact that people are going to mutilate you?

Well, I can take that as long as we can get the cover out. And I really don't know what the chances are of that.

You don't worry about the nuts across the street?

No, no, I know it won't be very comfortable walking around with all the lorry drivers whistling and that, but it'll all die. Next year it'll be nothing, like miniskirts or bare tits. It isn't anything. We're all naked really. When people attack Yoko and me, we know they're paranoiac. We don't worry too much. It's the ones that don't know, and you know they don't know—they're just going round in a blue fuzz. The thing is, the album also says: Look, lay off, will you? It's two people—what have we done?

Lenny Bruce once compared himself to a doctor, saying that if people weren't sick, there wouldn't be any need for him.

That's the bit, isn't it? Since the Beatles started being more natural in public—the four of us—we've really had a lot of knocking. I mean, we're always natural. I mean, you can't help it. We couldn't have been where we are if we hadn't done that. We wouldn't have been us either. And it took four of us to enable us to do it; we couldn't have done it alone and kept that up. I don't know why I get knocked more often. I seem to open me mouth more often, something happens, I forget what I am till it all happens again. I mean, we just get knocked—from the underground, the pop world—me personally. They're all doing it. They've got to stop soon.

Couldn't you go off to your own community and not be bothered with all of this?

Well, it's just the same there, you see. India was a bit of that, it was a taste of it—it's the same. So there's a small community, it's the same gig, it's relative. There's no escape.

Your show at the Fraser Gallery gave critics a chance to take a swipe at you.

Oh, right, but putting it on was taking a swipe at them in a way. I mean, that's what it was about. What they couldn't understand was that—a lot of them were saying, well, if it hadn't been for John Lennon nobody would have gone to it, but as it was, it was *me* doing it. And if it had been Sam Bloggs it would have been nice. But the point of it was—it was me. And they're using that as a reason to say why it didn't work. Work as what?

Do you think Yoko's film of you smiling would work if it were just anyone smiling?

Yes, it works with somebody else smiling, but she went through all this. It originally started out that she wanted a million people all over the world to send in a snapshot of themselves smiling, and then it got down to lots of people smiling, and then maybe one or two and then me smiling as a symbol of today smiling—and that's what I am, whatever that means. And so it's me smiling, and that's the hang-up, of course, because it's me again. But they've got to see it someday—it's only me. I don't mind if people go to the film to see me smiling because it doesn't matter, it's not harmful. The idea of the film won't really be dug for another fifty or a hundred years probably. That's what it's all about. I just happen to be that face.

It's too bad people can't come down here individually to see how you're living.

Well, that's it. I didn't see Ringo and his wife for about a month when I first got together with Yoko, and there were rumors going around about the film and all that. Maureen was saying she really had some strange ideas about where we were at and what we were up to. And there were some strange reactions from all me friends and at Apple about Yoko and me and what we were doing—"Have they gone mad?" But of course it was just us, you know, and if they are puzzled or reacting strangely to us two being together and doing what we're doing, it's not hard to visualize the rest of the world really having some amazing image.

International Times *recently published an interview with Jean-Luc Godard . . .*

Oh yeah, right, he said we should do something. Now that's sour grapes from a man who couldn't get us to be in his film [*One Plus One*, in which the Stones appear], and I don't expect it from people like that. Dear Mr. Godard, just because we didn't want to be in the film with you, it doesn't mean to say that we aren't doing any more than you. We should do whatever we're all doing.

But Godard put it in activist political terms. He said that people with influence and money should be trying to blow up the establishment and that you weren't.

What's he think we're doing? He wants to stop looking at his own films and look around.

Time magazine came out and said, look, the Beatles say "no" to destruction.

There's no point in dropping out because it's the same there and it's got to change. But I think it all comes down to changing your head and, sure, I know that's a cliché.

What would you tell a Black Power guy who's changed his head and then finds a wall there all the time?

Well, I can't tell him anything, 'cause he's got to do it himself. If destruction's the only way he can do it, there's nothing I can say that could influence him, 'cause that's where he's at, really. We've all got that in us, too, and that's why I did the "out and in" bit on a few takes and in the TV version of "Revolution"—"Destruction, well, you know, you can count me out, and in," like yin and yang.

I prefer "out." But we've got the other bit in us. I don't know what I'd be doing if I was in his position. I don't think I'd be so meek and mild. I just don't know.

(1968)

JOHN LENNON
The Last *Rolling Stone* Interview

"WELCOME TO THE INNER SANCTUM!" says John Lennon, greeting me with high-spirited, mock ceremoniousness in Yoko Ono's beautiful cloud-ceilinged office in their Dakota apartment. It's Friday evening, December 5, 1980, and Yoko has been telling me how their collaborative new album, *Double Fantasy*, came about: Last spring, John and their son, Sean, were vacationing in Bermuda while Yoko stayed home "sorting out business," as she puts it. She and John spoke on the phone every day and sang each other the songs they had composed in between calls.

"I was at a dance club one night in Bermuda," John interrupts as he sits down on a couch and Yoko gets up to bring coffee. "Upstairs, they were playing disco, and downstairs, I suddenly heard 'Rock Lobster' by the B-52's for the first time. Do you know it? It sounds just like Yoko's music, so I said to meself, 'It's time to get out the old ax and wake the wife up!' We wrote about twenty-five songs during those three weeks, and we've recorded enough for another album."

"I've been playing side two of *Double Fantasy* over and over," I say, getting ready to ply him with a question. John looks at me with a time- and interview-stopping smile. "How are you?" he asks. "It's been like a reunion for us these last few weeks. We've seen Annie Leibovitz. She took my first *Rolling Stone* cover photo. It's been fun seeing everyone we used to know and doing it all again—we've all survived. When did *we* first meet?"

"I met you and Yoko on September 17, 1968," I say, remembering the first of our several meetings. I was just a lucky guy, at the right place at the right time. John had decided to become more "public" and to demystify his Beatles persona. He and Yoko, whom he'd met in November 1966, were preparing for the Amsterdam and Montreal bed-ins for peace and were soon to release *Two Virgins*, the first of their experimental record collaborations. The album cover—the infamous frontal-nude portrait of them—was to grace the pages of *Rolling Stone's* first-anniversary issue. John had just discovered the then-impoverished San Francisco-based magazine, and he'd agreed to give *Rolling Stone* the first of his "coming-out" interviews. As "European editor," I was asked to visit John and Yoko and to take along a photographer (Ethan Russell, who later took the photos for the *Let It Be* book that accompanied the English release of the album). So, nervous and excited, we met John and Yoko at their temporary basement flat in London.

First impressions are usually the most accurate, and John was graceful, gracious, charming, exuberant, direct, witty, and playful; I remember noticing how he wrote little reminders to himself in the wonderfully absorbed way that a child paints the sun. He was due at a recording session in a half hour to work on the White Album, so we agreed to meet the next day to do the interview, after which John and Yoko invited me to attend the session for "Back in the U.S.S.R." at Abbey Road Studios. Only a performance of Shakespeare at the Globe Theatre might have made me feel as ecstatic and fortunate as I did at that moment.

Every new encounter with John brought a new perspective. Once, I ran into John and Yoko in 1971. A friend and I had gone to see *Carnal Knowledge*, and afterward we bumped into the

Lennons in the lobby. Accompanied by Jerry Rubin and a friend of his, they invited us to drive down with them to Ratner's delicatessen in the East Village for blintzes, whereupon a beatific, long-haired young man approached our table and wordlessly handed John a card inscribed with a pithy saying of the inscrutable Meher Baba. Rubin drew a swastika on the back of the card, got up, and gave it back to the man. When he returned, John admonished him gently, saying that that wasn't the way to change someone's consciousness. Acerbic and skeptical as he could often be, John Lennon never lost his sense of compassion.

Almost ten years later, I am again talking to John, and he is as gracious and witty as the first time I met him. "I guess I should describe to the readers what you're wearing, John," I say. "Let me help you out," he offers, then intones wryly: "You can see the glasses he's wearing. They're normal plastic blue-frame glasses. Nothing like the famous wire-rimmed Lennon glasses that he stopped using in 1973. He's wearing needle-cord pants, the same black cowboy boots he'd had made in Nudie's in 1973, a Calvin Klein sweater, and a torn Mick Jagger T-shirt that he got when the Stones toured in 1970 or so. And around his neck is a small, three-part diamond heart necklace that he bought as a makeup present after an argument with Yoko many years ago and that she later gave back to him in a kind of ritual. Will that do?

"I know you've got a Monday deadline," he adds, "but Yoko and I have to go to the Record Plant now to remix a few of Yoko's songs for a possible disco record. So why don't you come along and we'll talk in the studio."

"You're not putting any of your songs on this record?" I ask as we get into the waiting car. "No, because I don't make that stuff." He laughs and we drive off. "I've heard that in England some people are appreciating Yoko's songs on the new album and are asking why I was doing that 'straight old Beatles stuff,' and didn't I know about punk and what's going on—'You were great then; "Walrus" was hip, but this *isn't* hip, John!' I'm really pleased for Yoko. She deserves the praise. It's been a long haul. I'd love her to have the A side of a hit record and me the B side. I'd settle for it any day."

"It's interesting," I say, "that no rock 'n' roll star I can think of has made a record with his wife or whomever and given her fifty percent of the disc."

"It's the first time we've done it this way," John says. "It's a dialogue, and we have resurrected ourselves, in a way, as John and Yoko—not as John ex-Beatle and Yoko and the Plastic Ono Band. It's just the two of us, and our position was that, if the record didn't sell, it meant people didn't want to know about John and Yoko—either they didn't want John anymore or they didn't want John with Yoko or maybe they just wanted Yoko, whatever. But if they didn't want the two of us, we weren't interested. Throughout my career, I've selected to work with—for more than a one-night stand, say, with David Bowie or Elton John—only two people: Paul McCartney and Yoko Ono. I brought Paul into the original group, the Quarrymen; he brought George in and George brought Ringo in. And the second person who interested me as an artist and somebody I could work with was Yoko Ono. That ain't bad picking."

When we arrive at the studio, the engineers begin playing tapes of Yoko's "Kiss Kiss Kiss," "Every Man Has a Woman Who Loves Him" (both from *Double Fantasy*) and a powerful new disco song (not on the album) called "Walking on Thin Ice," which features a growling guitar lick by Lennon based on Sanford Clark's 1956 song, "The Fool."

"Which way could I come back into this game?" John asks as we settle down. "I came back from the place I know best—as unpretentiously as possible—not to prove anything but just to enjoy it."

"I've heard that you've had a guitar on the wall behind your bed for the past five or six years, and that you've only taken it down and played it for *Double Fantasy*. Is that true?"

"I bought this beautiful electric guitar, round about the period I got back with Yoko and had the baby," John explains. "It's not a normal guitar; it doesn't have a body; it's just an arm and this tubelike, toboggan-looking thing, and you can lengthen the top for the balance of it if you're sitting or standing up. I played it a little, then just hung it up behind the bed, but I'd look at it every now and then, because it had never done a professional thing, it had never really been played. I didn't want to hide it the way one would hide an instrument because it was too painful to look at— like, Artie Shaw went through a big thing and never played again. But I used to look at it and think, 'Will I ever pull it down?'

"Next to it on the wall I'd placed the number 9 and a dagger Yoko had given me—a dagger made out of a bread knife from the American Civil War to cut away the bad vibes, to cut away the past symbolically. It was just like a picture that hangs there but you never really see, and then recently I realized, 'Oh, goody! I can finally find out what this guitar is all about,' and I took it down and used it in making *Double Fantasy*.

"All through the taping of 'Starting Over,' I was calling what I was doing 'Elvis Orbison': 'I want you I need only the lonely.' I'm a born-again rocker, I feel *that* refreshed, and I'm going right back to my roots. It's like Dylan doing *Nashville Skyline*, except I don't have any Nashville, you know, being from Liverpool. So I go back to the records I know—Elvis and Roy Orbison and Gene Vincent and Jerry Lee Lewis. I occasionally get tripped off into 'Walruses' or 'Revolution 9,' but my far-out side has been completely encompassed by Yoko.

"The first show we did together was at Cambridge University in 1968 or '69, when she had been booked to do a concert with some jazz musicians. That was the first time I had appeared un-Beatled. I just hung around and played feedback, and people got very upset because they recognized me: 'What's *he* doing here?' It's always: 'Stay in your bag.' So, when she tried to rock, they said, 'What's *she* doing here?' And when I went with her and tried to be the instrument and not project—to just be her band, like a sort of Ike Turner to her Tina, only her Tina was a different, avant-garde Tina—well, even some of the jazz guys got upset.

"Everybody has pictures they want you to live up to. But that's the same as living up to your parents' expectations, or to society's expectations, or to so-called critics who are just guys with a typewriter in a little room, smoking and drinking beer and having their dreams and nightmares, too, but somehow pretending that they're living in a different, separate world. That's all right. But there are people who break out of their bags."

"I remember years ago," I say, "when you and Yoko appeared in bags at a Vienna press conference."

"Right. We sang a Japanese folk song in the bags. 'Das ist really you, John? John Lennon in zee bag?' Yeah, it's me. 'But how do we know ist you?' Because I'm telling you. 'Vy don't you come out from this bag?' Because I don't want to come out of the bag. 'Don't you realize this is the Hapsburg palace?' I thought it was a hotel. 'Vell, it is now a hotel.' They had great chocolate cake in that Viennese hotel, I remember that. Anyway, who wants to be locked in a bag? You have to break out of your bag to keep alive."

"In 'Beautiful Boys'," I add, "Yoko sings: 'Please never be afraid to cry . . . / Don't ever be afraid to fly . . . / Don't be afraid to be afraid.' "

"Yes, it's beautiful. I'm often afraid, and I'm not afraid to be afraid, though it's always scary. But it's more painful to try *not* to be yourself. People spend a lot of time trying to be somebody else, and I think it leads to terrible diseases. Maybe you get cancer or something. A lot of tough guys die of cancer, have you noticed? Wayne, McQueen. I think it has something to do—I don't know, I'm not an expert—with constantly living or getting trapped in an image or an illusion of themselves, suppressing some part of themselves, whether it's the feminine side or the fearful side.

"I'm well aware of that, because I come from the macho school of pretense. I was never really a street kid or a tough guy. I used to dress like a Teddy boy and identify with Marlon Brando and Elvis Presley, but I was never really in any street fights or down-home gangs. I was just a suburban kid, imitating the rockers. But it was a big part of one's life to look tough. I spent the whole of my childhood with shoulders up around the top of me head and me glasses off because glasses were sissy, and walking in complete fear, but with the toughest-looking little face you've ever seen. I'd get into trouble just because of the way I looked; I wanted to be this tough James Dean all the time. It took a lot of wrestling to stop doing that. I still fall into it when I get insecure. I still drop into that I'm-a-street-kid stance, but I have to keep remembering that I never really was one."

"Carl Jung once suggested that people are made up of a thinking side, a feeling side, an intuitive side, and a sensual side," I mention. "Most people never really develop their weaker sides and concentrate on the stronger ones, but you seem to have done the former."

"I think that's what feminism is all about," John replies. "That's what Yoko has taught me. I couldn't have done it alone; it had to be a female to teach me. That's it. Yoko has been telling me all the time, 'It's all right, it's all right.' I look at early pictures of meself, and I was torn between being Marlon Brando and being the sensitive poet—the Oscar Wilde part of me with the velvet, feminine side. I was always torn between the two, mainly opting for the macho side, because if you showed the other side, you were dead."

"On *Double Fantasy*," I say, "your song 'Woman' sounds a bit like a troubadour poem written to a medieval lady."

"'Woman' came about because, one sunny afternoon in Bermuda, it suddenly hit me. I saw what women do for us. Not just what my Yoko does for me, although I was thinking in those personal terms. Any truth is universal. If we'd made our album in the third person and called it *Fred and Ada* or *Tommy* and had dressed up in clown suits with lipstick and created characters other than us, maybe a Ziggy Stardust, would it be more acceptable? It's not our style of art; our life is our art. . . . Anyway, in Bermuda, what suddenly dawned on me was everything I was taking for granted. Women really are the other half of the sky, as I whisper at the beginning of the song. And it just sort of hit me like a flood, and it came out like that. The song reminds me of a Beatles track, but I wasn't trying to make it sound like that. I did it as I did 'Girl' many years ago. So this is the grown-up version of 'Girl.'

"People are always judging you, or criticizing what you're trying to say on one little album, on one little song, but to me it's a lifetime's work. From the boyhood paintings and poetry to when I die—it's all part of one big production. And I don't have to announce that this album is part of a larger work; if it isn't obvious, then forget it. But I did put a little clue on the beginning of the record—the bells . . . . the bells on 'Starting Over.' The head of the album, if anybody is interested, is a wishing bell of Yoko's. And it's like the beginning of 'Mother' on the *Plastic Ono* album, which had a very slow death bell. So it's taken a long time to get from a slow church death bell to this sweet little wishing bell. And that's the connection. To me, my work is one piece."

"All the way through your work, John, there's this incredibly strong notion about inspiring people to be themselves and to come together and try to change things. I'm thinking here, obviously, of songs like 'Give Peace a Chance,' 'Power to the People,' and 'Happy Xmas (War Is Over).' "

"It's still there," John replies. "If you look on the vinyl around the new album's [the twelve-inch single "(Just Like) Starting Over"] logo—which all the kids have done already all over the world from Brazil to Australia to Poland, anywhere that gets the record—inside is written: ONE WORLD, ONE PEOPLE. So we continue.

"I get truly affected by letters from Brazil or Poland or Austria— places I'm not conscious of all the time—just to know somebody is there, listening. One kid living up in Yorkshire wrote this heartfelt letter about being both Oriental and English and identifying with John and Yoko. The odd kid in the class. There are a lot of those kids who identify with us. They don't need the history of rock 'n' roll. They identify with us as a couple, a biracial couple, who stand for love, peace, feminism, and the positive things of the world.

"You know, give peace a chance, not shoot people for peace. All we need is love. I believe it. It's damn hard, but I absolutely believe it. We're not the first to say, 'Imagine no countries' or 'Give peace a chance,' but we're carrying that torch, like the Olympic torch, passing it from hand to hand, to each other, to each country, to each generation. That's our job. We have to conceive of an idea before we can do it.

"I've never claimed divinity. I've never claimed purity of soul. I've never claimed to have the answer to life. I only put out songs and answer questions as honestly as I can, but *only* as honestly as I can—no more, no less. I cannot live up to other people's expectations of me because they're illusionary. And the people who want more than I am, or than Bob Dylan is, or than Mick Jagger is . . .

"Take Mick, for instance. Mick's put out consistently good work for twenty years, and will they give him a break? Will they ever say, 'Look at him, he's number one, he's thirty-six and he's put out a beautiful song, "Emotional Rescue," it's up there'? I enjoyed it, lots of people enjoyed it. So it goes up and down, up and down. God help Bruce Springsteen when they decide he's no longer God. I haven't seen him—I'm not a great 'in'-person watcher—but I've heard such good things about him. Right now, his fans are happy. He's told them about being drunk and chasing girls and cars and everything, and that's about the level they enjoy. But when he gets down to facing his own success and growing older and having to produce it again and again, they'll turn on him, and I hope he survives it. All he has to do is look at me and Mick. . . . I cannot be a punk in Hamburg and Liverpool anymore. I'm older now. I see the world through different eyes. I still believe in love, peace, and understanding, as Elvis Costello said, and what's so funny about love, peace, and understanding?"

"There's another aspect of your work, which has to do with the way you continuously question what's real and what's illusory, such as in 'Look at Me,' your beautiful new 'Watching the Wheels'—what are those wheels, by the way?—and, of course, 'Strawberry Fields Forever,' in which you sing: 'Nothing is real.' "

"Watching the wheels?" John asks. "The whole universe is a wheel, right? Wheels go round and round. They're my own wheels, mainly. But, you know, watching meself is like watching everybody else. And I watch meself through my child, too. Then, in a way, *nothing* is real, if you break the word down. As the Hindus or Buddhists say, it's an illusion, meaning all matter is floating atoms, right? It's *Rashomon*. We all see it, but the agreed-upon illusion is what we live in. And the hardest thing is facing yourself. It's easier to shout 'Revolution' and 'Power to the People' than it is to look at yourself and try to find out what's real inside you and what isn't, when you're pulling the wool over your own eyes. That's the hardest one.

"I used to think that the world was doing it to me and that the world owed me something, and that either the conservatives or the socialists or the fascists or the communists or the Christians or the Jews were doing something to me; and when you're a teenybopper, that's what you think. I'm forty now. I don't think that anymore, 'cause I found out it doesn't fucking work! The thing goes on anyway, and all you're doing is jacking off, screaming about what your mommy or daddy or society did, but one has to go through that. For the people who even bother to go through that—most assholes just accept what is and get on with it, right?—but for the few of us who did question what was going on . . . I have found out personally—not for the whole world!—that I am responsible for it, as well as them. I am part of them. There's no separation; we're all one, so in that respect, I look at it all and think, 'Ah, well, I have to deal with me again in that way. What is real? What is the illusion I'm living or not living?' And I have to deal with it every day. The layers of the onion. But that is what it's all about.

"The last album I did before *Double Fantasy* was *Rock 'n' Roll*, with a cover picture of me in Hamburg in a leather jacket. At the end of making that record, I was finishing up a track that Phil Spector had made me sing called 'Just Because,' which I really didn't know—all the rest I'd done as a teenager, so I knew them backward—and I couldn't get the hang of it. At the end of that record—I was mixing it just next door to this very studio—I started spieling and saying, 'And so we say farewell from the Record Plant,' and a little thing in the back of my mind said, 'Are you *really* saying farewell?' I hadn't thought of it then. I was still separated from Yoko and still hadn't had the baby, but somewhere in the back was a voice that was saying, 'Are you saying farewell to the whole game?'

"It just flashed by like that—like a premonition. I didn't think of it until a few years later, when I realized that I had actually stopped recording. I came across the cover photo—the original picture of me in my leather jacket, leaning against the wall in Hamburg in 1962—and I thought, 'Is this it? Do I start where I came in, with "Be-Bop-A-Lula"?' The day I met Paul I was singing that song for the first time onstage. There's a photo in all the Beatles books—a picture of me with a checked shirt on, holding a little acoustic guitar—and I am singing 'Be-Bop-A-Lula,' just as I did on that album, and there's the picture in Hamburg and I'm saying goodbye from the Record Plant.

"Sometimes you wonder, I mean really wonder. I know we make our own reality and we always have a choice, but how much is preordained? Is there always a fork in the road and are there two preordained paths that are equally preordained? There could be hundreds of paths where one could go this way or that way—there's a choice and it's very strange sometimes . . . . And that's a good ending for our interview."

Jack Douglas, co-producer of *Double Fantasy*, has arrived and is overseeing the mix of Yoko's songs. It's two-thirty in the morning, but John and I continue to talk until four as Yoko naps on a studio couch. John speaks of his plans for touring with Yoko and the band that plays on *Double Fantasy*; of his enthusiasm for making more albums; of his happiness about living in New York City, where, unlike England or Japan, he can raise his son without racial prejudice; of his memory of the first rock'n'roll song he ever wrote (a takeoff on the Dell Vikings' "Come Go with Me," in which he changed the lines to: "Come come come come / Come and go with me / To the peni-tentiary"); of the things he has learned on his many trips around the world during the past five years. As he walks me to the elevator, I tell him how exhilarating it is to see Yoko and him looking and sounding so well. "I love her, and we're together," he says. "Goodbye, till next time."

"After all is really said and done / The two of us are really one," John Lennon sings in "Dear Yoko," a song inspired by Buddy Holly, who himself knew something about true love's ways. "People asking questions lost in confusion / Well I tell them there's no problem, only solutions," sings John in "Watching the Wheels," a song about getting off the merry-go-round, about letting it go.

In the tarot, the Fool is distinguished from other cards because it is not numbered, suggesting that the Fool is outside movement and change. And as it has been written, the Fool and the clown play the part of scapegoats in the ritual sacrifice of humans. John and Yoko had never given up being Holy Fools. In a recent *Playboy* interview, Yoko, responding to a reference to other notables who had been interviewed in that magazine, said: "People like Carter represent only their country. John and I represent the world." I am sure many readers must have snickered. But three nights after our conversation, the death of John Lennon revealed Yoko's statement to be astonishingly true. "Come together over me," John had sung, and people everywhere in the world came together.

(1980)

RAY DAVIES

THE KINKS—WITH THEIR LEAD SINGER, POET, and composer Ray Davies—were in the forefront of the English rock renaissance, singing songs like "You Really Got Me" and "All Day and All of the Night" (later lifted by the Doors in "Hello, I Love You"). The Kinks had a #1 record with "Waterloo Sunset," after which, except in the eyes of an ecstatic group of devotees, they seemed to fade into the background.

"The world keeps going 'round," Ray Davies once sang, and every once in a while you hear the Kinks and wonder where they've been. Ray Davies used to write gutsy songs about not sleeping at night and getting tired waiting. His directness led him down a quiet and lonesome path that most people turned off as the world turned on. With the release of the Kinks' eighth album, Arthur, you might feel like catching up.

Many of Ray Davies's songs have set me thinking of the Taoist saint who fished with a pin and a single silk filament. The man caught multitudes of fish because he was perfectly attuned to— contemplating and participating in—the endless flowing. The means of Ray Davies's songs are small—like the persons he sings about—but the effect is that of a small and quiet radiance that would seem to belie the songs' subjects but which in fact lights them up from the inside. "Sunny Afternoon," "Waterloo Sunset," or "Sitting by the Riverside" suggest the world of T'ang Chinese poets conversing and drinking wine by moonlight or, closer to home, the streams and meadows of Izaak Walton's angler.

Afternoon tea with Ray Davies took place in the garden restaurant (a converted carriage house) of Kenwood House on Hampstead Heath, London, in November 1969. The setting might have been a Kinks song: gray-lit cool autumn afternoon, children playing, old persons sitting. Signs on the grass positively read: PLEASE STEP ON THE PATHS. And in the toilet, a little boy sang cheerily "I LIKE you, Daddy," as his embarrassed father outside muttered: "Get a move on." As Chekhov once said, almost defining Ray Davies's method, "I imagine people so they can tell me things about themselves."

After tea, we continued the interview on a bench on the heath, and just as Ray Davies was mentioning how he thought people hated the Kinks, the cassette machine broke down. On playback, you heard a sped-up Donald Duck, voice augmented by the sounds of a squadron of fighter planes reaching an explosion: then silence, as if the loosing of the apocalyptic beast had terminated the interview, even though Ray Davies and I continued to talk, tapes turning, microphones registering.

We concluded our conversation a couple of days later amid the pigeons in Trafalgar Square.

Before your first hit, "You Really Got Me," you recorded "Long Tall Sally" and "You Do Something to Me," the second of which sold something like 127 copies.

Really? Fantastic. How did you know that?

I checked it out.

Then it must be true . . . I was an art student, like thousands of others. Then I got together with my brother and a friend and we decided to go and play dates. The more we played, the more we wanted to do it. And it got to a stage when we wanted to do it all the time. Our repertoire consisted of rhythm and blues, Sonny Terry things.

For a while when you started, the Kinks were listened to as much as the Beatles and Stones.

No, we weren't, never. 'Cause I think we were more unpopular than they were. In the States, our old image is still lasting, since the last time we went there that's what they remember us doing—the heavy things, the chunk-chunk things, you couldn't really miss it. Those three chords were part of my life—G, F, B-flat—yeah, it is, it is, and I can't help noticing it. But there have been other things nearly as close to it which people haven't noticed, other songs we've done.

"See My Friends (Playing 'Cross the River)" moves from those chords to something closer to an Indian drone.

I got the idea from being in India. I always like the chanting. Someone once said to me, "England is gray and India *is* like a chant." I don't think England is that gray, but India is like a long drone. When I wrote the song, I had the sea near Bombay in mind. We stayed at a hotel by the sea, and the fishermen came up at five in the morning and they were all chanting. And we went on the beach and we got chased by a mad dog—big as a donkey.

It sounded as if you were singing about an English river.

I think it was the Indian Ocean.

A number of your earlier songs sound not like places, but like other songs: "I'll Remember," for example, like a Beatles song.

"I'll Remember"? No, no, bullshit. It's a song written on the sixth, Buddy Holly! I wrote it on a harmonica in Seattle, which is in Washington. I'll remember.

I liked "Love Me Do." When it came out, I thought it was an American surfing song. Totally unsurfer. But I did think it was an American group . . . I like surfers. Their imagery, it's great. And that floating feeling . . . I wrote "Holiday in Waikiki" at the Waikiki Hotel in Hawaii, and admittedly it's like Chuck Berry. We used to do a lot of his songs.

I think that songwriting changed when groups started spending more time in the studio. See, when groups were on the road, they used to go right in the studio and create the same kind of feeling they had on the road, and the stuff they used to cut was influenced by what they did at gigs. But then groups spent more time in the studio and started to change, the atmosphere changed.

When you're making a record, and if you spend more time over it, you have to record it a tone lower or cut the tones lower because you can't reach some of the notes, I find this. But when you go onstage, you have to put the key up and it really changes the whole thing.

A lot of our stuff recently has been routine for the studio, when it should have been routine for the stage, and that's why it sounds so different. I think the writing's the same, maybe, but it's the fact that we spend more time in the studio and less on the road that's changed the sound of it.

You create an easy driving feeling in "Sunny Afternoon." The guy's had to sell his yacht, his money's gone, and he wants to live life pleasantly. How much are you the person you're singing?

Not at all, really. I'm easy driving. But I'm not a person who loves to live pleasantly above everything else. I'm not that way at all. I might think that I'm that, but I'm not really that. I think the person in "Waterloo Sunset" is closer to me.

"Sunny Afternoon" was made very quickly, in the morning, it was one of our most atmospheric sessions. I still like to keep tapes of the few minutes before the final takes, things that happen before the session. Maybe it's superstitious, but I believe that if I had done things differently—if I had walked around the studio or gone out—it wouldn't have turned out the same way.

The bass player went off and started playing funny little classical things on the bass, more like a lead guitar; and Nicky Hopkins, who was playing piano on that session, was playing "Liza"—we always used to play that song. Little things like that helped us get into the feeling of the song.

At the time I wrote "Sunny Afternoon" I couldn't listen to anything. I was only playing the *Bringing It All Back Home* LP along with my Frank Sinatra and Glenn Miller and Bach—it was a strange time. I thought they all helped one another, they went into the chromatic part that's in the back of the song.

I once made a drawing of my voice on "Sunny Afternoon." It was a leaf with a very thick black outline—a big blob in the background—the leaf just cutting through it.

You sing a lot about sunsets and autumn.

I like autumn things. I did a record called "Autumn Almanac"—
I drew pictures of it and everything. After I wrote it, for a whole
month I was thinking about it. I wasted a lot of time, really,
because I was sweeping up dead leaves and putting them in the
sack. I'm susceptible to that sort of thing—to walls and flowers.
Walls. You can get probably something more from a wall than from
a person sometimes. It's just put somewhere. It's in line, in order,
it's in line with the horizon. Ah, ridiculous.

What I try to do probably doesn't come out. What I've worked
out, what I do—I might not be right—is to do something very
personal, and then suddenly I look at it, up in the air, I look at it. I
blow it up and look at it and then I come down again. A better man.

All my records—at one time they've been the most important
thing I've ever done. Even the ones that aren't hits. Even the ones that
sell 100 copies. At one time they've been the most important thing to
me. So I can't hear our records on the radio, I can't stand it, because
they sound to me so *out* of what everyone is doing. You know what I
mean? I get embarrassed doing television shows that have lots of
people on, compressed, like *Top of the Pops*, one group after another,
and we're right in the middle. I feel wrong, not inferior, just wrong. I
think we need a bit of time for people to get used to us.

*You've also sung about blue skies and suns. "Lazy Old Sun" has what
sounds like a hippo groan, almost joking up what you're saying.*

Unfortunately, the song just didn't come off, really. When you
look at it in writing, it's a lot better. I don't like a lot of the lines.
It's nicer when I think about it than when somebody tells me what
it's like. I know what I was getting to, but didn't quite get there. It
is a joke, it ended up as a joke, a very sad joke . . . too bad. At one
stroke it can sound jokey and the next minute I can believe it.

Are you worried about sentimentality in your songs?

I worry about it because I think other people think I worry. That's the only reason. I like looking at things, remembering things, I like that.

"Dead End Street" sets the theme for a number of your songs. "We are strictly second class." Cracks in the ceiling, sink leaking. At the end of the song, you sing: "Dead End Street / Head to my feet / I can feel it," bringing the personal and the social awareness together.

What you're saying, too, is that it's not only what other people are doing, it's what I'm doing, what I'm feeling. It's a little bit selfish as well. The Beatles are aware that Mr. So-and-so in Northampton is about to buy the record and listen to it while he's having his tea. I think they've always tried to keep that in mind. I'm a little more selfish. I like to do things that involve me a little bit. Sorry, I'm not answering your question directly. We do tend to think about what we're doing . . . too much. And that's what happened to "Dead End Street."

I'll tell you about "Dead End Street." It was about miners, to begin with, because we had a thing in England called Aberfan where a coal tip fell on a school in Wales—they dig for coal and they put all the slag and make a hill. It all fell down on a school and killed about a hundred little kids. That's where it all started. I wrote the song about that time, and all that time there were news flashes about Aberfan, and also it was the first year of the economic cutback. I felt it was like the depression days.

"Big Black Smoke" has that mood, too, about the girl who takes purple hearts and sleeps in bowling alleys.

Yeah, it was written at the same time. But it started off to be something different. The big black smoke was there, and I said,

"Why can't I just say 'Big Black Smoke'?" There are some songs that *sound* great. You don't know the words—you don't want to know the words—it's the way they roll off the tongue, they might mean anything. And when you look at the song sheet and the words say "I love you, baby" or something very ordinary, they just sound like something good. "Big Black Smoke" had that sound. But I had to put something around it. I had two lines: "Big black smoke" and "She took all her pretty-colored clothes," and the song revolves around those lines, really. Because the build-up to the song occurs when she comes into it, or when he comes into it, or when I come into it: "She took all her pretty-colored clothes." The beginning builds up to it, and from that line it fades out. There was the first draft, and then I got involved in the story. You've got to have something build up to that line: "She took all her pretty-colored clothes."

How did The Village Green Preservation Society *come about?*

Three years ago I wanted it to be *Under Milk Wood*, something like that, but I never got a chance to do it because we had to make albums. Somebody said to me that I preserve things, and I like village green and preservation society. The title track is the national anthem of the album, and I like Donald Duck, Desperate Dan, draught beer.

In "Animal Farm" you sing: "I want to be back there among the cats and the dogs and the pigs and the goats, where people are people and not just plain."

I like plain Janes. In "Waterloo Sunset" I wanted to use the names Bernard and Dorothy, but it wouldn't work. Terry [Stamp] and Julie [Christie] would have to dog themselves up a bit. They'd have to be less glamorous for a Waterloo Sunset movie. Plain Jane . . . I'd like to hear Burt Lancaster singing "Big Sky."

"Sitting by the Riverside" is similar to "Afternoon Tea" or "Waterloo Sunset." They have that loosened up, spaces between feeling.

That's the studio. Maybe people should have a winding down session before listening to our songs. Maybe they should be briefed. Or debriefed. I think they should be debriefed.

Listening to lots of your songs, you get a sense that there's a house on Dead End Street with big black smoke around, a guy upstairs with his Harry Rag, the cat always eating . . .

Do they all live together in a house?

Yes. Plastic Man and Dandy come around to visit. Do you intend to create this kind of world?

I'm not aware of trying to, but it might seem that way. I think on *The Village Green Preservation Society* they were all brothers and sisters. Nobody made love because it was all in the family. I don't think there's a love song on it. Our new record is literally about a family.

You make a perfect family where everyone's friends.

Yeah. The people I'd like to be with are over there—across the river. I'm not left out. I've got a choice, but the easiest one is the one I don't really want. There's a line that says: "Wish that I'd gone with her / She is gone / Now there's no one left but my friends." Yeah, she went over there and I stayed here. [*Silence.*]

Would you say something about your new opera, Arthur?

The opera is about the rise and fall of the British Empire, which people tend to associate me with [*laughter*]. You could sum up the British Empire in one song. I haven't written it, but it can be done, a little fifteen-minute thing [*laughter*]. But about the opera: I decided to make it about one person, someone who didn't really count, that's all, and mix it with a few people whom I knew, put them into one. I told Julian Mitchell, who wrote the script, a story about somebody I know. We liked it and worked on it and it came from there. He was easy to work with.

"Some Mother's Son" contains those beautiful lines: "But still the world keeps turning / Though all the children have gone away." The idea of childhood and the sun join each other in the song.

That's "Lazy Old Sun," see, that's the way it works. It didn't work in that song: "When I'm dead and gone your light will shine eternally." The idea was right to me, and there was a vehicle in "Some Mother's Son" for it to work.

I wrote the song in a kitchen. Wrote it at night, it's not a day song. I had a song which I liked, but which nobody else liked very much called "Wonder Boy," and the lines went: "Wonder Boy, some mother's son / Turn your sorrow into wonder." I had to use "some mother's son" again. It was just one line and it was gone and had to be explained, for me, I was interested in that line. And then I wanted to write about how soldiers must have been frightened fighting and killing each other, but they were just some mother's son. Apart from the line "Head blown up by some soldier's gun," the song could be about executives in an advertising agency.

What do you think of the people you sing about in "Shangri-La"?

I played "Shangri-La" to somebody, an old friend of mine, and I knew halfway through it that he was embarrassed by it because it was about him, and he realized it, and I didn't want him to realize it, and I can never sort of talk to him again. I wanted him to hear it, and then I realized: there he is.

I'm not laughing at those people in the song at all. They're brainwashed into that, they brainwash themselves. She says,

"That's it, I don't want a new dress," not because she really doesn't want it, but because she can't afford it. Their minds are like that; they're happy, really. It becomes a religion to them. The glory of being boring. It's a glory. He shows you his stamp collection. It's a sense of greatness he's got around him that you can't penetrate because you feel you might upset him, he's got that aura of *stuff*.

The chorus of "Shangri-La" is a bit of a chant—like "See My Friends." It's a religious thing. You accept it as your religion because you can't have anything else, and whatever you've got anyway is what you accept yourself. You let yourself believe it . . . No, perhaps not. If you lived there [*gestures toward Kenwood House*] and you accepted this, and this was as far as you could go, you'd be a lot happier. Well, no, perhaps not. See, I've tried living in a big house—and I can't. I'm going back to a little house. I don't think people really want to live in a posh house, as much as a rich person doesn't want to live in a slum. I don't like to say what I've got and be happy with it. I'd wear hobnail boots by my fire rather than slippers. I can't stand slippers cause they symbolize giving up to me. But at the same time, I love the people who are like that. But I hate what's handed down when people get into the state where that's all they want. And that can be anybody—toffs, toffs are the worst offenders. Top hats and walking sticks, Cary Grant's a toff. David Niven.

It's like the song "Princess Marina." My brother David said, "I don't know whether you like these people or you hate them." You don't really hate anybody, do you? You only hate people for an instant. They can't help it. "Princess Marina" starts pretty sad, maybe, then it goes into the bit about what it's all about—"I haven't got any money or anything," they're having a hard time. And then they sing the way they did in the music hall, because that's the way they used to express it: "Don't Have Any More, Mrs. Moore." There was a song about poverty. People think I'm taking it out on ordinary persons. But it's about all people. In fact, it's more about nobs and toffs, executives—"Yes, sir, No, sir, Three bags full, sir."

If people are second class, and if, when they start making it, they become dedicated followers of fashion, what alternative do they have, given the way things are?

Be like me and be unhappy . . . We went to Australia and they wanted to take pictures of us surfing, and I thought they only surfed in America. We rolled our trousers up and pulled our overcoats up. It was 100 degrees and we were sweating, but we refused to take our overcoats off. Why should we do it? Surfing in Australia! Rebel at any cost. That's what it seems like, but it isn't really. They'll probably play our song "Australia" at cabaret clubs with maracas and things. That'll be nice. Fabulous!

The singer in "Driving" sounds like the singer of "Sunny Afternoon."

Can't drive. I probably can. I'm probably a hustler. An American told me I was a hustler: I pretend I can't do things and I can, really. Is that what it means? I probably can drive, but I've never been behind a steering wheel . . . . The song was written for 1938 or '9. "Dead End Street" is written about now, but it could be about the Depression. "Driving" is about the thirties, but people still take the attitude: Let's just go driving and get away. I don't, 'cause I can't drive.

In "Yes Sir, No Sir," you wrote: "You're outside and there ain't no admission to our play." Again, these people aren't part of what's happening.

Superb line the way you said that . . . Nothing's happening [*laughter*].

"Now I've got children and I'm going gray / No time for talking I got nothing to say . . ."

Better with an American accent.

Nothin' to say. That's what you tell the cops.

Most certainly. I was in a lift in New York City and wanted to go to the fiftieth floor. A woman came in and wanted to go to the basement. She pressed basement and I said, I was in here first, I want the fiftieth floor, and she said, "Sue me." Great. I accepted it . . . A lot more casual, the Americans.

Sometimes they shoot you.

In England they just let you live [*laughter*]. That's the best way to die. The deadest way.

Grayness is beauty in boredom. I could have given Arthur a limp, I suppose, made him buy funny books, have a secret life. Then, that isn't the important thing—he'd have had control over his secret life, and he hasn't control over what's happening to him. But he thinks he does . . . . When we play the opera in America, I hope people will accept the opera as a musical thing. There's jamming—we do a lot of that, but people don't think we do, since we don't do it on record. As far as the next thing I'm doing, I'm leaving what I've done. That's why I didn't want pictures taken of me reminiscing. I'm not like that, really. I'm going to try something else next . . . . Someone will get me if I talk about it.

How do you go about writing?

Everything has been thrown at me, and paper boats float past me, but something more direct might hit me and leave its mark. I think the things I write about are the things I can't fight for. There are a lot of things I say that are really commonplace. I can't get rid of them. I go into something minute, then look at it, then go back into it.

Have you been influenced by any poetry?

I like a poet who has the same name as me, someone named Davies. And a crummy eight-line poem that ends up saying "And that lovely woman is my mother." There's a poem I like, too, whose first line goes "Imagine that life was an old man carrying flowers on his head." And it ends up by saying "And death liked flowers." I'm afraid that's as far as my poetic influences go.

How do you feel about the name of your group?

I went to a studio in a gray pullover and horrible tweed trousers, and the next day I went in an orange tie, and a bloke told me, "Now you really look like a Kink." Maybe it was an unfortunate name—the sadistic image or the things in your arm. It's a good name, in a way, because it's something people don't really want. I think people hate us, they think we betrayed them. Perhaps we have.

But when you recorded Live at Kelvin Hall *people were screaming and adoring you.*

Yeah, it was recorded at a cattle show. There was a large metal roof which gave that effect. Someone said that the audience was more in it than the group. The part I enjoyed was when everyone started singing "Sunny Afternoon."

They must love us really.

(1970)

BOB DYLAN
Interview #1

WE WERE DRIVING DOWN SUNSET BOULEVARD—Christmastime in L.A.—
looking for a place to eat, when Bob Dylan noticed Santa Claus,
surrounded by hundreds of stuffed, Day-Glo animals, standing and
soliciting on the street. "Santa Claus in the desert," he commented
disconcertedly; "it really brings you down."

A few minutes later, we passed a billboard that showed a photo
of George Burns pointing to a new album by John Denver and
praising it to the skies. "Did you see that movie they appeared in
together?" Dylan asked me. "I sort of like George Burns. What
was he playing?"

"I saw it on the plane coming out here. He played God," I said.

"That's a helluva role," Dylan replied.

Bob Dylan should know. For years he has been worshiped—and
deservedly so. His songs are miracles, his ways mysterious and
unfathomable. In words and music, he has reawakened, and thereby
altered, our experience of the world. In statement ("He not busy being
born is busy dying") and in image ("My dreams are made of iron
and steel / With a big bouquet of roses hanging down / From the
heavens to the ground") he has kept alive the idea of the poet and

artist as vates—the visionary eye of the body politic—while keeping himself open to a conception of art that embraces and respects equally Charles Baudelaire and Charley Patton, Arthur Rimbaud and Smokey Robinson.

"Mystery is an essential element in any work of art," says the director Luis Buñuel in a recent New Yorker profile by Penelope Gilliatt. "It's usually lacking in film, which should be the most mysterious of all. Most filmmakers are careful not to perturb us by opening the windows of the screen onto their world of poetry. Cinema is a marvelous weapon when it is handled by a free spirit. Of all the means of expression, it is the one that is most like the human imagination. What's the good of it if it apes everything conformist and sentimental in us? It's a curious thing that film can create such moments of compressed ritual. The raising of the everyday to the dramatic."

I happened to read these words during my flight to Los Angeles in December of 1977—having just finished watching the conventional and sentimental in-flight movie—hardly knowing then that, just a day later, I would be seeing a film that perfectly embodied Buñuel's notion of the possibilities of cinema.

Renaldo and Clara—an audacious and remarkable four-hour movie that opened in January 1978—is Bob Dylan's second film. His first, Eat the Document, was a kind of antidocumentary, a night journey through the disjointed landscapes of Dylan's and the Band's 1966 world tour, a magic swirling ship of jump cuts, "ready for to fade." It was a fascinating work. But to remain on a given level, no matter how exalted, is a sin, a spiritual teacher once said. And just as it is impossible for Bob Dylan "to sing the same song the same way twice"—as he himself puts it—so his new film is a departure from Eat the Document, as it announces the arrival of a visionary cinematic free spirit.

Conceived over a period of ten years, and edited down by Howard Alk and Dylan from 100 hours of footage, Renaldo and Clara was shot during the 1975–76 Rolling Thunder Revue, whose participants made up a cast that included Bob Dylan (Renaldo), Sara Dylan (Clara), Joan Baez (the Woman in White), Ronnie Hawkins (Bob Dylan), Ronee Blakly (Mrs. Dylan), Jack Elliott (Longheno de Castro), Bob Neuwirth (the Masked Tortilla), Allen Ginsberg (the Father), David Blue (David Blue), and Roger McGuinn (Roger McGuinn).

WHO ARE YOU, BOB DYLAN? was the headline in the French newspaper read by Jean-Pierre Léaud in Jean-Luc Godard's Masculin-Féminin. And the mystery of Renaldo and Clara is: "Who is Bob Dylan?" "Who is Renaldo?" and "What is the relationship between them?"

I decided to ask Bob Dylan himself.

"There's Renaldo," he told me, "there's a guy in whiteface singing on the stage, and then there's Ronnie Hawkins playing Bob Dylan. Bob Dylan is listed in the credits as playing Renaldo, yet Ronnie Hawkins is listed as playing Bob Dylan."

"So Bob Dylan," I surmise, "may or may not be in the film."

"Exactly."

"But Bob Dylan made the film."

"Bob Dylan didn't make it. I made it."

"I is another," wrote Arthur Rimbaud, and this statement is certainly demonstrated by Renaldo and Clara, in which characters in masks and hats—often interchangeable—sit in restaurants and talk, disappear, reappear, exchange flowers, argue, visit cemeteries, play music, travel around in trains and vans and, in one exhilarating scene, dance around at the edge of a beautiful bay, where they join hands and begin singing an American Indian/Hindu Indian–sounding chant to the accompaniment of a bop-shoo-op-doo-wah-ditty chorus—a spiritual and rock 'n' roll reunion.

To the anagogic eye, however, the film seems to be about just one man—who could pass for the Jack of Hearts, the leading actor of Dylan's song "Lily, Rosemary, and the Jack of Hearts," a card among cards, an image among images—and just one woman. Together they find themselves in the grip of a series of romantic encounters that are reenactments of the Great Mystery, culminating in the confrontation of the Woman in White (Joan Baez), Clara (Sara Dylan), and Renaldo (Bob Dylan)—a meeting at the border of myth and reality. Using his physical image and name as the raw material of the film, Bob Dylan—like the Renaissance kings of masque and spectacle—moves daringly and ambiguously between fiction, representation, identification, and participation.

Renaldo and Clara, of course, is a film filled with magnificently shot and recorded concert footage of highly charged Dylan performances of songs like "It Ain't Me, Babe," "A Hard Rain's A-Gonna Fall," and "Knockin' on Heaven's Door"—the last of whose delicate and eerie instrumental breaks make you feel as if you were entering the gates of paradise itself. Avoiding all of the cinematic clichés of pounding-and-zooming television rock 'n' roll specials, the cameras either subtly choreograph the songs, revealing structures and feelings, or else look at the white-faced Dylan and the accompanying painted musicians in rapturous and intensely held close-ups.

Around these musical episodes Dylan has woven a series of multilayered and multileveled scenes—unconsciously echoing similar movements in films by Jean Cocteau, John Cassavetes, and especially Jacques Rivette—each of which lights up and casts light on all the others. Scenes and characters duplicate and mirror each other, are disassociated and recombined, all of them, in the words of the director, "filled with reason but not with logic." Thus, when Clara says to Renaldo: "I am free . . . I can change," it brings back to us the words spoken earlier on by Renaldo to the Woman in White: "I haven't changed that much. Have you?" to which the Woman in White replies, "Maybe."

And then there are the correspondences and the doubled worlds. The scenes in the bordello—with Joan Baez and Sara Dylan playing prostitutes and Allen Ginsberg playing a kind of Buddhist john—become an image of something like Vajra Hell, the Tantric Buddhist idea of the unbreakable diamond netherworld. And a musician blocking someone's way backstage becomes the Guardian at the Gates.

What is most adventurous and mysterious about Renaldo and Clara, however, is the way it counterpoints music with action, lyrics with dialogue, songs with other songs. In one scene, for example, Rodeo (Sam Shepard) is trying to win over Clara, and on the soundtrack you hear, almost subliminally, what sounds like the chord progression of "Oh, Sister," but which you later realize is "One Too Many Mornings"—as if the songs themselves were trying to communicate with each other, as if they were saying goodbye to each other:

You're right from your side,

I'm right from mine.

We're both just too many mornings

An' a thousand miles behind.

In another scene, members of the Rolling Thunder Revue join in a reception with members of the Tuscarora Indian tribe, while on the soundtrack we hear Dylan's haunting rehearsal-tape version of Curtis Mayfield's "People Get Ready." And, finally, in another scene, Renaldo hurries nervously down a city street, panhandling and making some kind of furtive French connection with the Masked Tortilla (Bob Neuwirth), to the accompaniment of Dylan's version of "Little Moses," above which we hear powerfully spoken lines from poet Anne Waldman's "Fast Speaking Woman" ("I'm the Druid Woman / I'm the Ibo Woman / I'm the Buddha Woman / I'm the Vibrato Woman").

"Your films make one wonder what's going on in people's minds," says Penelope Gilliatt to Buñuel, to which he responds: "Dreams, and also the most everyday questions: 'What time is it?' 'Do you want to eat?' " And, in spite of the compression and density of most of the scenes in Renaldo and Clara, there is also a presentational immediacy and clarity that fixes the scenes in one's mind—like a very special dream one wants to remember.

"I expect this will be a very small film," Buñuel said during the shooting of his recent That Obscure Object of Desire—which might, in fact, have served as the title of Renaldo and Clara. "One needs just a hole to look out of," Buñuel continued, "like a spider that has spun its web and is remembering what the world outside was like. This hole is the secret of things. An artist can provide an essential margin of alertness."

Renaldo and Clara is a long film—and a much-maligned and neglected film—but it is really an intimate and evanescent one. "Art is the perpetual motion of illusion," says Bob Dylan in the interview that follows, which took place a week before Christmas 1977 in Los Angeles. "The highest purpose of art," Dylan commented, "is to inspire. What else can you do? What else can you do for anyone but inspire them?"

If someone asked me what Renaldo and Clara was about, I'd say: "Art and life, identity and God—with lots of encounters at bars, restaurants, luncheonettes, cabarets, and bus stations."

Do you want to see it again? Would it be helpful for you to see it again?

You think I'm too confused about the film?

No. I don't think so at all. It isn't just about bus stations and cabarets and stage music and identity—those are elements of it. But it is mostly about identity—about everybody's identity. More important, it's about Renaldo's identity, so we superimpose our own vision on Renaldo: it's his vision and it's his dream.

You know what the film is about? It begins with music—you see a guy in a mask, you can see through the mask he's wearing, and he's singing "When I Paint My Masterpiece." So right away you know there's an involvement with music. Music is confronting you.

So are lines like: "You can almost think that you're seein' double."

Right. Also on a lyrical level. But you still don't really know . . . and then you're getting off that, and there seems to be a tour. You're hearing things and seeing people . . . it's not *quite* like a tour, but there's some kind of energy like being on a tour. There's a struggle, there's a reporter—who later appears in the restaurant scenes.

All right, then it goes right to David Blue, who's playing pinball and who seems to be the narrator. He's Renaldo's narrator, he's Renaldo's scribe—he belongs to Renaldo.

Yet David Blue talks not about Renaldo but about Bob Dylan and how he, David Blue, first met Dylan in Greenwich Village in the late fifties.

They seem to be the same person after a while. It's something you can only feel but never really know. Any more than you can know whether Willie Sutton pulled all those bank jobs. Any more than you can know who killed Kennedy for sure.

And right away, David Blue says: "Well, what happened was that when I first left my parents' house, I bought *The Myth of Sisyphus.*" Now, that wasn't really the book, but it was pretty close. It was actually *Existentialism and Human Emotions.* So that's it: This film is a post-existentialist movie. We're in the post-existentialist period. What is it? That's what it is.

What could be more existentialist than playing pinball? It's the perfect existentialist game.

It is. I've seen rows and rows of pinball players lined up like ducks. It's a great equalizer.

What about the emotions in Existentialism and Human Emotions?

Human emotions are the great dictator, in this movie as in all movies . . . I'll tell you what I think of the emotions later. But getting back to David Blue: he's left his home, and right away you're in for something like a triple dimension. Just ten minutes into the movie he says: "I got in the bus. I went down to New York, walked around for four hours, got back on the bus, and went home." And that is exactly what a lot of people are going to feel when they walk into the movie theater: they got on the bus, walked around for four hours, and walked home.

There's another guy, later in the film, who walks out into the night and says to a girl: "This has been a great mistake."

Yeah. You can pick any line in a movie to sum up your feeling about it. But don't forget you don't see that guy anymore after that . . . he's gone. And that means Renaldo isn't being watched anymore because *he* was watching Renaldo.

Talking about mistakes and seeing double: it's fascinating how easy it is to mistake people in the film for one another. I mistook you, for instance, for the guy driving the carriage (maybe it was you); for Jack Elliott; and I even mistook you for you.

The Masked Tortilla is mistaken for Bob Dylan, Bob Dylan is mistaken for Renaldo. And . . . *Bob Dylan is the one with the hat on.* That's who Bob Dylan is—he's the one with the hat on.

Almost every man in the film has a hat on.

Right.

All those disguises and masks.

The first mask, as I said, is one you can see through. But they're all masks. In the film, the mask is more important than the face.

All the women in the film seem to turn into one person, too, and a lot of them wear hats. It reminds me of "The Ballad of Frankie Lee and Judas Priest":

> *He just stood there staring*
>
> *At that big house as bright as any sun,*
>
> *With four and twenty windows*
>
> *And a woman's face in ev'ry one.*

This film was made for you [*laughing*]. Did you see the Woman in White who becomes a different Woman in White? One's mistaken for the other. At first she's only an idea of herself—you see her in the street, later in the carriage . . . I think the women in the movie are beautiful. They look like they've stepped out of a painting. They're vulnerable, but they're also strong-willed.

"Breaking just like a little girl."

That's the child in everyone. That's the child in everyone that has to be confronted.

"Just Like a Woman" always seemed to me to be somehow about being born: "I can't stay in here . . . I just can't fit." So by confronting the child in you, saying goodbye to childhood, you're born into something bigger . . . In a way, it's a frightening song.

It always was a frightening song, but that feeling needs to be eliminated.

I was thinking of what looked like a Yiddish cabaret filled with older women listening intently to Allen Ginsberg reading passages from "Kaddish," his great elegy to his mother.

Those women are strong in the sense that they know their own identity. It's only the layer of what we're going to reveal in the next film, because women are exploited like anyone else. They're victims just like coal miners.

The poet Robert Bly has written about the image of the Great Mother as a union of four force fields, consisting of the nurturing mother, like Isis (though your Isis seems more ambiguous); the Death Mother (like the woman in "It's All Over Now, Baby Blue"); the Ecstatic Mother (like the girl in "Spanish Harlem Incident"); and the Stone Mother who drives you mad (like Sweet Melinda who leaves you howling at the moon in "Just Like Tom Thumb's Blues"). Traces of these women seem to be in this film as well.

The Death Mother is represented in the film, but I don't know what I should say or can say or shouldn't say about who is who in the movie. I mean, *who* is the old woman everyone calls Mama— the woman who sings, plays guitar, and reads palms? She reads Allen's palm, saying: "You've been married twice." And me, later on I'm looking at the gravestone marked HUSBAND, and Ginsberg asks: "Is that going to happen to you?" And I say: "I want an unmarked grave." But of course I'm saying this as Renaldo.

In Tarantula you wrote your own epitaph:
Here lies bob dylan
killed by a discarded Oedipus
who turned
around
to investigate a ghost
and discovered that
the ghost too was more than one person.

Yeah, way back then I was thinking of this film. I've had this picture in mind for a long time—years and years. Too many years . . . Renaldo is oppressed. He's oppressed because he's born. We don't really know who Renaldo is. We just know what he isn't. He isn't the Masked Tortilla. Renaldo is the one with the hat, but he's not wearing a hat. I'll tell you what this movie is: it's like life exactly, but not an imitation of it. It transcends life, and it's not like life.

That paradox is toppling me over.

I'll tell you what my film is about: it's about naked alienation of the inner self against the outer self—alienation taken to the extreme. And it's about integrity. My next film is about obsession. The hero is an arsonist . . . but he's not really a hero.

Renaldo and Clara *seems to me to be about obsession, too.*

That's true, but only in the way it applies to integrity.

The idea of integrity comes across in a lot of your songs and in lines like: "To live outside the law, you must be honest" and "She doesn't have to say she's faithful, / Yet she's true, like ice, like fire."

We talked about emotions before. You can't be a slave to your emotions. If you're a slave to your emotions you're dependent on your emotions, and you're only dealing with your conscious mind. But the film is about the fact that you have to be faithful to your subconscious, unconscious, superconscious—as well as to your conscious. Integrity is a facet of honesty. It has to do with knowing yourself.

At the end of the film, Renaldo is with two women in a room (the Woman in White and Clara), and he says: "Evasiveness is only in the mind—truth is on many levels . . . . Ask me anything and I'll tell you the truth." Clara and the Woman in White both ask him: "Do you love her?" as they point to each other—not: "Do you love me?"

Possessiveness. It was a self-focused kind of question. And earlier, one of the women in the whorehouse talks about the ego-protection cords she wears around her neck. Do you remember that? . . . In the scene you mentioned, did you notice that Renaldo was looking at the newspaper which had an article on Bob Dylan and Joan Baez in it? Joan Baez and Bob Dylan at this point are an illusion. It wasn't planned that way. Joan Baez without Bob Dylan isn't too much of an illusion because she's an independent woman and her independence asserts itself. But Joan Baez with Bob Dylan *is*.

So at the moment you open up that newspaper, art and life really come together.

Exactly.

*And what about the moment when Joan Baez, looking at Clara, says:
"Who is this woman?" and you cut to your singing "Sara"? Talk about
art and life!*

It's as far as you can take it—meaning personally and generally.
Who is this woman? Obviously, this woman is a figment of the
material world. Who is this woman who has no name? Who is this
woman, she says . . . who is this woman, as if she's talking about
herself. Who this woman is is told to you, earlier on, when you see
her coming out of the church carrying a rope. You know she means
business, you know she has a purpose.

Another way of putting it is: The singer's character onstage is
always becoming Renaldo. By singing "Sara," the singer comes as
close to Renaldo as he can get. It brings everything as close as
possible without two becoming one.

*It was pretty amazing to see you use your personal life and the myth
of your life so nakedly in that scene with Renaldo and the two women.*

Right, but you're talking to me as a director now.

Still, you do have that scene with Joan Baez and Sara Dylan.

Well, Sara Dylan here is working as Sara Dylan. She has the
same last name as Bob Dylan, but we may not be related. If she
couldn't have played the role of Clara, she wouldn't have done it.

*Some people will obviously think that this film either broke up your
marriage or is a kind of incantation to make your marriage come back
together.*

Either one of those statements I can't relate to. It has nothing
to do with the breakup of my marriage. My marriage is over. I'm
divorced. This film is a film.

Why did you make yourself so vulnerable?

You must be vulnerable to be sensitive to reality. And to me being vulnerable is just another way of saying that one has nothing more to lose. I don't have anything but darkness to lose. I'm way beyond that. The worst thing that could happen is that the film will be accepted and that the next one will be compared unfavorably to this one.

Strangely, the scene where the two women confront Renaldo reminds me of King Lear, *in which each of the daughters has to say how much she loves her father.*

You're right. Renaldo sees himself as Cordelia.

I've always interpreted some of The Basement Tapes *as being concerned with ideas from King Lear: "Too much of nothing / Can make a man abuse a king"; "Oh what dear daughter 'neath the sun / Would treat a father so, / To wait upon him hand and foot/And always tell him, 'No'?"*

Exactly. In the later years it changed from "king" to "clown."

King Lear had a fool around him, too, and when the fool leaves, Cordelia comes back. She takes his place, and he takes hers.

The roles are all interchangeable.

Jesus is a very strong figure in Renaldo and Clara. There's that song by you called "What Will You Do When Jesus Comes?" There's the woman who says to you in the restaurant: "There's nowhere to go. Just stand and place yourself like the cross and I'll receive you." And then there are the shots of the huge cement crucifix in the Catholic grotto.

Right. Jesus is the most identifiable figure in Western culture, and yet he was exploited, used and exploited. We all have been.

There's also that scene, near the end of the film, where Allen Ginsberg takes you around to see the glassed-in sculptures of the Stations of the Cross—and we see Jesus killed for the second time and then buried under the weight of the cross. On one level, the film is about the Stations of the Cross, isn't it?

Yeah, you're right, like the double vision having to be killed twice. Like why does Jesus really die?

Spiritually or politically?

Realistically . . . Because he's a healer. Jesus is a healer. So he goes to India, finds out how to be a healer, and becomes one. But see, I believe that he overstepped his duties a little bit. He accepted and took on the bad karma of all the people he healed. And he was filled with so much bad karma that the only way out was to burn him up.

In my film, we're looking at masks a lot of the time. And then when the dream becomes so solidified that it has to be taken to the stage of reality, then you'll see stone, you'll see a statue—which is even a further extension of the mask: the statue of Mary in front of the statue of Jesus-on-the-cross in the crucifix grotto.

Throughout the film, I also noticed the continual reappearance of the red rose. Every woman has a rose.

It has a great deal to do with what's happening in the movie. Do you remember the woman in the carriage? She's bringing a rose to Renaldo, who gives it back to her.

But then it appears in your hat when you're singing.

By that time it's all fallen apart and shattered, the dream is gone . . . it could be anywhere after that.

There's another scene like that in which Mick Ronson is blocking Ronnie Hawkins's way to a backstage area. He seemed like some kind of guardian.

He's the Guardian of the Gates. But scenes like these work in terms of feeling. It's like with Tarot cards—you don't have to be confused as to what they mean . . . someone else who knows can read them for you.

"Nothing is revealed," you sing at the end of "The Ballad of Frankie Lee and Judas Priest." Is anything revealed at the end of Renaldo and Clara?

Yeah, I'll tell you what the film reveals: This film reveals that there's a whole lot to reveal beneath the surface of the soul, but it's unthinkable . . . That's exactly what it reveals. It reveals the depths that there are to reveal. And that's the most you can ask, because things are really very invisible. You can't reveal the invisible. And this film goes as far as we can to reveal that.

Under a statue of Isis in the city of Saïs is the following inscription: "I am everything that was, that is, that shall be . . . Nor has any mortal ever been able to discover what lies under my veil."

That's a fantastic quotation. That's true, exactly. Once you see what's under the veil, what happens to you? You die, don't you, or go blind?

I wanted to tie in two things we've talked about: the idea of integrity and the idea of Jesus. In your song "I Want You," you have the lines:

Now all my fathers, they've gone down,
True love they've been without it.
But all their daughters put me down
'Cause I don't think about it.

These are some of my favorite lines of yours, and to me they suggest that real desire is stronger than frustration or guilt.

I know. It's incredible you find that there. I know it's true. And in *Renaldo and Clara* there's no guilt. But that's why people will take offense at it, if they are offended by it in any way, because of the lack of guilt in the movie. None at all.

This brings us back to Jesus.

Jesus is . . . well, I'm not using Jesus in the film so much as I'm using the *concept* of Jesus—the idea of Jesus as a man, not the virgin birth.

But what about the concept of masochism associated with Jesus?

That's what happened to Jesus. People relate to the masochism, to the spikes in his hand, to the blood coming out, to the fact that he was crucified. What would have happened to him if he hadn't been crucified? That's what draws people to him. There are only signals of that in this film—like a fingernail blade at one point.

What about the line in "Wedding Song": "Your love cuts like a knife"?

Well, it's bloodletting, it's what heals all disease. Neither aggression nor anger interests me. Violence only does on an interpretive level, only when it's a product of reason.

People are attracted to blood. I'm personally not consumed by the desire to drink the blood. But bloodletting is meaningful in that it can cure disease. But we didn't try to make a film of that nature. This film concerns itself with the dream. There's no blood in the dream, the dream is cold. This film concerns itself with the depth of the dream—the dream as seen in the mirror . . . . For some reason I've just thought of my favorite singer.

Who is that?

Om Kalsoum—the Egyptian woman who died a few years ago. She was my favorite.

What did you like about her?

It was her heart.

Do you like dervish and Sufi singing?

Yeah, that's where my singing really comes from . . . except that I sing in America. I've heard too much Leadbelly, really, to be too much influenced by the whirling dervishes.

Now that we somehow got onto this subject, what musicians do you like at the moment?

I think Alice Cooper is an overlooked songwriter. I like Ry Cooder. And I like Dave Mason's version of something which is on the jukebox right now.

Rock 'n' roll ended with Phil Spector. The Beatles weren't rock 'n' roll either. Nor the Rolling Stones. Rock 'n' roll ended with Little Anthony and the Imperials. Pure rock 'n' roll. Rock 'n' roll ended in 1959.

When did it begin for you?

1954.

What is there now?

Programmed music. Quadruple tracking.

I came across something you wrote a while back:

> Desire . . . never fearful
> finally faithful
> it will guide me well
> across all bridges
> inside all tunnels
> never failin'.

I even remember where I wrote that. I wrote that in New Hampshire. I think I was all alone.

Here's something else you wrote:

> Mine shall be a strong loneliness
> dissolvin' deep
> t' the depths of my freedom
> an' that, then, shall
> remain my song.

You seem to have stayed true to that feeling.

I haven't had any reason to stray.

In "The Times They Are A-Changin'" you sing: "He that gets hurt / Will be he who has stalled." What has kept you unstalled?

I don't know. Mainly because I don't believe in this life.

The Buddhist tradition talks about illusion, the Jewish tradition about allusion. Which do you feel closer to?

I believe in both, but I probably lean to allusion. I'm not a Buddhist. I believe in life, but not this life.

What life do you believe in?

Real life.

I wanted to read to you two Hasidic texts that somehow remind me of your work. The first says that in the service of God, one can learn three things from a child and seven from a thief. "From a child you can learn: 1) always to be happy; 2) never to sit idle; and 3) to cry for everything one wants. From a thief you should learn: 1) to work at night; 2) if one cannot gain what one wants in one night, to try again the next night; 3) to love one's coworkers just as thieves love each other; 4) to be willing to risk one's life even for a little thing; 5) not to attach too much value to things even though one has risked one's life for them—just as a thief will resell a stolen article for a fraction of its real value; 6) to withstand all kinds of beatings and tortures but to remain what you are; and 7) to believe that your work is worthwhile and not be willing to change it."

Who wrote that?

A Hasidic rabbi.

Which one?

Dov Baer, the Maggid of Mezeritch.

That's the most mind-blazing chronicle of human behavior I think I've ever heard . . . . How can I get a copy of that? I'll put it on my wall. There's a man I would follow. That's a real hero. A real hero.

Another Hasidic rabbi once said that you can learn something from everything. Even from a train, a telephone, and a telegram. From a train, he said, you can learn that in one second one can miss everything. From a telephone you can learn that what you say over here can be heard over there. And from a telegram that all words are counted and charged.

It's a cosmic statement. Where do you get all of these rabbis' sayings? Those guys are really wise. I tell you, I've heard gurus and yogis and philosophers and politicians and doctors and lawyers, teachers of all kinds . . . and these rabbis really had something going.

They're like Sufis, but they speak and teach with more emotion.

As I said before, I don't believe in emotion. They use their hearts, their hearts don't use them.

In one second missing everything on a train . . . do you think that means that you can miss the train or miss seeing something from the train window?

That's a statement of revelation. I think it means that in one moment you can miss everything because you're not there. You just watch it, and you know you're missing it.

What about the telephone—what you say here is heard over there?

That means you're never that far away from the ultimate God.

And words being counted and charged.

That's very truthful, too. That everything you say and think is all being added up.

How are you coming out?

You know, I'll tell you: lately I've been catching myself. I've been in some scenes, and I say: "Holy shit, I'm not here alone." I've never had that experience before the past few months. I've felt this strange, eerie feeling that I wasn't all alone, and I'd better know it.

Do you watch what you say?

I always try to watch what I say because I try not to say anything I don't mean. Music, too, is truthful. Everything's okay, you put on a record, someone's playing an instrument—that changes the vibe. Music attracts the angels in the universe. A group of angels sitting at a table are going to be attracted by that.

So we always get back to the music in the film. We made a point of doing it, as if we had to do it. You're not going to see music in the movies as you do in this film. We don't have any filler. You don't see any doors close or any reverse shots which are just there to take up time until you get to the next one. We didn't want to take time away from other shots.

I know this film is too long. It may be four hours too long—I don't care. To me, it's not long enough. I'm not concerned how long something is. I want to see a set shot. I *feel* a set shot. I don't feel all this motion and boom-boom. We can fast cut when we want, but the power comes in the ability to have faith that it is a meaningful shot.

You know who understood this? Andy Warhol. Warhol did a lot for American cinema. He was before his time. But Warhol and Hitchcock and Sam Peckinpah and Tod Browning . . . they were important to me. I figured Godard had the accessibility to make what he made, he broke new ground. I never saw any film like *Breathless*, but once you saw it, you said: "Yeah, man, why didn't I do that, I could have done that." Okay, he did it, but he couldn't have done it in America.

Renaldo and Clara, *in a way, is a culmination of a lot of your ideas and obsessions.*

That may be true, but I hope it also has meaning for other people who aren't that familiar with my songs, and that other people can see themselves in it, because I don't feel so isolated from what's going on. There are a lot of people who'll look at the film without knowing who anybody is in it. And they'll see it more purely.

Eisenstein once wrote: "The Moscow Art Theater is my deadly enemy. It is the exact antithesis of all I am trying to do. They string their emotions together to give a continuous illusion of reality. I take photographs of reality and then cut them up so as to produce emotions."

What we did was to cut up reality and make it more real.

In "Wedding Song" you sing: "I love you more than ever / Now that the past is gone." But in "Tangled Up in Blue" you sing: "But all the while I was alone / The past was close behind."

We allow our past to exist. Our credibility is based on our past. But deep in our soul we have no past. I don't think we have a past, any more than we have a name. You can say we have a past if we have a future. Do we have a future? No. So how can our past exist if the future doesn't exist?

So what are the songs on Blood on the Tracks *about?*

The present.

Why did you say, "I love you more than ever / Now that the past is gone"?

That's delusion. That's gone.

And what about "And all the while I was alone / The past was close behind"?

That's more delusion. Delusion is close behind.

What do you think makes Blood on the Tracks *so intense?*

Willpower. Willpower is what makes it an intense album . . . but certainly not anything to do with the past or the future. Willpower is telling you that we are agreeing on what is what.

What about "Idiot Wind"?

Willpower.

Why have you been able to keep so in touch with your anger throughout the years, as revealed in songs like "Can You Please Crawl Out Your Window?" and "Positively 4th Street"?

Willpower. With strength of will you can do anything. With willpower you can determine your destiny.

Can you really know where your destiny is leading you?

Yeah, when you're on top of your game . . . . Anger and sentimentality go right next to each other, and they're both superficial. Chagall made a lot of sentimental paintings. And Voltaire wrote a lot of angry books.

I know I'm being nostalgic, but I loved hearing you sing "Little Moses" in Renaldo and Clara.

I used to play that song when I performed at Gerdes Folk City. It's an old Carter Family song, and it goes something like:
Away by the waters so wide
The ladies were winding their way,
When Pharoah's little daughter
Stepped down in the water
To bathe in the cool of the day.
And before it got dark,

She opened the ark,

And saw the sweet infant so gay.

Then little Moses grows up, leads the Jews—it's a great song. And I thought it fit pretty well into the movie.

Everybody's in this film: the Carter Family, Hank Williams, Woody Guthrie, Beethoven. Who is going to understand this film? Where are the people to understand this film—a film which needs no understanding?

Who understands "Sad-Eyed Lady of the Lowlands"?

I do . . . . It's strange. I finally feel in the position of someone whom people want to interview enough that they'll fly you into town, put you up in a hotel, pay all your expenses, and give you a tour of the city. I'm finally in that position.

I once went to see the king of the Gypsies in southern France. This guy had twelve wives and a hundred children. He was in the antique business and had a junkyard, but he'd had a heart attack before I'd come to see him. All his wives and children had left. And the Gypsy clan had left him with only one wife and a couple of kids and a dog. What happens is that after he dies they'll all come back. They smell death and they leave. That's what happens in life. And I was very affected by seeing that.

Did you feel something like that in the past five years?

You're talking about 1973? I don't even remember 1973. I'm talking about the spring of 1975. There was a lack of targets at that time. But I don't remember what happened last week.

But you probably remember your childhood clearly.

My childhood is so far away . . . it's like I don't even remember being a child. I think it was someone else who was a child. Did you ever think like that? I'm not sure that what happened to me yesterday was true.

But you seem sure of yourself.

I'm sure of my dream self, I live in my dreams, I don't really live in the actual world.

> "I'll let you be in my dreams
> if I can be in yours.
> I said that."
> —Bob Dylan, 1963

(1977)

BOB DYLAN
Interview #2

ON THE EVENING OF SEPTEMBER 15, 1978, the Boston Red Sox were in New York City trying to get back into first place. In New Orleans, just before Muhammad Ali made his comeback, TV commentator Howard Cosell introduced the fighter by quoting from the song "Forever Young": "May your hands always be busy / May your feet always be swift / May you have a strong foundation / When the winds of changes shift." And in Augusta, Maine, the composer of that song inaugurated a three-month tour of the United States and Canada that included sixty-five concerts in sixty-two cities.

According to an Associated Press review of the opening night, Bob Dylan drove a packed house of 7,200 into "shrieks of ecstasy . . . His audience in the Augusta Civic Center was a mixture of people who first knew Dylan as an angry young poet in the early sixties and high-school students more accustomed to punk rock. Dylan satisfied both, although his veteran fans seemed the happiest."

After a highly successful series of concerts in Japan, Australia, New Zealand, and Western Europe earlier this year, it might seem peculiar to think of Dylan's latest American tour as a kind of comeback. But, at least in this country, Dylan has recently been the recipient of some especially negative reviews, both for his film Renaldo and Clara (which, incidentally, was warmly greeted at this year's Cannes Film Festival), and his latest album, Street-Legal. This billingsgate, moreover, has come from a number of Dylan's "veteran fans." In the Village Voice, seven reviewers—a kind of firing squad—administered justice to the film with a fusillade of abuse. And Rolling Stone, in its two August issues, featured a column and review that pilloried the album. Yet Street-Legal seems to me one of Dylan's most passionate, questing, and questioning records.

I ran into Dylan in the hallway of his Portland motel at noon on September 17—an hour before the entourage was to take off for New Haven. He was heading to breakfast and wasn't looking forward to it. "I ran into a girl last night," he told me as we walked to the dining room, "whom I knew in the Village in 1964. She figured the food wouldn't be too good up here, so she said she'd bring some with her this morning. But I haven't seen her."

Then, just after we had sat down and were told that breakfast wasn't being served any longer, a woman appeared next to us with the promised feast in a basket. We ate, saved the muffins to give to the band later on, and went out to catch the Scenicruiser bus that was to drive us to the local airport for the flight—on a chartered Bac III jet—to New Haven, where the group was to perform that night at the Veterans' Memorial Coliseum.

Dylan and I sat at the back of the bus. The musicians and tour organizers listened to a cassette recording of Ray Charles and the

Raelettes. As the bus started, I foolhardily tried to interest Dylan in a theory I had about "Changing of the Guards"—namely, that the song could be seen to have a coded subtext revealed by the characters of various tarot cards—the Moon, the Sun, the High Priestess, the Tower and, obviously, the King and Queen of Swords—the two cards Dylan specifically mentions. My idea was that the attributes associated with these images make up the "plot" of the song.

"I'm not really too acquainted with that, you know," he warded me off. (What was that tarot card doing on the back of the jacket of Desire? I wondered.) Undaunted, I mentioned that it had been said that tarot diviners discover the future by intuition, with "prophetic images drawn from the vaults of the subconscious." Didn't Dylan think that a song like "Changing of the Guards" wakens in us the images of our subconscious? Didn't songs like that and "No Time to Think" suggest the idea of spirits manifesting their destiny as the dramatis personae of our dreams?

Dylan wasn't too happy with the drift of the discussion and fell silent. "I guess," I said, "there's no point in asking a magician how he does his tricks."

"Exactly!" Dylan responded cheerfully.

"Okay," I said, "we have to start someplace. What about the first line of 'Changing of the Guards'? Does 'sixteen years' have anything to do with the number of years you've been on the road?"

"No," Dylan replied, "sixteen is two short of eighteen years. Eighteen years is a magical number of years to put in time. I've found that threes and sevens . . . well, things come up in sevens . . . What am I saying? I mean, what am I saying?"

The Bus

When I tell Rolling Stone *what we've been talking about, they may not believe it.*

They had the nerve to run the reviews they did on *Street-Legal*—why should I give them an interview, anyway?

Are you going to kick me off the bus?

No, it's your interview. It's okay. But if you were doing it for another magazine, it'd be okay, too.

Think I should go somewhere else with it?

Yeah—*Business Week.*

[The tape of Ray Charles and the Raelettes that has been counterpointing our banter has now given way to Joe Cocker's Mad Dogs and Englishmen.*] It's strange, but I noticed in your last two performances that your phrasing and the timbre of your voice at certain points resemble those of Little Anthony, Smokey Robinson, and Gene Chandler. Are you aware of this?*

No. When your environment changes, you change. You've got to go on, and you find new friends. Turn around one day and you're on a different stage, with a new set of characters . . . Just look outside the window at the picket fences and the pine trees. New England falls are so beautiful, aren't they? Look at those two kids playing by the train tracks. They remind me of myself. Both of them.

Did you ever lie down on the tracks?

Not personally. I once knew someone who did.

What happened?

I lost track of him. . . . You should describe in your interview this village we're passing through. It's real special. Go ahead, describe it.

There's a little pond at the edge of the road . . .

. . . and here's the Stroudwater Baptist Church. We just turned the corner and are heading on down . . . I'll tell you in a minute. What do you call this kind of architecture? . . . Look at the ducks over there . . .

. . . and that little waterfall.

This is Garrison Street, we've just passed Garrison Street— probably never will again.

Clothes on the line behind that house.

Yeah, clothes on the line. Someone's frying chicken—didn't Kris Kristofferson say something like that? You don't see this in New York City . . . well, maybe at McDonald's. [The bus pulls into the airport.] This may be our last chance to talk, so I hope we've got it down right.

The Plane

Let's find something to talk about.

Maybe I should ask a question that someone I know wanted to ask you.

Ask me.

Okay, why are you doing this tour?

Well, why did I do the last one? I'm doing this one for the same reason I did the last one.

And what reason was that?

It was for the same reason that I did the one before that. I'm doing this tour for one reason or another, I can't remember what the reason is anymore.

Articles about the tour always mention that you're doing it for the money.

They always say that. There are more important things in the world than money. It means that to the people who write these articles, the most important thing in the world is money. They could be saying I'm doing the tour to meet girls or to see the world. Actually, it's all I know how to do. Ask Muhammad Ali why he fights one more fight. Go ask Marlon Brando why he makes one more movie. Ask Mick Jagger why he goes on the road. See what kind of answers you come up with. Is it so surprising I'm on the road? What else would I be doing in this life—meditating on the mountain? Whatever someone finds fulfilling, whatever his or her purpose is—that's all it is.

You recently said that you do new versions of your older songs because you believe in them—as if to believe in something is to make it real.

They *are* real, and that's why I keep doing them. As I said before, the reason for the new versions is that I've changed. You meet new people in your life, you're involved on different levels with people. Love is a force, so when a force comes in your life—and there's love surrounding you—you can do anything.

When you introduce the singers onstage as your childhood sweethearts, your present girlfriend, your former girlfriend—is that literal?

Oh, of course.

May I list some of the themes I found on Street-Legal?

Yeah.

Here goes: Survival, homelessness, trust, betrayal, sacrifice, exile, tyranny, and victimization.

All right, those things go through all of my songs because I feel those things. And those feelings touch me, so naturally they're going to appear in the songs.

There's a lot of talk about magic in Street-Legal: *"I wish I was a magician / I would wave a wand and tie back the bond / That we've both gone beyond" in "We Better Talk This Over"; "But the magician is quicker and his game / Is much thicker than blood" in "No Time to Think."*

These are things I'm really interested in, and it's taken me a while to get back to it. Right through the time of *Blonde on Blonde* I was doing it unconsciously. Then one day I was half-stepping, and the lights went out. And since that point, I more or less had amnesia. Now, you can take that statement as literally or metaphysically as you need to, but that's what happened to me. It took me a long time to get to do consciously what I used to be able to do unconsciously.

It happens to everybody. Think about the periods when people don't do anything, or they lose it and have to regain it, or lose it and gain something else. So it's taken me all this time, and the records I made along the way were like openers—trying to figure out whether it was this way or that way, just what *is* it, what's the simplest way I can tell the story and make this feeling real.

So now I'm connected back, and I don't know how long I'll be there because I don't know how long I'm going to live. But what comes now is for real and from a place that's . . . I don't know, I don't care who else cares about it.

John Wesley Harding was a fearful album—just dealing with fear, but dealing with the devil in a fearful way, almost. All I wanted to do was to get the words right. It was courageous to do it because I could have *not* done it, too. Anyway, on *Nashville Skyline* you had to read between the lines. I was trying to grasp something that would lead me on to where I thought I should be, and it didn't go nowhere—it just went down, down, down. I couldn't be anybody but myself, and at that point I didn't know it or want to know it.

I was convinced I wasn't going to do anything else, and I had the good fortune to meet a man in New York City [the art teacher Norman Raeben] who taught me how to see. He put my mind and my hand and my eye together in a way that allowed me to do consciously what I unconsciously felt. And I didn't know how to pull it off. I wasn't sure it could be done in songs because I'd never written a song like that. But when I started doing it, the first album I made was *Blood on the Tracks*. Everybody agrees that that was pretty different, and what's different about it is that there's a code in the lyrics and also there's no sense of time. There's no respect for it: you've got yesterday, today, and tomorrow all in the same room, and there's very little that you can't imagine not happening.

From that point I went on to *Desire*, which I wrote with Jacques Levy. And I don't remember who wrote that. And then I disappeared for a while. Went on the Rolling Thunder tour, made *Renaldo and Clara*—in which I also used that quality of no-time. And I believe that that concept of creation is more real and true than that which *does* have time.

When you feel in your gut what you are and then dynamically pursue it—don't back down and don't give up—then you're going to mystify a lot of folks. Some people say, "I don't like him anymore." But other people do, and my crowd gets bigger and bigger. But who cares, really? If you fall down and you're hurting, you care about that immediate situation—if you have the energy to care. Who *really* cares? It's like that line—how does it go?— "Propaganda, who really cares?"

The Dressing Room

I ran into Dylan backstage half an hour before a sound check at the Veterans' Memorial Coliseum in New Haven. He invited me into his room, where we concluded our talk.

What do you think of all the criticisms of Street-Legal?

I read some of them. In fact, I didn't understand them. I don't think these people have had the experiences I've had to write those songs. The reviews didn't strike me as being particularly interesting one way or another, or as compelling to my particular scene. I don't know who these people are. They don't travel in the same crowd, anyway. So it would be like me criticizing Pancho Villa.

The reviews in this country of Renaldo and Clara *weren't good, either. The writers went out of their way to call you presumptuous, pretentious, and egocentric.*

These people probably don't like to eat what I like to eat, they probably don't like the same things I like, or the same people. Look, just one time I'd like to see any one of those assholes try and do what I do. Just once let one of them write a song to show how they feel and sing it in front of ten, let alone 10,000 or 100,000 people. I'd like to see them just try that one time.

Some of these critics have suggested that you need more sophisticated record production.

I probably do. The truth of it is that I can hear the same sounds that other people like to hear, too. But I don't like to spend the time trying to get those sounds in the studio.

So you're really not a producer type?

I'm not. Some musicians like to spend a lot of time in the studio. But a lot of people try to make something out of nothing. If you don't have a good song, you can go into the studio and make it appear to be good, but that stuff don't last.

You've had producers—Tom Wilson, Bob Johnson, Don De Vito . . .

But that wasn't all that sophisticated. I mean, John Hammond produced my first record, and it was a matter of singing into a microphone. He'd say, "It sounded good to me," and you'd go on to the next song. That's still the way I do it.

Nowadays, you start out with anything *but* the song—the drum track, for instance—and you take a week getting the instruments all sounding the way they should. They put down the rhythm track or whatever sound they want to hear in the ghost tracks. If you have a good song, it doesn't matter how well or badly it's produced. Okay, my records aren't produced that well. I admit it.

Personally, I love the "primitive" sound of Buddy Holly demo tapes or the original Chuck Berry discs.

But in those days they recorded on different equipment, and the records were thicker. If you buy one of my early records—and you can't today—they weren't like Saran Wrap, as they are now. There was quality to them . . . and the machinery was different and the boards were different. The Beach Boys did stuff on two-track in the garage.

You've got a bigger sound now—on record and onstage—than you've ever had before.

I do—and I might hire two more girls and an elephant—but it doesn't matter how big the sound gets as long as it's behind me emphasizing the song. It's still pretty simple. There's nothing like it in Vegas—no matter what you've heard—and it's anything but disco. It's not rock 'n' roll—my roots go back to the thirties, not the fifties.

On this tour, you've again been changing some of the radically new versions of songs that I heard you perform in Europe this past summer.

Yeah, we've changed them around some—it's a different tour and a different show. The band has to relearn the songs, but they're fast and the best at that.

Do you write songs now with them in mind?

I've had this sound ever since I was a kid—what grabs my heart. I had to play alone for a long time, and that was good because by playing alone I had to write songs. That's what I didn't do when I first started out, just playing available songs with a three-piece honky-tonk band in my hometown. But when I was first living in New York City—do you remember the old Madison Square Garden? Well, they used to have gospel shows there every Sunday, and you could see everyone from the Five Blind Boys, the Soul Stirrers, and the Swan Silvertones to Clara Ward and the Mighty Clouds of Joy. I went up there every Sunday. I'd listen to that and Big Bill Broonzy. Then I heard the Clancy Brothers and hung out with them—all of their drinking songs, their revolutionary and damsel-in-distress songs. And I listened to Jean Ritchie, Woody Guthrie, Leadbelly.

What about the doo-wop groups?

They played at shows, and those artists didn't have to be onstage for more than twenty minutes. They just got on and got off, and that was never what I wanted to do. I used to go to the Brooklyn Fox a lot, but the band I liked the best at that time was Bobby Blue Bland's, and I heard them at the Apollo. But the people whose floors I was sleeping on were all into the Country Gentlemen, Uncle Dave Macon, the Stanley Brothers, Bill Monroe. So I heard all that, too.

You seem to like music that's real and uncorrupted, no matter what its tradition. But some of your folk-music followers didn't care much for your own musical changes.

But don't forget that when I played "Maggie's Farm" electric at Newport, that was something I would have done years before. They thought I didn't know what I was doing and that I'd slipped over the edge, but the truth is . . . Al Kooper and Michael Bloomfield remember that scene very well. And what the newspapers say happened didn't actually happen that way. There wasn't a whole lot of resistance in the crowd. Don't forget they weren't equipped for what we were doing with the sound. But I had a legitimate right to do that.

The Beatles and the Rolling Stones were already popular in this country at that time, though.

I remember hanging out with Brian Jones in 1964. Brian could play the blues. He was an excellent guitar player—he seemed afraid to sing for some reason—but he could play note for note what Robert Johnson or Son House played.

In songs like "Buckets of Rain" or "New Pony," you seem just to go in and out of musical traditions, pick up what you want and need, and transform them as you please.

That's basically what I do, but so do the Stones. Mick and Keith knew all that music. America's filled with all kinds of different music.

Someone once said that "discovery," in poetry is a situation in which "the mind unites with a figure of its own devising as a means toward understanding the world." I've seen you tell people who don't know you that some other person standing nearby is you.

Well sure, if some old fluff ball comes wandering in looking for the real Bob Dylan, I'll direct him down the line, but I can't be held accountable for that. I didn't create Bob Dylan. Bob Dylan has always been here . . . always was. When I was a child, there was Bob Dylan. And before I was born, there was Bob Dylan.

Why did you have to play that role?

I'm not sure. Maybe I was best equipped to do it.

Sometimes your parents don't even know who you are. No one knows but you. Lord, if your own parents don't know who you are, who else in the world is there who would know except you? Sometimes I think I'm a ghost. Don't you have to have some poetic sense to be involved in what we're talking about? It's like what you were saying about people putting my record down. I couldn't care less if they're doing that, but, I mean, who are these people, what qualifications do they have? Are they poets, are they musicians? You find me some musician or poet, and then maybe we'll talk. Maybe that person will know something I don't know, and I'll see it that way. That could happen. I'm not almighty. But my feelings come from the gut, and I'm not too concerned with someone whose feelings come from his head. That don't bother me none.

This criticism has been going on for a long time. It's like a lover: you like somebody, and then you don't want to like them anymore because you're afraid to admit to yourself that you like them so much. . . . I don't know, you've just got to try, try to do some good for somebody. The world is full of nonsupporters and backbiters— people who chew on wet rags. But it's also filled with people who love you.

(1978)

MICK JAGGER

A certain prudent man, when he felt himself to be in love, hung a little bell round his neck to caution women that he was dangerous. Unfortunately for themselves they took too much notice of it; and he suffered accordingly.

—A. R. ORAGE

I'VE BEEN MISSING THE ROLLING STONES FOR YEARS—ever since they released Exile on Main Street, as a matter of fact. Of course, I've seen them on their occasional concert tours—which have become more and more circuslike—and enjoyed a number of their mid-seventies songs ("Star Star," "If You Really Want to Be My Friend," "Time Waits for No One," "Fool to Cry," "Memory Motel"). But during their post-Exile period, the Stones seem to have been around more in body than in spirit.

But now we have Some Girls—an album that draws on, in a remarkably unhackneyed way, the Stones' love for blues, the Motown sound, for country music, and Chuck Berry, and that combines and transforms these elements into the group's most energized, focused, outrageous, and original record since the days of Between the Buttons, Beggar's Banquet, Let It Bleed, and

Exile on Main Street. *And it is an album that crystallizes the Stones'*
perennial obsession with "some girls"—both real and imaginary.

After years of standing in the shadows, the soul survivors are back
on their own, with no direction home, sounding just like . . . the
Rolling Stones.

You've been a Rolling Stone for about fifteen years. How does it feel?

What a funny question! It's a long time, maybe too long. Maybe
it's time to restart a cycle—yeah, restart a five-year cycle.

Maybe we can start talking about "Miss You," which you've released
in three versions: a 45 disc, an LP track, and a twelve-minute version
on which there's a fantastic harmonica solo by a guy named Sugar
Blue, who plays like a snake charmer.

Yeah, my friend Sandy Whitelaw discovered him playing in the
Paris Métro. He's a blues harpist from America, and he plays not
only in the subway but in a club called La Vielle Grille. He's a very
strange and talented musician.

The lines in the song about being called up at midnight by friends
wanting to drag you out to a party remind me of "Get Off of My
Cloud."

I've a limited number of ideas [*laughing*].

You once sang: "I only get my rocks off while I'm dreaming."

I don't dream more than anybody else. But dreams are a great
inspiration for the lowliest rock 'n' roll writer to the greatest
playwrights. Chaucer was a great one for dreams. He was a great
one for explaining them and making fun of the astrological
explanations. He used to take the piss out of most of them, but

some of them he took seriously. Shakespeare, too, knew a lot about early English witchcraft and religion, and Chaucer had some sort of similar knowledge. Today we have psychiatrists to interpret dreams.

Have you ever been to one?

Never, not once. I've read a lot of Jung, and I would have gone to see him because he was interesting . . . . Anyway, dreams are very important, and I get good ideas from them. I don't jot them down, I just remember them—the experiences of them—they're so different from everyday experiences.

In "Moonlight Mile" there's the beautiful line, "I'm hiding sister and I'm dreaming."

Yeah, that's a dream song. Those kinds of songs with kinds of dreamy sounds are fun to do, but not all the time—it's nice to come back to reality.

What about the girl with the faraway eyes on your new album ("Faraway Eyes")? The lines "And if you're downright disgusted and life ain't worth a dime / Get a girl with faraway eyes" make it sound as if this dreamy truck-stop girl from Bakersfield, California, is really real.

Yeah, she's real, she's a real girl.

Is she a girl you know?

Yeah, she's right across the room . . . little bleary-eyed.

Well, there's no one else here except for that poster of a Japanese girl. Is that whom you mean?

Naw, she's not in a truck stop.

Right, she's standing under a parasol, in fact.... Let me have another glass of wine and maybe I'll see her, too!

You know, when you drive through Bakersfield on a Sunday morning or Sunday evening—I did that about six months ago—all the country-music radio stations start broadcasting black gospel services live from L.A. And that's what the song refers to. But the song's really about driving alone, listening to the radio.

I sense a bit of a Gram Parsons feeling on "Faraway Eyes"—country music as transformed through his style, via Buck Owens.

I knew Gram quite well, and he was one of the few people who really helped me to sing country music—before that, Keith and I used to just copy it off records. I used to play piano with Gram, and on "Faraway Eyes" I'm playing piano, though Keith is actually playing the top part—we added it on after. But I wouldn't say this song was influenced specifically by Gram. That idea of country music played slightly tongue in cheek—Gram had that in "Drugstore Truck Drivin' Man," and we have that sardonic quality, too.

The title of your new album is the title of one of your most powerful and outrageous songs—"Some Girls"—and I wanted to ask you about some of the girls in your songs. Here are a few lines taken at random from several of your older albums: "Who's that woman on your arm / All dressed up to do you harm?" ("Let It Loose"); "Women think I'm tasty / But they're always trying to waste me" ("Tumbling Dice"); "But there is one thing I will never understand / Some of the sick things a girl does to a man" ("Sittin' on a Fence").

I didn't write all those lines, you know [*laughing*].

All right, we'll reduce the charge. But obviously, in your songs of the mid-sixties, you were at pains to accuse girls of being deceptive, cheating, greedy, vain, affected, and stupid. It was a list of sins. Whether you were singing about rejecting the girl ("Out of Time," "Please Go Home") or about the girl rejecting you ("All Sold Out," "Congratulations") or about both ("High and Dry," "Under My Thumb"), almost all the songs from that period . . .

Most of those songs are really silly, they're pretty immature. But as far as the heart of what you're saying, I'd say . . . any bright girl would understand that if I were gay I'd say the same things about guys. Or if I were a girl I might say the same things about guys or other girls. I don't think any of the traits you mentioned are peculiar to girls. It's just about people. Deception, vanity . . . . On the other hand sometimes I do say nice things about girls [*laughing*].

Some of those other girls—Ruby Tuesday, Child of the Moon, or the girls in songs like "She's a Rainbow" and "Memory Motel"—are all very elusive and mystical.

Well, the girl in "Memory Motel" is actually a real, independent American girl. But they are mostly imaginary, you're right. . . . Actually, the girl in "Memory Motel" is a combination. So was the girl in "Faraway Eyes." Nearly all of the girls in my songs are combinations.

What about in "Till the Next Good-bye"?

No, she was real [*laughing*], she was real . . . . If you really want to know about the girls on the new album: "Some Girls" is all combinations. "Beast of Burden" is a combination. "Miss You" is an emotion, it's not really about *a* girl. To me, the feeling of longing is what the song is—I don't like to interpret my own fucking songs— but that's what it is.

You mentioned Jung before, and it seems to me that your "dream" girls are what Jung called anima figures. Do you ever think in those terms?

My anima is very strong. . . . I think it's very kind. . . . What you're saying, though, is that there are two different types of girls in my songs: there's the beautiful dreamy type and the vicious bitch type. There are also one or two others, but, yeah, you're right—there are two kinds of girls . . . only I never thought about it before.

You don't have too many girls in your songs that share both qualities.

Ah, I see, I'm not integrating them properly. Maybe not. Maybe "Beast of Burden" is integrated slightly: I don't want a beast of burden, I don't want the kind of woman who's going to drudge for me. The song says: I don't need a beast of burden, and I'm not going to be your beast of burden, either. Any woman can see that that's like my saying that I don't want a woman to be on her knees for me. I mean, I get accused of being very antigirl, right?

Right.

But people really don't listen, they get it all wrong; they hear "Beast of Burden" and say, *"Argggh!"*

They sure heard "Under My Thumb" ("Under my thumb's a squirming dog who's just had her day").

That's going back to my teenage years!

Well, it's both a perverse and brilliant song about power and sex.

At the time there was no feminist criticism because there was no such thing, and one just wrote what one felt. Not that I let it hinder me too much now. . . . Did you hear about the dinner honoring Ahmet Ertegun [president of Atlantic Records]? Some feminists were giving out leaflets saying what terrible things he'd done, saying that the Average White Band's new cover depicts a naked woman standing in a steaming bath of water, which could cause "enormous pain and possible death" [*laughing*]—things like that.

How about your woman-in-bondage poster for your Black and Blue *album? Many people may have a deep masochistic streak, but that poster and some of your songs certainly seem hung up on that.*

Yeah, we had a lot of trouble with that particular poster. As far as the songs go, one talks about one's own experience a lot of the time. And you know, a lot of bright girls just take all of this with a pinch of salt. But there are a lot of women who *are* disgraceful, and if you just have the misfortune to have an affair with one of those . . . it's a personal thing.

And the "squirming dog" image.

Well, that was a joke. I've never felt in that position vis-à-vis a person—I'd never want to really hurt someone.

What about the groupies on the road ready for anything? What about "Star Star"?

Exactly! That's real, and if girls can do that, I can certainly write about it because it's what I see. I'm not saying all women are star fuckers, but I see an awful lot of them, and so I write a song called that. I mean, people show themselves up by their own behavior, and just to describe it doesn't mean you're antifeminist.

That bondage poster, though, was pretty blatant.

Well, there are a lot of girls into that, they dig it, they want to be chained up—and it's a thing that's true for both sexes.

But why use it to advertise a record?

I don't see why not. It's a valid piece of commercial art, just a picture.

Would you show yourself getting whipped and beaten?

Sure, if I thought it was more commercial than a beautiful girl!

People are obviously going to take a few of these songs on the new LP as being about your domestic situation.

Well, I actually mention "my wife" in "Respectable."

"Get out of my life, go take my wife—don't come back." And there's also: "You're a rag trade girl, you're the queen of porn / You're the easiest lay on the White House lawn."

Well, I just thought it was funny. "Respectable" really started off as a song in my head about how "respectable" we as a band were supposed to have become. "We're" so respectable. As I went along with the singing, I just made things up and fit things in. "Now we're respected in society . . . " I really meant *us*. My wife's a very honest person, and the song's not "about" her.

But people will probably take this song, as well as the album, to be about you, in the same way they took Blood on the Tracks *to be about Dylan or John Lennon's "I don't believe in Beatles" song to be about him.*

But it's very rock 'n' roll. It's not like "Sara." "Respectable" is very lighthearted when you *hear* it. That's why I don't like divorcing the lyrics from the music. 'Cause when you actually hear it sung, it's not what is, it's the way we do it. "Get out of my life, go take my wife—don't come back" . . . it's not supposed to be taken seriously. If it were a ballad, if I sang it like: *"Pleeese, taaake* my wiiiiife"—you know what I mean?—well, it's not that, it's just a shit-kicking rock 'n' roll number.

Keith Richards once said something to the effect that rock 'n' roll really is subversive because the rhythms alter your being and perceptions. With your words and your rhythms, your stuff could do and has done that, don't you think?

Rhythms are very important. But subvert what?

Well, Keith Richards's implication was that words could be used to lie, but that what the Stones did was just to let you see clearly the way things were. And that that vision—or so I inferred—was what was subversive.

Maybe Keith did mean that. Music is one of the things that changes society. That old idea of not letting white children listen to black music is true, cause if you want white children to remain what they are, they mustn't.

Look at what happened to you [laughing].

Exactly! You get different attitudes to things . . . even the way you walk . . .

And the way you talk.

Right, and the way you talk. Remember the twenties when jazz in Europe changed a lot of things. People got more crazy, girls lifted up their dresses and cut their hair. People started to dance to that music, and it made profound changes in that society. . . . That sounds awfully serious!

To keep on the semiserious keel for a second, the song "Some Girls" seems to be about what happens when hundreds of idealized twenties girls—like the ones drawn by Guy Peelaert on your It's Only Rock 'n' Roll *album—decide to come to life, and, like maenads, try to eat you up, destroy you—taking your money and clothes and giving you babies you don't want.*

Well, it could be a bad dream in a way. I had a dream like that last night, incidentally, but there were dogs as well as girls in it.

Maybe you can call your next album Some Dogs.

[*Laughing*] I'd get in trouble with the anti-dog defamation league.

I wonder what the girls and women, of all races, are going to think of lines like: "Chinese girls, they're so gentle—they're really such a tease."

I think they're all well covered—everyone's represented [*laughing*]. Most of the girls I've played the song to *like* "Some Girls." They think it's funny; black girlfriends of mine just laughed. And I think it's very complimentary about Chinese girls, I think they come off better than English girls. I really like girls an awful lot, and I don't think I'd say anything really nasty about any of them.

Are you running for president?

[*Laughing*] The song's supposed to be funny. I remember that when I wrote it, it was very funny. 'Cause we were laughing, and the phone was ringing, and I was just sitting in the kitchen and it was just coming out . . . and I thought I could go on forever!

The first time I heard it, I started making up my own lyrics: "Green girls get me anxious / Blue girls get me sad / Brown girls get me silly / And red girls make me mad." It's like a kid's song.

[*Laughing*] That's why I said it wasn't serious, it's just anything that came to my head.

Do you remember the Beach Boys' "California Girls"?

Yeah, I love that song.

Well, it seems to me that instead of all the girls in your song being California girls, they've all turned into a different type of girl, and certainly from another state.

I know what you mean. I never thought of it like that. I never thought that a rock critic of your knowledge and background could ever come out with an observation like that [*laughing*].

You mean it's pretentious?

Not at all. It's a great analogy. But like all analogies, it's false [*laughing*].

On your It's Only Rock 'n' Roll *album you did a great version of the Temptations' "Ain't Too Proud to Beg," and now you're doing a version of "Just My Imagination."*

It's like a continuation, and I've always wanted to do that song—originally as a duet with Linda Ronstadt, believe it or not. But instead we just did our version of it—like an English rock 'n' roll band tuning up on "Imagination," which has only two or three chords . . . it's real simple stuff.

I like the lines: "Soon we'll be married and raise a family / Two boys for you, what about two girls for me?" There are those girls *in there again.*

Yeah, I made that up. In reality the girl in the song doesn't even know me—it's a dream . . . and we're back where we started this conversation.

"Of all the girls in New York she loves me true" is one of the lines from "Imagination." And in fact the entire album is full of New York City settings and energy.

Yeah, I added the New York reference in the song. And the album itself is like that because I was staying in New York part of last year, and when I got to Paris and was writing the words, I was thinking about New York. I wrote the songs in Paris.

It's a real New York record.

Hope they like it in South Jersey [*laughing*].

There's the gay garbage collector on Fifty-third Street in "When the Whip Comes Down," Central Park in "Miss You," the sex and dreams and parties and the schmattas *on Seventh Avenue in "Shattered"— and there's a distinct Lou Reed–cum–British vaudeville tone to some of your singing on "Shattered."*

Every time I play guitar my engineer, Chris Kimsey, says: "Oh, here comes Lou Reed again." But I think a lot of English singers do that—there's a kind of tradition, it's natural. In "Shattered," Keith and Woody [Ron Wood] put a riff down, and all we had was the word "shattered." So I just made the rest up and thought it would sound better if it were half talked.

I'd written some of my verses before I got into the studio, but I don't like to keep singing the same thing over and over, so it changed. And I was noticing that there were a lot of references to New York, so I kept it like that. *Some Girls* isn't a "concept" album, God forbid, but it's nice that some of the songs have connections with each other—they make the album hold together a bit. . . . But then there's the girl with faraway eyes!

(1978)

VAN MORRISON

SPEAKING OF VAN MORRISON, the German filmmaker Wim Wenders once said: "I know of no music that is more lucid, feelable, hearable, seeable, touchable, no music you can experience more intensely than this." And Wenders added: "Not just moments, but extended and long periods of experience that convey the feel of what films could be: a form or perception that no longer hurls itself blindly on meanings and definitions, but allows the sensuous to take over and grow. Where indeed something does become indescribable."

In his indescribable songs, Van Morrison draws you, trancelike, into a world of mystery and beauty. It is a world of fields and gardens wet with rain, country fairs and magic nights, gypsies with hearts on fire, boats in the harbor, cool evening breezes, and rivers ever flowing—a world where, to quote from his song "Streets of Arklow," "our souls were clean and the grass did grow."

William Butler Yeats once suggested that the ancient Celts lived in a world where anything might flow and change, and become any other thing: "They had imaginative passions because they did not live within our own straight limits, and were nearer to ancient chaos, every man's desire, and had immortal models about them. The hare that ran by among the dew might have sat up on his haunches when the first man was made, and the poor bunch of rushes under their feet might have been a goddess laughing among the stars; and with but a little magic, a little waving of the hands, a little murmuring of the lips, they too could become a hare or a bunch of rushes, and know immortal love and immortal hatred."

Van Morrison's "little murmuring of the lips" reveals the richest and most expressive voice in rock music. Reviewing Morrison's *Moondance* album many years ago, Ralph J. Gleason quoted a remark of John McCormick, the the Irish tenor, to the effect that what made a great voice different from a merely good one was "the yarrrrragh in your voice." In a perceptive elaboration of this remark, Greil Marcus wrote: "The yarrrrragh is Van Morrison's version of Leadbelly, of jazz, of blues, of poetry. It is a mythic incantation, and he will get it, or get close to it, suggest it, with horns (no white man working in popular music can arrange horns with the precision and grace of Van Morrison), strings, in melody, in repetition (railing the same word, or syllable, ten, twenty, thirty times until it has taken his song where he wants it to go). To Morrison the yarrrrragh is the gift of the muse and the muse itself. He has even written a song about it, 'Listen to the Lion.' Across eleven minutes, he sings, chants, moans, cries, pleads, shouts, hollers, whispers, until finally he breaks away from language and speaks in Irish tongues, breaking away from ordinary meaning until he has loosed the lion inside himself. He begins to roar: he *has that sound, that yarrrrragh, as he has never had it before. He is not singing it, it is singing him."*

As a composer, writer, and performer, Van Morrison seems almost possessed—a medium through which the voices of bards and mystics ("Blake and the Eternals," as he calls them), of children and lovers pure of heart, of rivers and mountains, and of blues, gospel, jazz, and Celtic musicians meet and interfuse. In the words of the English Theosophist composer Cyril Scott: "Today, as we enter this new Age, we seek, primarily through the medium of inspired music, to diffuse the spirit of unification and brotherhood, and thus quicken the vibration of this planet." Van Morrison attempts to do just this in his beautiful visions and his chants for (and of) healing, all filled with the "light of the Master's eyes":

Saw you shining in the sun this morning
Saw you shining in the moon at night
Saw you shining in the sun this morning
Saw you shining in the moon at night
Ancient of Days . . .

Felt you stirring in my heart this morning
Felt you moving in my heart at night
Felt you stirring in my heart this morning
Felt you moving in my heart at night
Ancient of Days . . .

In 1974 Van Morrison gave up performing and releasing albums, dropping out of sight in order—as he says in the following interview—to get his "energy together, doing things I like to do, and just living as if I were nobody instead of somebody." He reappeared in 1976 to give an electrifying performance at The Last Waltz concert, and last year he released a somewhat sluggish LP, A Period of Transition (which did, however, contain two vintage Morrison songs—"Flamingos Fly" and "Heavy Connection"). But today, Van Morrison is again proving that he is "one of the few originals left in rock." His latest LP, Wavelength, is a ravishing work, and he is now on his first nationwide tour in five years. Accompanied by a brilliant band of five instrumentalists and two background vocalists, Morrison's recent performance in San Francisco revealed him in total control of his vocal powers, as he presented—without a trace of theatrics—one of the most passionate and inspiring sets I've heard since the concerts of Ray Charles and Otis Redding more than a decade ago.

Off stage, and at first meeting, Van Morrison seems to be a shy, private, occasionally moody and melancholic person who has little time for small talk and less time for "significant" inquiries about his life and poetry. He finds interviews distasteful and, one discovers, even painful. Rather than use the interview format to project some intended image, and rather than undermine both the format and the image—as other public "personalities" sometimes do—Van Morrison makes it clear that he prefers to be left alone to compose and perform his songs.

Any interviewer would be advised—to use one of the singer's own images—not to push the river. Not being well enough forewarned, I met up, in early October, with Van Morrison in Sausalito, California, where he currently resides, and discovered his sentiments concerning interviews in—appropriately and ironically—the following interview.

I've heard that one of the first and biggest influences in your life was Leadbelly.

He was my guru. Somebody once sent me a poster of him—a huge poster of Leadbelly just beaming down with a twelve-string guitar. I framed it and put it up on the wall, and I've had it on the wall everywhere I've been. I always take pictures with me all over the world—I have a poster of Them, too—and as long as I have these certain photographs on the wall, I could be anywhere.

And this Leadbelly picture on the wall—well, one day in Los Angeles I was looking at it and was thinking, "I've got to get rid of this, it's doing me in." So I took it down and was about to throw it out. At that moment I was fiddling around with the radio—I wanted to hear some music—and I tuned in this station, KP something, and "Rock Island Line" by Leadbelly came on. So I just turned around, man, and very quietly put the picture back on the wall.

"Keep your picture at the station of the Rock Island Line." He was telling you something.

That's it. I heard his records first when I was ten or eleven, and I thought it was the greatest thing since Swiss cheese [*laughing*]. The energy, the way he was singing, the guitar—it was the vibe of the whole thing. "Rock Island Line," "Backwater Blues," "Bring a Little Water, Sylvie," "Bo Weevil," "Christmas Day," and "Ellis Speed"—"Come on and all take heed, / Tell you about the death of Ellis Speed."

I once heard recordings by the McPeake Family Singers, a traditional Irish folk group from Belfast, and was deeply moved by them—much as you were moved by Leadbelly.

I heard the McPeakes at a party years ago, and their version of "Wild Mountain Thyme" just blew me out of my gourd. The way they did that was ridiculous, I'd never heard anything like it . . . with Da McPeake, the younger kids, the pipes.

Is that a Scottish or an Irish song?

We don't know. It's both. I probably did my version of the song ["Purple Heather"] because I heard theirs.

Your song "Country Song" sounds very nostalgic and very Irish, too.

That was the inspiration. . . . Most of *Astral Weeks* and *Veedon Fleece* was written in Ireland and recorded here. The songs on the other records were done mostly in this country. But nowadays I go between two places—the United States for recording and working and organizing, and Ireland for inspiration and composing.

You've said that you've been influenced by Leadbelly and other kinds of American black music—as if in Ireland you're drawn to this country, and in the States you're drawn back home.

You find that you're pulled by different things at different times. You find that something is pulling you that you have to get to because it's telling you different things about yourself. And I just kind of go where the pull is strongest at the time.

So Ireland is stronger for you in terms of writing?

I think it always is, because it's my roots, really. I don't have those business distractions there.

Do you still have friends in Ireland?

Yeah, I've got a few, both in Belfast and Dublin. I see people I used to grow up with, people I played with in bands, and it brings back into perspective what you're doing. It brings you back to reality. In my new band, Peter Bardens was formerly with Them, and I've known him a long time. Peter Van Hooke is a Dutch drummer, and I've worked with him on an American tour. Herbie Armstrong, who's on rhythm guitar, and I used to play together with a guy named Brian Rossi a long time ago at Plaza Macka ballroom in Belfast—and in other show bands at that period. I'm going back to my roots, really—I mean, if I turn around in the middle of a set and look at Herbie . . . I mean, how can I take this whole thing seriously?

I didn't know you played in show bands.

A lot of people only think of Them, but I had a whole other career. The Monarchs and various show bands. When I started out, I had my own skiffle group. A lot of bands.

You've been a musician since you were really young.

Yeah, short pants. I went for that before I went for anything else. You just walk into it totally blind.

I heard that your mother was a singer and that your father was a blues-music fan.

Yeah, he was into jazz and blues records. But my mother was a great singer—and still is. She could sing anything from Al Jolson to "Ave Maria."

In one of your new songs, "Take It Where You Find It," you sing: "Change, change come over, / Change come over, / Talkin' about a change." What change do you think has come over you? People have been wondering what you've been doing during the past few years.

I've gone through quite a few big changes in the last couple of years as far as how I'm relating to what I'm doing. Because in 1974 I was completely at the end of my rope. I was doing gigs, I was uptight, I wasn't getting anything out of it. I felt like I was a robot, and I had a lot of tension—there was tension in my shoulders, my neck, my feet. All this sort of stuff.

And I remember I was in Belgium, sitting in my hotel room looking out the window, and I was thinking, "This isn't worth it, man." I'd done two American and two European tours in the 1973–74 period. And these record-company people were always earbending with their line: "He never works." That was their typical line, and I blew that one out the window. So I was just kind of sitting thinking that I had all those people, doing these gigs, and something wasn't right. I wasn't getting off, it wasn't what I had planned my life to be like. I wasn't going to let show business control my life. So I decided to take a break, get my shit together, and think about what I was doing being in this music business—it was becoming oppressive. I wanted to shift out of it for a while.

Was the time between 1974 and now a kind of fertile void for you, or did you just flip out?

No, I didn't flip out. I've never flipped out, I'm too crazy to flip out. People who change their minds a lot don't flip out. It's those who have one kind of fixation that do that. My mind changes too much. No, it was a conscious decision. Like I was somebody sitting there looking at the movie, and I wanted to change the movie.

What about the audience watching the movie? What about your audience?

Well, the thing is, if you're not together, you can't do it. I wasn't happy in any way—I wasn't writing—so I didn't have anything to give anybody.

You were pretty courageous to do what you did.

The usual thing happened, you know: the William Morris Agency called me up every three days and said, "What are you doing?" "Doing a break, what do you think I'm doing?" I was traveling in England, Ireland, Scotland, Los Angeles, Switzerland—all over the place. I was just kind of living life as opposed to *being* somebody, being like Van Morrison or somebody. I was just looking at things, getting my energy together, doing things I like to do, and just living as if I were nobody instead of somebody. I have to be nobody so I can live my life.

It's like the writer who talks about how important it is to learn how to get lost in a city in order to see things again clearly.

That's it.

In "Wavelength," you have the lines: "I heard the Voice of America / Callin' on my wavelength / Singin', Come back baby / Come back, come back."

It's got several meanings. When I was growing up in Belfast, I used to listen to Radio Luxembourg and the Voice of America, which broadcast from Frankfurt. And these lines are about returning to Europe and getting back to my roots, because being brought up in Europe is completely different from being brought up in America—it's a completely different ballgame. So that's what that's about.

In "Take It Where You Find It," you sing: "Lost dreams and found dreams in America."

I wrote that on a plane from Los Angeles to San Francisco and carried it around with me for a long time—it didn't make any sense to me at all. I knew people were going to ask what it was about. And not really knowing or even caring what it was about, I tried changing it to "Lost dreams and found dreams in Skundtharpe" or "the Bahamas" or anywhere. I tried to change it, but it never fit—that line kept sticking. When I played it on the piano I couldn't get away from it. And the rest of the song I wrote later on.

Some of these lines, especially "You will build on whatever is real / And wake up each day / To a new waking dream," suggest a sense of things that are common to a lot of your songs.

You get this thing coming through—it comes through in different spaces and time, and you don't really know what it is. If you're receptive to it, you channel in and you write it down.

You said that in 1974 your body's energy was all blocked up. In "Kingdom Hall" now, you sing about "good body music" and about clearing inhibitions away. Almost all your songs are full of deep and lively feelings about dancing.

When I started out, I was playing dance music. I was in dance bands, and people were on the floor dancing. And that's really what I wanted to do, when I started in this game—play dance music. And I just found myself getting further and further away from the dance thing with concerts and all that. And I wanted to get back to it.

A philosopher once suggested that even thoughts could be expressed in dance, that dancing could be a form of thinking.

I see it as a way of not thinking, really. I see dancing as just dancing. When you're really into playing music, the words become irrelevant because you're in that space. And I feel that way about dancing—it goes beyond words.

But a lot of your most danceable songs have very beautiful lyrics.

I don't know, this thing about lyrics—I'm just catching on to this. If you get some of the facts together . . . I mean, I sell records in places where they don't speak English. And I've experienced listening to Greek singers, for instance, and not knowing what the words are, but I get a story and a feeling from it even though I haven't a clue to what's being said. So if English-language songs can sell in non-English-speaking countries and people can be touched by them, then we can see how irrelevant the words are.

Sometimes it seems that you let the words dance when you sing them, you release them, and they take off in their own directions.

The only time I actually work with words is when I'm writing a song. After it's written, I release the words; and every time I'm singing, I'm singing syllables. I'm just singing signs and phrases.

I wanted to speak to you about water, about how images of it appear in many of your songs—rivers flowing and, as you sing in "And It Stoned Me," "Oh, the water . . . let it run all over me."

I've never thought about it, but now that you mention it . . . water is a healing thing. But I never thought about the fact that many of my songs are about water.

In "Redwood Tree," a boy and his dog go out looking for a rainbow. Then the boy and his father go out looking for the lost dog. And the question that's asked in the song is: What have they learned?

The thing is, we've become so serious, we get too heavy about all this—what everything means. I was sitting one day feeling very heavy, and my daughter, who's eight years old, came up to me and started cracking up. And then I started cracking up when I realized it. I'm sitting here thinking that this is all serious, and it's not.

You're the one who wrote: "Well, I'm caught one more time / Up on Cyprus Avenue." That's serious.

Well, that's what I'm saying, we get too serious about it all.

Is there something wrong about being serious?

Yeah, I think there's something's wrong with being serious.

In "Come Here My Love," you sing: "In fathoms of my inner mind / I'm mystified by this mood, / This melancholy feeling that just don't do me good."

That's it, that says it right there, that's what I'm talking about: I am *mystified*.

The song continues: "Come here my love and I will lift my spirits high for you, / I'd like to fly away and spend a day or two / Just contemplating fields and leaves and talking about nothing."

That's it. Talking about absolutely nothing.

That must be why interviews bother you, because people like myself insist on talking to you about something.

Interviews tend to drain you—you have to backtrack and make something out of the past which is dead.

Then the song continues, almost like Walt Whitman: "Just laying down in shades of effervescent odors and shades of time and tide, / Then flowing through, become enraptured by the sights and sounds and intrigue of nature's beauty, / Come along with me and take it all in." I suppose if I were in the countryside with you, I'd probably ask you about the flowers and birds and bees, not about who Madame George really is.

Right.

Some people have interpreted "Madame George" to be about a boy's father who's in drag, the madam of a bordello in which the boy hangs out and does errands and from which he eventually runs away.

If you're writing something, you get ideas from all over the place. And the songs aren't necessarily about you or what you're involved in or what you're doing. Some of them might be about me or about somebody I knew when I was four years old. You write about other situations, you get ideas from everywhere. These songs are kinds of cameo stories or whatever, and that's about it. It's whatever it means to you. Something I wrote ten years ago means different things to me now. It means what it means now. I've forgotten a lot of this. It's the past, and the past is dead.

When I was a kid of maybe ten or eleven, I thought I wanted to be a rock 'n' roll singer, and there was a certain dream there. The dream was that this kid had some goal or ambition. And that dream was lived out—I did whatever my dream was. But the thing is, you grow up and you're not that kid anymore. So you have different goals and ambitions, sometimes you don't have any ambitions, sometimes you find you don't really have *that* ambition. We have these different stages, and it's called life. Obviously the dream of the kid isn't the dream of the adult, because you change. You're not always a teenager, you're not always in your thirties or forties. And at certain points you look back and you realize: I'm not there anymore, what do I want to be now, what's my goal?

For me, I realized that when I became twenty-eight or twenty-nine I'd lived out a certain thing, and that was the dream of the kid. The boy had his vision, but the man had a different one, and it's your option whether you want to change your vision of life. And it was time for me, as an adult, to have another dream. And I realized I didn't have any ambition.

What's your dream right now?

I don't have any at all.

(1978)

GEORGE BALANCHINE
On Music

GEORGE BALANCHINE (1904–83) WAS GENERALLY CONSIDERED to be the greatest choreographer of modern times. He studied music and dance in St. Petersburg and made his dancing debut at the age of ten as a cupid in the Maryinsky Theatre Ballet Company production of The Sleeping Beauty. He later served as ballet master for Serge Diaghilev's famous Ballets Russes de Monte Carlo. At the end of 1933, he traveled to the United States, where, along with the distinguished dance connoisseur and man of letters Lincoln Kirstein, he helped to found both the School of American Ballet and the New York City Ballet, of which he was the artistic director.

For this continually inspiring company, Balanchine created scores of masterpieces, including Serenade, The Four Temperaments, Jewels, A Midsummer Night's Dream, and Vienna Waltzes, whose "dance evolutions and figures"—in the words of the late poet and critic Edwin Denby—were "luminous in their spacing, and of a miraculous musicality in their impetus." Among the greatest of his works were his more than thirty ballets to the scores of Igor Stravinsky, with whom he was associated beginning in 1925, when he choreographed a revised version of the composer's Song of the Nightingale. In the collaborations between these two Russian masters, one became ineluctably conscious of "seeing" music and "hearing" movements, as music and dance revealed sound and light to be two manifestations of one vibrational source.

I was fortunate enough to meet with and interview George Balanchine on two occasions. The first time was in July of 1978 at the opening of the New York City Ballet's annual summer season in Saratoga Springs, New York. The second time occurred exactly four years later in July of 1982, during one of the final performances of the City Ballet's Stravinsky Centennial Celebration, held during that month. It was to be Balanchine's final interview. Several months later he entered New York City's Roosevelt Hospital, suffering from progressive cerebral disintegration. He died on April 30, 1983.

Mr. B (as Balanchine was known to his colleagues) held at bay almost all kinds of visionary and speculative theorizing about his work, preferring to talk about himself as a craftsman rather than a creator, and comparing himself to a cook and a cabinetmaker (he was apparently extremely adept at both endeavors) and even, as he did once with me, to a horse!

Both of my conversations with George Balanchine concerned themselves with music. As the composer George Perle writes in his liner notes to the marvelous A Balanchine Album (Nonesuch Records): "Balanchine was an accomplished musician, but he was much more than this. Just as the words of a Schubert Lied have become Schubert's words, whoever the poet may have been, so the music of a Balanchine ballet becomes Balanchine's composition, *not because he has appropriated it, but because he seems to have magically reexperienced the creative act, to have relived the decisions, the choices, and eliminations that the composer has lived through in bringing it into being."*

Witty, gracious, childlike, and charming, Balanchine conversed with me, both in 1978 and 1982, in his inimitable, idiosyncratic English. During our second conversation, I noticed that Balanchine's mind would occasionally wander, and that he would respond to one question with the answer to another. When asked about Stravinsky's childhood, for example, he proceeded to talk about his own. But as the following two interviews both make clear, Balanchine always refused to dwell on the past or the future. ("I'm not interested in later on. I don't have any later on. We all live in the same time forever.") And the only way to pay tribute to the spirit of this twentieth-century genius is simply to regard his ballets as eternally new creations.

(Part 1)

Of all the art forms, music and dance seem to be the closest—like brother and sister, or like lovers. And whenever I think of your ballets, I hear the dancers and see the music.

Anything that doesn't belong to the world of words, you can't explain. People say, "What do you feel when you look at this?" We always have to compare with something else. "Is it beautiful?" "Yes." "Well, how beautiful?" "Like a rose, like a taste, like a wine." "And what does wine taste like?" "Like grass." It's always something else. So you describe my ballets in terms of hearing; and you're a writer, so you write. I myself don't have a writing style . . . not at all. Just a few words that I need to remember things.

The French poet Stéphane Mallarmé once talked about a dancer "writing with her body."

Naturally. But not with words. You see, I got a message. Each one of us is here to serve on this earth. And probably I was sent here to see and to hear—that's all I can do. I can't see something that doesn't exist. I don't create or invent anything, I assemble. God already made everything—colors, flowers, language—and somehow there had to be a Mother. Our business is to choose. The more you choose, the more amazing everything is. But I can't explain what I do.

How do you explain a piece by Anton Webern? You can say, mechanically, that it's twelve-tone music, but that doesn't mean anything to anybody. It's like saying something is a four-part fugue, but after a while, people listening to it lose hold of it. So the beginning of my ballet *Episodes* to Webern's music Symphony [Opus 21] is canonic. I had to try to paint or design time with bodies in order to create a resemblance between the dance and what was going on in sound.

The nineteenth-century theorist Eduard Hanslick said: "Music is form moving in sounds." This would also seem to be your definition of dance.

Absolutely. You have to have sound in order to dance. I need music that's possible to move to. You have to hear the music—the timbre and the use of the sound. Music is like an aquarium with the dancers inside it. It's all around you, like fish moving through water.

Some choreographers take an important piece and then give the ballet an inappropriate title—a Brahms piano concerto, say, and then call it a "Rainbow" ballet by Brahms. He didn't write a rainbow. I, personally, can't do dances to a Brahms symphony or to

Beethoven—perhaps little moments from a specific piece. But you can't take one of their symphonies and dance to it.

You've choreographed much Stravinsky, but never Le Sacre du Printemps.

It's impossible, terrible. Nobody can do it. And Stravinsky's *Les Noces* is impossible, too, and it shouldn't be done. The words are tough Russian words, and when at the end of the piece the Bridegroom, very drunk, screams out that he and his Bride will live together forever and that everyone will be jealous of their good life . . . well, he's unhappy when he sings that, because the marriage will be a disaster. He's never seen her and she's never seen him. It's a tragedy, really, when you hear this sung in Russian—those words and that almost funeral music.

Speaking of Stravinsky, someone once described him at a Nadia Boulanger class in Paris, sitting at a piano and "inventing a chord"— playing a chord, then taking one note out and putting another in until he had something very special. Don't you do the same thing?

Absolutely. There's gesture and timing, and I leave things alone or take something out, put something else in instead. I can't take a formula and do just anything with it. Naturally, in a few seconds I can create very banal movements with a formula, but to do something important, to occupy time and space with bodies— several bodies that stop in time and pass—you have to look at them and say: "Not right now, don't do that, get out, do it this way." You have to put things together like a gefilte fish. That's how I do it.

In the second pas de deux *of your ballet* Stravinsky Violin Concerto, *I get the sense of inert matter being formed—the artist shaping his materials. The dancers' last gestures, especially, suggest this. Did you have this idea in mind?*

To me, it's the music that wants you to do certain things. Dance has to look like the music. If you use music simply as an accompaniment, then you don't hear it. I occupy myself with how not to interfere with the music. And at the end of this pas de deux I made a gesture as if to say, "How do you do, Stravinsky?" That music is very Russian—reminiscent of old, nostalgic Russian folk songs—and I know what Stravinsky meant, I understood and felt it.

It's very difficult to make a gesture such that it looks like a sound. It's also like your asking and making a question—two people addressing the world. So, at the conclusion, I made a little bow to Stravinsky. And I also did that in the duet to the *Symphony in Three Movements*—there's a little Balinese-type gesture (Stravinsky loved Balinese culture), like a prayer, and that, too, was for the composer.

Stravinsky's body is gone, but he's still here. What could he leave, his nose? He left me a cigarette case and other things. But the music is really what he left, and when his music plays, he's right here.

There are at least two basic ideas concerning the nature of dance. The first of these is conveyed in a statement by Saint Augustine: "All the dancer's gestures are signs of things, and the dance is called rational, because it aptly signifies and displays something over and above the pleasure of the senses." The second is revealed in a statement by the Sufi poet Rumi: "Whosoever knoweth the power of the dance, dwelleth in God."

To me, these are two ways of saying the same thing. Now, the dervishes don't perform specifically for the sake of money or beauty, but, personally, I have to do ballets that will attract a public. If people don't come, we don't have a company, dancers and musicians can't get paid. Once they have a salary, they can eat—and then we can tell them: "Don't eat, get thin, do this, put on some makeup, you look like hell!" *Train* them. And then you can do certain dances that aren't meant specifically to entertain the public.

In the great ballroom finale of Vienna Waltzes, *you've created a ballet that entertains but that also suggests a world of waltzing dervishes!*

I agree.

And in the midst of these whirling dancers is the heroine, who just as she seems about to awake—both sexually and spiritually—swoons and faints like the archetypal Victorian maiden.

Or like some of the characters in Turgenev . . . yes, there it is! Hegel once said that people want to see their lives onstage. That means, for example, that one man might think: "I'm married, my wife and children have left me, and I'm unhappy and feel that I'm going to kill myself." And that's what I think art is—people should play for me my story. Another guy has a bad stomach. So everyone has a different story. Look at *Jesus Christ Superstar*: people say it's very good, they think they get something from it, but they get nothing from it, it's miserable. That's no way to find God—going to sleep, having a drink.

I've always wanted to know whether or not you like rock 'n' roll.

It's not my cup of tea, I'm too old. Jazz is my time—and some Gershwin and Rodgers and Hart. But I'm not really American yet. I can't understand rock 'n' roll words: "Auh-uh-er-er-you-er . . ." The boy and girl meet and then never meet again . . . and then . . . what

... "you went away" ... er ... "you and I holding hands ..." I don't understand it.

Getting back to dance and how you choreograph: When you first hear the opening intervals of a piece of music—Webern's Symphony—*do you immediately visualize these intervals, or feel them in your body?*

No, I feel something can be done, but if I don't try it out, then I can never do it. You can't sit down and think about dancing, you have to get up and dance. You take people and move them and see if their movements correspond to the music. And I have to know the music. In Webern's Symphony I made the dancers turn upside down at one point in order to parallel the use of the musical inversion. And near the ending of Stravinsky's *Movements for Piano and Orchestra* I have dancers marking the composer's returning twelve-tone row ... but now slowed down, spread and stretched out. These certain things I do, naturally, but as little as possible. I don't imitate the notes of a piece.

When you listen to music, you can hear lots of notes in one ear, but you can't see collected movements, as if they were a pill that goes into your eye and dissolves immediately. Léonide Massine used to have people dancing everywhere—he called it contrapuntal ballet. "Contra," which means "against," actually—in reality—means "together." As I've said many times, the movements of arms, head, and feet are contrapuntal to the vertical position of the body.

Writing about Webern's use of retrograde canons, the composer Ernst Krenek once pointed to something extremely fascinating. As Krenek stated it: "The accuracy and elegance with which the reversibility of these models is worked out emanate from a peculiar fascination, seeming to suggest a mysterious possibility for circumventing the one-

way direction of time." Does this have any relationship to what you feel about Webern's music or about the way you choreograph a work like Symphony?

Even if it's so, you can't and shouldn't try to effect this. Several years ago I read an article about the reverse-time sense, and I think that the world must have this sense. In the usual time sense, everything decays—what is young gets older and separates—and the world, as we know it, is like that. But there's another world where all this decayed material, in our time sense, goes into . . . whatever it is and reverses. It's as if you're born dead, get younger, and die at birth. Not only that . . . it may be that this time sense is going on at the same time as the other one. Why not? It's everything at once. As you've reminded me before, I still believe what I once said: "I'm not interested in later on. I don't have any later on. We all live in the same time forever." . . . Of course, they talk about the Black Hole. But think: the Black Hole will probably disintegrate, too, because it's part of our world. So the Black Hole feeds himself—it's a *he*, probably, the Black Hole—he eats up the light . . . and then when he's completely fed, he'll explode like mad!

Some of the endings of your Stravinsky ballets, in particular, feel so strongly to me like beginnings that I look forward to the endings.

Like beginnings. Yes. But remember, we have to be thinking of this on the level of particles. And you don't really become aware of it, you only think of it that way. I think that the reverse-time sense is true because I've always thought that it couldn't be that everything goes in just one direction. We know Andromeda goes one way and continues to go that way until it becomes dust. But what else? What about on the level of subatomic particles? I feel something, but as Bottom the Weaver says in *A Midsummer Night's Dream*, "My eye cannot hear and my ear cannot see."

In my ballets, of course, there's an order. A dance must start and go somewhere. I can't start until I know why I have to do something. "Why this?" I say. "Why this way?" If I don't know why, I can't start a ballet. Physically, I do. But before that, I must know, I must be sure why *this* is *that* way. It's inside of me—I have to feel inside of me that this little bundle is right and that it represents something clear, with a beginning, middle, and end.

The painter Paul Klee once wrote about the idea of male sperm impregnating the egg as a way of describing the formal energy of art: "Works as form-determining sperm: the primitive male component."

I don't believe in this at all. It sounds like the painter Pavel Tchelitchew, who once described this idea in reverse. I've often said that the ballet that I represent makes the woman most important. If the woman didn't exist, there wouldn't be a ballet. It would be a man's ballet company, like Maurice Béjart's. That's a good example. There are, of course, women in his company, but it's the men—the way they look—who are most important. His *Le Sacre*, by the way, is the best anyone has done. It has a certain impact, I think, and I was amazed how almost right—physically and musically—his version was. But in my ballet, the man is a consort and the woman is the queen. Terpsichore is our muse, and little Apollo's head is covered with curls. Ballet is a feminine form, it's matriarchal. And we have to serve her.

It's strange, though—when I see your pas de deux, *especially those in* Agon, Stravinsky Violin Concerto, Duo Concertant, Pithoprakta, *I pay less attention, finally, to the fact that there's a man and a woman dancing, but rather start thinking of things like identity, personality, separation, reflections, duplications.*

That's right. Some people, though, see in these pas de deux only pure man-woman relationships: "The woman didn't have any guts, the man wasn't sexy enough." This isn't my business. And what you're saying is absolutely right. Strange things happen. In the Webern [*Episodes*] pas de deux. for example, it's like a roof . . . raindrops on a crystal roof.

In a pas de deux *like that I get a sense of two, or many, parts of myself, and I feel the dance as a kind of energy or electric field, lighting up my emotions.*

That's what it is. It exists.

These pas de deux *always seem to be distillations and compressions of the whole ballet, incorporating everything that occurs before and after it and raising it to an extraordinary level. "Ripeness is all," Shakespeare said. Moments of ripeness. Which reminds me of the beautiful* pas de deux *in the second act of* A Midsummer Night's Dream.

When Bottom the Weaver is transformed into an ass, he says: "The eye of man hath not heard, the ear of man hath not seen, man's hand is not able to taste, his tongue to conceive, nor his heart to report what my dream was." It sounds silly, but it's full of double and triple meanings. And I think that at moments like this, Shakespeare was a Sufi. It reminds me of Saint Paul's First Epistle to the Corinthians [1 Corinthians 2:9]: "Eye hath not seen, nor ears heard, neither have entered into the heart of man, the things which God hath prepared for them that love him." What Bottom says sounds as if the parts of the body were quarreling with each other. But it's really as if he were somewhere in the Real World. He loses his man's head and brain and experiences a revelation.

And then what happens? Bottom wants to recite his dream, which "hath no bottom," to the Duke after his and his friends' play-within-a-play is over, but the Duke chases them away. And the really deep and important message was in that dream.

At one point, when I was choreographing the ballet, I said to myself: "In the last act, I'll make a little entertainment and then a big vision of Mary standing on the sun, wrapped in the moon, with a crown of twelve stars on her head and a red dragon with seven heads and ten horns . . . the Revelation of St. John!"

Why didn't you do it?

Well, because then I thought that nobody would understand it, that people would think I was an idiot.

"The lunatic, the lover and the poet / Are of imagination all compact,"
Shakespeare says elsewhere in the play.

That's it. I knew it was impossible. I wished I could have done it. But instead, in the second act, I made a pretty—not silly or comic—pas de deux to a movement from an early Felix Mendelssohn string symphony [*Symphony No. 9 in* C]—something people could enjoy.

But that pas de deux *is so mysterious and calm . . . perhaps you did, in fact, give us Bottom's dream.*

It doesn't matter what it is. What's important is that it's pretty and makes you happy to see it. What it is—a flower or a girl or a dance or music—you can do what you want with it, you can talk about it, take it home with you, think about it, and say it represents this or that . . . that's fine.

So the inexplicability of dance is similar to Bottom's vision.

Absolutely.

128

You seem to choreograph these pas de deux *with a feeling of adoration and of devotion, and the result is a kind of rapturous grace.*

Naturally, I do it that way . . . but I don't tell anybody. When I was a child, I heard about a kind of enormous water lily—it was called Victoria Regina—that opens only once every hundred years. It's like wax, and everything is in there, everything lives . . . by itself, and it doesn't tell anybody anything. It goes to sleep and then comes back again. It doesn't say, "Look at me, now I'm going to wake up, I'm going to jump . . . Look, Ma, I'm dancing!" But if you happen to be around, and are ready, you'll probably see something.

It's like the time capsule with everything in it. Or like the seed that, when you plant it, becomes an enormous tree with leaves and fruit. Everything was in that little seed, and so everything can open. The tree of dance is like that. It just takes a long, long time to blossom.

(1978)

(Part 2)

Someone once suggested that painting is not a profession but actually an extension of the art of living. Do you think that might be said about dancing?

It's probably true. You see, all I am is a dancer. It started long ago, you know. At first, I didn't want to dance, but I was put in the Imperial Ballet School in Russia. I got accustomed to it and began to like it. Then I was put onstage; everyone was well dressed in blue on a beautiful stage, and I liked participating. And it became a kind of drug. I don't know myself except as a dancer. Even now, though I'm old, I still can move, or at least I can tell exactly how it feels to move, so that I can teach and stage ballets.

You can ask a horse why he's a horse, but he just lives a horse's life. It's like the story of the horse that goes to a bar: The barman serves him, and when he leaves, the people say, "But that was a horse!" And the barman just replies, "I know, and he never takes a chaser!" So it's very difficult to explain why I do what I do. I don't live any other life. It's like a chess player who has a chess player's head.

I can teach and explain to pupils what to do better, but not because there's a reason. I got experience from wonderful teachers in Russia, and then I just started working with my body and discovered that *this* was better than *that*. I improved, I could turn, I could do everything. Now I know *why* it's this way and not that way. But that's all. People like Stravinsky and Vladimir Nabokov studied Roman law or Latin or German. They knew everything, and I didn't know anything! . . . Actually, though, I do remember that, along with my training as a dancer, I had to recite speeches by Chekhov and Aleksandr Griboyedov, and only today do I remember these. When I talk to myself now, I can recite them and appreciate that beautiful language.

You once said: "Choreography is like cooking or gardening. Not like painting, because painting stays. Dancing disintegrates. Like a garden. Lots of roses come up, and in the evening they're gone. Next day, the sun comes up. It's life. I'm connected to what is part of life."

I don't care about my past. At all. I know people like La Karinska [*Barbara Karinska, former head of the NYCB costume shop*], who have everything, but who only talk about the past: "I remember how I was, I was pretty, I was this and that." I don't give a damn about the past. And the future . . . I wouldn't know what that is. To me, today is everything. Of course, I remember how to cook, I remember the dough that smelled so good. Today comes from the past, but in reality, it's all one thing to me.

The New York City Ballet is this year [1982] celebrating the 100th anniversary of Igor Stravinsky's birth with a series of old and new ballets set to his music. You and Stravinsky were always collaborators, and it is generally agreed that there was some kind of special affinity you had with his music, and he with your choreography—as if you were soul mates.

It's difficult for me to talk about soul—I just don't know. I know, however, that I liked his music, and I felt how it should be put into movement. But our affinity with each other didn't have so much to do with soul but rather with understanding and eating food! We often had large dinners with "hookers" [*Mr. Balanchine's term for a shot of vodka or whiskey*] and caviar, and finally we got so that we could say dirty things, like everybody else [*laughing*]. But when we met to talk about his music, he'd play something and say, "This should be *this* way"—slow, fast, whatever. That's always what he did, ever since I first worked with him on *The Song of the Nightingale* in 1924 or '25.

What was your first impression of Stravinsky?

First of all, I had great respect for him; he was like my father, since he was more than twenty years older than I. Stravinsky started playing the piece on the piano—*tha ta ta ta, tha tum ta tum* . . . So I choreographed all that, and one day, Diaghilev came to see what I'd been up to and exclaimed: "No, that's the wrong tempo. Much slower!" So I changed the whole thing. Stravinsky came again, we played the piece slowly, and he said, "No, it's not right!" And I said that Mr. Diaghilev had told me to change it. Stravinsky jumped. So I rearranged the choreography again. I didn't know—I was very young, I'd never even heard the piece, I'd just come from Russia! And Matisse, whom I met . . . I didn't know who the heck Matisse was. Raphael, yes, but not Matisse! I didn't speak a word of French, but he seemed like a nice man with a beard.

Anyway, I worked with Stravinsky again on *Apollo*, and then I came to America. . . . Oh, yes, I remember meeting him in Nice, and that was easy because he spoke Russian. I had lunch at his house with his priest and the priest's wife—white clergy were allowed to marry, but not black clergy. My uncle was archbishop of Tbilisi, by the way. And I remember that the first time he learned he was going to be a monk, he went down on the floor and was covered with black crepe. So, at that moment, he was dead to the world. Then the people helped him get up, and they took him away.

You yourself were an altar boy at church.

Yes, and I liked it. And at home, I even played priest with two chairs beside me. I liked the ceremony and the way the priests dressed. I was five or six then.

But you became a choreographer instead. Do you think there's a connection?

There is. Our church services were elaborate, like productions. They really were like plays with beautiful singing and choruses . . .You know, I've just finished choreographing Stravinsky's *Perséphone*, and at the end, I bring the boys onstage—the chorus is there and nobody's doing anything—and I light them from the bottom up, so you can see their faces, as if they're candles in church.

So your childhood love of church influenced your ballets.

Oh, yes.

Stravinsky was religious. Are you?

I don't tell anyone, but I go to church by myself.

Stravinsky used to say that he believed in the Devil.

Not the Devil. The devil exists, but not the Devil. The devil only stands for the negative.

Stravinsky once wrote: "What are the connections that unite and separate music and dance? In my opinion, the one does not serve the other. There must be a harmonious accord, a synthesis of ideas. Let us speak, on the contrary, of the struggle between music and choreography."

Absolutely! Struggle means to be together. It's not so easy to unite and to be together. When you're *immediately* together, it's [*clasps hands*] and you evaporate. Stravinsky's right.

You see, if you look at the dances that most dance makers or ballet masters make, the music is used as background, basically . . . like movie music or television music. Who are the ballet masters?

Unsuccessful dancers. Not all of them, but hundreds and hundreds everywhere. They open a school and teach badly because they didn't dance very well themselves. But to be a choreographer, you must be a great dancer—maybe not great, but better than the dancers who come to you. Because you have to invent and teach these people something that they don't know. Otherwise, you use the steps of somebody else.

I remember that with the GI Bill of Rights, the government would send us people they didn't want to take into the army, and they paid us to take them—we *had* to take them. Sixty boys would come to us. And there was one young man who approached me and asked how one became a choreographer. Well, I told him it was very difficult: You had to learn how to dance very well, better than all other dancers. And then, God blesses you, gives you something, helps you to refine what's there. And he replied: "I want to be a choreographer first. I don't want to learn anything. I want to sit and tell everybody what to do." Lots of boys were like that.

So it's no use even to talk about it. It's like everybody wants to write a book. I've even written a book, but I didn't really write it: I sat down and conversed with a nice writer, and he wrote something. So not everybody should be a choreographer. To take music and just use it as a background and have people dance to it . . . it's not right if it doesn't represent anything.

So struggle means respecting dance and music.

Yes, struggle means you have to be right in the way you put them together.

Then each of your works with Stravinsky is a struggle with his music?

Absolutely. After he finished the scores, he gave them to me. I would visit his home in California, and we'd talk. "What do you want to do?" he'd ask, and I'd say, "Supposing we do *Orpheus*." "How do you think *Orpheus* should be done?" "Well," I'd say, "a little bit like opera. Orpheus is alone, Eurydice is dead, he cries, an angel comes and takes him to the underworld, and then Orpheus returns to earth. But he looks back, and she disappears forever."

Well, we tried to do that. And Stravinsky said, "I'll write the end first; I sometimes have an appetite to write the end first." And that's what he did, with the two horns—it's a beautiful thing, sad, hair flowing. We couldn't have a river on the stage, but it suggests something like that.

Then he asked, "Now, how to begin?" And I said, "Eurydice is in the ground, she's already buried, Orpheus is sad and cries—friends come to visit him, and then he sings and plays." "Well," Stravinsky asked, "how long does he play?" And I started to count [*snaps fingers*], the curtain goes up. "How long would you like him to stand without dancing, without moving? A sad person stands for a while, you know." "Well," I said, "maybe at least a minute." So he wrote down "minute." "And then," I said, "his friends come in and bring something and leave." "How long?" asked Stravinsky. I calculated it by walking. "That will take about two minutes." He wrote it down.

And it went on like that. He'd say, "I want to know how long it should be." "It could be a little longer," I'd tell him, "but at least it's not forever!" And later he played one section for me, and I said, "It's a little bit too short." "Oh, oh," he'd sigh, "I already orchestrated it, and it's all finished . . . Well, I'll do something, I know what to do." "Ah, thank you!" I replied. Things like that, you see: "How long?" he'd say. "One minute and twenty seconds," I'd tell him. "Twenty-one," he'd say, and smile. And I'd agree, "Fine, twenty-one!"

Stravinsky is more complicated than I am, because the body doesn't have the possibilities that music has in terms of speed. A pianist can play fast, but the body can't go that quickly. The body's different from music. Supposing you start moving fast, like sixty-fourth notes. But you can't, you can't see it. Eyes can't really see peripherally, the movement passes and is gone. So we have to calculate movements. To hear and to see isn't the same thing. You have to have extremely fantastic eyes to see everything.

But perhaps it's better not to talk about. Horses don't talk, they just go! We want to win the race. And how? With energy, training, and dancing!

(1982)

PIERRE BOULEZ

"*I BELIEVE A CIVILIZATION THAT CONSERVES,*" the French composer and conductor Pierre Boulez once stated, "*is one that will decay because it is afraid of going forward and attributes more importance to memory than the future. The strongest civilizations are those without memory—those capable of complete forgetfulness. They are strong enough to destroy because they know they can replace what is destroyed. Today our musical civilization is not strong: it shows clear signs of withering.*"

Along with Karlheinz Stockhausen and Luciano Berio, Pierre Boulez (who was born in 1925 in Montbrison, France) is probably the most important European composer since World War II—the creator of such extraordinary works as Le Marteau Sans Maître, Pli Selon Pli, Éclat-Multiples, Rituel, and Notations for Orchestra. He has always been an audacious, recusant, and outspoken avant-garde polemicist, who once, as a student—accompanied by ten like-minded noisy compatriots—invaded a Stravinsky concert to protest that composer's "reactionary neoclassicism." An early and ardent advocate of "serialism" (a procedure in which musical parameters such as pitch, dynamics, and rhythm are predetermined by the composer), Boulez dismissed Arnold Schoenberg—the founder of the "Twelve-Tone School"—as a failed revolutionary in an infamous 1951 article entitled "Schoenberg Is Dead." And he more than once rhetorically suggested that it would be no loss if the opera houses of the world were blown up.

All this from a man who would eventually conduct astonishing and illuminating performances of Wagner's Ring cycle at Bayreuth, Pelléas and Mélisande at Covent Garden, and Wozzeck and Lulu at the Paris Opera. But Boulez has also stated: "I am not much given to settling down in positions that have already been won. You must always keep questioning yourself." And he has done so, both in his recent, partly electronic compositions such as . . . explosante/fixe . . . and Répons and as a conductor of the music of Debussy, Ravel, Stravinsky, Schoenberg, Alban Berg, Webern, Charles Ives, and Edgard Varèse. In fact, with his profound sense of rhythmic precision, timbral clarity, and structural definition, Boulez, as chief conductor of the BBC Symphony Orchestra and musical director and chief conductor of the New York Philharmonic, gradually revealed himself as our preeminent interpreter of twentieth-century music. As the first and current director of IRCAM (Institut de Recherche et de Coordination Acoustique/Musique), the subterranean musical research center of Centre Georges Pompidou, moreover, Boulez has single-handedly put Paris at the forefront of contemporary musical life, a position it has not occupied since the Middle Ages and the first part of our century. As a composer, conductor, writer, teacher, and administrator, Boulez is "beyond question"—in the opinion of the English music critic Peter Heyworth—"one of the dominant musical figures of our time."

Concerning his notion of what he considers most valuable in musical creation, Boulez once said: "I like a work to be a labyrinth—one should be able to lose oneself in it. A work whose course reveals itself completely at one hearing is flat and lacking in mystery. The mystery of a work resides precisely in its being valid at many different levels. Whether it be a book, a picture, or a piece of music, these polyvalent levels of interpretation are fundamental to my conception of the work." In today's musically fractious world—whose fruitful diversity happily compensates for its state of divisiveness—not every composer would concur with Boulez's musical credo. Yet it is, I believe, one worth heeding and admiring—both for its preceptual rigor and for the musical richnesses and resonances it allows, and even argues for, under its seemingly detached, formal, and protective aesthetic shield.

I interviewed Boulez—who speaks a characteristically rapid, precise, and lucid English—in his underground office at IRCAM in April 1984. The subject of our discussion: the state of contemporary music.

The state of contemporary music seems to me to be unusually similar to that of contemporary architecture. As the critic Ada Louise Huxtable, writing in The New York Review of Books, *recently stated: "There is no* Zeitgeist *demanding recognition and fealty, no unifying force or sentiment, no greater public good, no banner around which architects can rally. They can go in any direction and follow any muse. This is surely one of the most open, challenging, promising, and dangerous moments in the history of the building art." Don't you think that this is true of the composing art as well?*

Yes and no. When I hear about the "Return to Romanticism," for example, I recall that the real romantics of the nineteenth century were extremely adventurous. But what I see in many of today's musical currents is simply a dead solution—a kind of self-protection against what is going on right now. There are, on the contrary, some other directions which seem to me more alive—the creation of new material and new aspects of sound, for instance. There are still some composers who recognize the adventure and who aren't afraid of going somewhere without knowing exactly where they will finish. And to me this is very important. The previous generation of composers was very adventurous, but that of the neoclassical 1930s, say, reflected the end of invention. And I think that right now we are witnessing the same kind of protective phenomenon. Ada Louise Huxtable mentioned the word *Zeitgeist*, but I would use the word *angst* in this case. Because there is a kind of anxiety in trying to find a refuge in old values that are no longer relevant.

The American composer Jacob Druckman recently [1983] programmed a series of contemporary music concerts for the New York Philharmonic subtitled, "Since 1968 a New Romanticism?" (There was a question mark in there.)

The question mark was very important, too!

And Druckman classified music as being either Apollonian—logical, rational, chaste—or Dionysian—sensual, mysterious, ecstatic. But if one thinks of a composition such as your own Livre Pour Cordes— *just to take one of numerous examples—it's obvious how simplistic and artificial Druckman's classification really is.*

This distinction between Dionysian and Apollonian is one that was made long ago by Nietzsche, and it had a meaning at that time. But these terms, which are very important, are now devalued to the point where they just become simple market words. For me, the deep problem of music is not whether it is either rational or ecstatic, but whether and how it allows you to express yourself. And if you're a complicated self, you express yourself in more complicated terms. In poetry, Mallarmé was expressing himself in a much more difficult way than Verlaine—all human minds aren't built on the same model. The opposition, then, is really between that of being understood or not being understood by the mass, between being complex or not complex, between having a vocabulary which is really very easy or one that is less easy to grasp. That's much more the problem; and hiding behind false categories is, to me, simply that.

Frank Zappa, who performs rock 'n' roll for the masses, recently completed an orchestral score entitled The Perfect Stranger *that you conducted in Paris.* [Boulez has since recorded this score with the Ensemble Inter Contemporain.]

Yes, he didn't want to be imprisoned in jail, in his musical ghetto. I think this kind of exchange is important. Because in the "classical" realm, we, too, are in a kind of ghetto and suffer under the weight of all these traditions, with their constraints of spirit and ways of thinking. I think it's very good to be in touch with people who have other concepts, and maybe they'll be freed of *their* concepts by meeting us, and vice versa.

You once stated: "Nothing could be more fruitful than this perpetual modification of perspective, of hypotheses, in the face of musical reality. . . . I am not much given to settling down in positions that have already been won. You must always keep questioning yourself." So your view of music is basically a dialectical one.

Completely. But I don't give up my principles, since to me that's just laziness.

So you wouldn't follow, say, George Rochberg's lead in giving up "twelve-tone" music and composing like Gustav Mahler instead.

Definitely not. Because I think Mahler has done it much better than Mr. Rochberg will ever do.

Sometimes I think that a dyed-in-the-wool conservative composer like Samuel Barber wrote better "Romantic" music than most of today's so-called neoromanticists.

Yes, because for him that was genuine—that was his way of thinking, his way of expressing himself. All right, his music wasn't terribly advanced, but at least it was honest. And what I fear in this type of "neoromanticism" is its deep dishonesty—dishonesty with oneself and with the audience—and, ultimately, an avoidance of real musical problems.

It is a commonplace that the modernist architectural movement of the first part of the century valued the notions of "function," "purification," and "salvation through design"; distrusted historical allusion and ornament; and emphasized planes, solids, and voids, thereby eliminating reference to the outside world. Similarly, in early twentieth-century music we find the case of Anton Webern, whose works you once called the "threshold of the music of the future," practicing and preaching an aesthetic that focused on "natural musical laws"; on symmetries, analogies, and groupings; and on "the unity and utmost relatedness of all component parts." But nowadays you find an architect like Robert Venturi praising "elements which are hybrid rather than pure, compromising rather than clean, distorted rather than straightforward, ambiguous and equivocal rather than direct and clear. I am for messy vitality," Venturi states, "over obvious unity." And many of today's composers would certainly agree with these sentiments.

But I don't necessarily disagree with Venturi's point of view. Because, as a matter of fact, the excess of purity always brings an excess of impurity. You can see that very well throughout the history of architecture. Baroque architecture was very impure in this sense—and also very interesting—but this doesn't mean that Baroque architecture should simply be opposed to Romanesque architecture just because the latter is very simple and the former is overcharged. No, I find it a bit childish to put things in this black-and-white manner.

Of course, with Webern you had an excess of purity, but it was necessary in his case—maybe because of his personality, first of all—but also because the birth of the new language was very difficult, and it couldn't accept ornamentation at that moment. But to prolong this ascetic attitude out of context would be unnatural today, since now you need something that is more ornate, richer in texture, more contrasted—a kind of enrichment of this language. But it doesn't mean that because you wish to enrich the thinking of your predecessors, you therefore have to go back to *their* predecessors—that because you don't want the Mies van der Rohe approach you have to return to the nineteenth century. It seems really stupid to me that in order to avoid a present danger, you adopt the dangers of the previous generation. In this way, you don't go forward and rethink a situation. And it doesn't work. This was like Stravinsky in the twenties saying: "I want to be 'classical,' so I will imitate the style of Bach." That was a completely useless reaction. And I can already see now that our "new" postmodernist buildings are as dead . . . even deader than the ones they wanted to replace.

As Ada Louise Huxtable has asked: "How many false columns and gables, how many cut-out oculi *and post-Palladian screens, how many deco touches and diagonal plans, how much ad hoc jumble does it take to add up to a predictable postmodernist cliché?"*

Exactly. I call that the aesthetical supermarket. You can have fruits from China, vegetables from Brazil, and think you're having a really good meal. But it's nothing to do with art.

That doesn't sound like such a bad meal to me!

It all depends on what you mix!

What about the important and often fruitful influence of Asiatic and early Western musical ideas, techniques, and textures on works as different as, say, Steve Reich's Tehillim *and your own* Éclat—*not to forget the obvious and earlier example of Debussy?*

Definitely, but you're always influenced by something; and when you discover a new culture you're going to be affected by it. But it's one thing to grasp the exterior part and quite another to understand the spirit of that influence. Even Debussy spoke of Japanese theater as if there were nothing complicated about it— he thought you just needed a couple of noises and voices shouting somewhere and you could then create the greatest tragedy in the world! But he didn't realize that Japanese theater was absolutely ritualistic and governed by more laws than anything we have in the West.

A great deal of misunderstanding occurs when you approach another civilization because, looking at it from outside, you miss or misspell the laws. But I find that these misunderstandings are often very fruitful, since what you see in another culture is what you want that other culture to reveal about what you *yourself* are doing and searching for. And then suddenly, you find something in common and you take from this culture what you most need. When you're creative, you look at everything in life as a predator. Even the most trivial things can strike you as exactly the thing you were waiting for just at that moment. Newton's apple, for example, didn't make him think of his computations. But he was thinking of them, and then this trivial occurrence led him in the right direction. And I think that we all are waiting for Newton's apple to fall on our heads!

Debussy once wrote: "Discipline must be sought in freedom and not within the formulas of an outworn philosophy." And many people have criticized the so-called "serial" compositions of the fifties and sixties for not heeding Debussy's advice and trying rather to find freedom in discipline.

I think that's too simple a distinction. Because the procedures of a composer are very closely related to the period in which he's living. Now, although Debussy's vocabulary was new, the elements—the perfect triads, etc.—were not. Debussy was free with regard to the network of musical relationships, but he was not with regard to the construction of the objects themselves. So for him the problem was simply to free the objects of the kind of constraints they'd previously been bound by.

Now, in our time, especially in the fifties, you had a new vocabulary and you didn't want any familiar musical objects to be there, so you had to construct them. And then you understood that you couldn't build objects without laws. Debussy built his chords based on "known" laws—they were used constantly, so he didn't have to think about them. But in the fifties you had to think about the methods of building these objects, so therefore the situation wasn't at all the same. Debussy's world was coherent, and he brought fantasy to it; while our world was incoherent, and we had to bring coherence to it . . . but without losing fantasy. And this was a problem that wasn't easy to solve. Because if you were too much engulfed in the methodology, then you lost complete spontaneity. The great composers throughout history have always tried to find a balance between spontaneity and strength of ideas. The stronger they were and the kinds of constraints they created for themselves enabled them to bring their imaginations into a world they would never have reached otherwise.

Philip Glass once stated that the compositions written in the fifties by you, Stockhausen, and Henri Pousseur, among others, seemed "creepy" both to him and to many of his generation.

Yes, but fights between generations are natural because you have always to find yourself, your own personality. It happens in families, it happens in life generally, so why not in the arts?

But polemics aside—which may be amusing but not finally terribly interesting—I think simply that suddenly there was a reaction against what was the "action" before. I wonder what it will be like in twenty years. Because in 1944 and 1945, for example, all the people of the Paris school—Francis Poulenc, Georges Auric, and so on—were saying that Schoenberg was out of fashion and old hat. And they were writing music of the third category— entertainment music, light music—and it had an audience. But as a matter of fact, what remains in history—entertainment music or music that is more demanding and interesting because it brings out more of the human experience? If you want a kind of supermarket aesthetic, okay, do that, nobody will be against it, but everybody will eventually forget it because each generation will create its own supermarket music—like produce that after eight days is rotten and you can't eat it anymore and have to toss it away. And, therefore, I'm always astonished that composers speak in terms of quantity, i.e., "Music is valid if it has more than two thousand people listening to it." For me, that's no criterion of validity. And when composers say that they've found a direct approach to an audience, what is that really? The "direct approach" is usually an experience that the audience has already had but with a new coat of paint on it, so to speak—that's all. And that's not a new experience. I find that very superficial and an avoidance of the real problems and symptomatic of a kind of amnesia that has forgotten about the catastrophes of previous years—the "stereophonic" year, the "chance" year, the "formless" year, the "novel tone colors" year. Even the works of a movement like neoclassicism are hardly performed anymore. So I'm afraid that some of the composers who are the excitement of today will not be the excitement of tomorrow; their works are, as they say in German, *Plakate*—advertising posters.

To be more specific, you have said that today's popular minimalist/repetitive composers make pieces in which the musical material "moves without moving." But, in fact, many of these compositions have an immediate and moving effect on its audience.

I don't want to be derogatory, but I think that that type of music appeals to an extremely primitive perception, and it reduces the elements of music to one single component—periodicity. You have a chord changing slowly, and the rest of the components are either completely ignored or reduced to just a minimum of minimums. And people suddenly say, "Ah, my God! I understand modern music!" But it's not modern whatsoever. It's simply like a detail of a painting that's been enlarged many times, and there's no substance to it whatsoever. If an audience wants to get high with this kind of music rather than with another product, that's okay with me. But I don't consider that a very high level of enjoyment.

Now, you can be obsessive in music without being simplistic. In Stravinsky, for instance, you have a lot of repetitive patterns—I'm thinking particularly of *Les Noces*—but they are manipulated in much more interesting ways. The music is rather reduced in its components, but it has a dialectic and a kind of evolution that makes things live. On the contrary, when you've heard two minutes of one of these recent minimal works, you know very well where it goes. And I find that, for me, if there's no surprise, then I'm no longer interested in it. Similarly, when you see light sculptures based on periodicity and are told that you won't have a similar periodicity for another two hundred years, well, who's interested in looking at that? That's just being passive. To me it's like cows in front of a train. And there are people who listen to music in this way.

It's frequently been said about totally serialized compositions, though, that if every musical event is different, then everything becomes and sounds the same.

I dealt with this problem myself, long ago—in 1955, in fact. And certainly, if you're constantly varying the parameters of composition, nobody can distinguish anything. The French philosopher Gilles Deleuze has said that perception is based on repetition and difference. And that's why I think it's necessary to have a certain form of repetition, because perception requires articulation fields to let you know where you are. And you can know where you are only when you can recognize similarities. But some things should only *seem* similar, because if they're too much alike then they'll repeat themselves, and the fourth time will be exactly the same as the third, and the third like the second. And if you can foresee this, the work is dead. Immediately. Because as soon as you can predict the combinations, it's superfluous for the composer to proceed with them. So why do it? For me what's interesting is to present material that is evolving and then, from time to time, to bring back the model . . . but not in exactly the same way. So that a listener has to wonder, "Do I recognize it? Don't I recognize it? I'm not sure anymore. But I know that it has something to do with it." And in *this* sense I like ambiguity—to get back to Robert Venturi's comment. But the kind of ambiguity that's simply a matter of games and style doesn't interest me at all.

This, for me, is the difference between, for instance, the late Picasso and, say, Jackson Pollack. You look at one of Picasso's later paintings for two minutes, and you know very well how it's been done, you've understood everything. But if you observe the best works of Pollack, you're puzzled and you try to see and explore his labyrinth; and that makes the work interesting and sustains your attention. Of course, you can be lost at first, but after a kind of acquaintance with the painting, you've lived with it and it changes. But the simplistic works, in their relationships with you, don't change. And that's their death.

Another example in this respect is Kafka, because he also constructs a kind of labyrinth where the logic is perfect, but it leads you into areas that are completely unexpected, such that you think you're going one way and then you wind up in the other direction. And I've found that when you're composing a work, it's exactly the same—you don't want to know at the onset where you'll be at the end of the score. You have a vague idea, of course, but it's not a matter of going in a straight line, you have all kinds of divigations.

You've spoken about the legendary Chinese landscape painter who disappeared into his canvas. And in many of your works, you seem to create moments of almost Oriental transparency and particularity that are then counterbalanced by moments of chaos—suggesting a movement from hyperconsciousness to the realm of the unconscious.

I myself like this kind of approach, so it's reflected in what I'm doing. And since this is what I like in painting and literature, I also want to express it in music, because it's certainly my personality—to be crystal clear in the sense that sometimes the crystal reflects yourself and other times you can see through the material. So the work suggests a hiding and opening at the same time. And what I want most to create is a kind of deceiving transparency, as if you are looking in very transparent water and can't make an estimation of the depths.

And when you stir things up . . .

That's when you begin to know.

Schoenberg once asserted: "Either what we do is music or what the French do is music. But both cannot be music." If one takes a wider view of the history of modern music, however, it seems clear that a lot of the sectarianism and partisanship reflected in Schoenberg's remark overlooks some important similarities between seemingly "antithetical" compositions such as Schoenberg's Farben *and Olivier Messiaen's* Chronochromie, *Debussy's* Les Parfums de la Nuit *and Berg's* Three Pieces for Orchestra, *Varèse's* Ionization *and Elliott Carter's* Double Concerto, *and even certain works by Webern and Morton Feldman.*

I find that composers tend to concentrate their attention on very specific aspects of music. But, of course, if they're very gifted, they can't neglect the other aspects; and even if these aspects aren't consciously always on their minds, composers still work unconsciously with them. We can say that a composer has a very solid center and then a kind of diffuse surrounding, and he's responsible for the center but less directly responsible for the test. That's the influence of the outside world and of other composers.

Even if they have their own territory really well guarded, all composers have buffer zones. And some of the musical aspects of these zones do relate in surprising ways to the works of other composers, such that there are similarities that even the composers themselves might be surprised by.

I've even felt a connection between the rhythmic aspects of the music of Schoenberg and Paul Hindemith, though it would undoubtedly have surprised and shocked both of them to hear that said.

Definitely. *Moses and Aaron* is Hindemith's greatest opera—an opera that Hindemith might have dreamt of writing but was never able to do . . . I'm sure of that. But don't forget the period of the thirties was neoclassicist, and neoclassicism's vocabulary implied certain kinds of rhythmical patterns, distribution of voices, and so on. And, in this case, Schoenberg was more refined and more effective than Hindemith, since the latter worked on a more primitive level. But I'm sure that Schoenberg wrote the best works of Hindemith!

Referring to the music of Charles Ives, John Cage once asked: "Does it emerge? Or do we enter in?" And Cage suggested that the former was most often the case, stating: "The difference is this: Everybody hears the same thing if it emerges. Everybody hears what he alone hears if he enters in." But if one thinks of supposedly "emerging" compositions like Elliot Carter's string quartets or your own Pli Selon Pli, *it's obvious that each listener will hear and discover quite different things in such richly layered works.*

Proust once said—and of course he phrased it more brilliantly than I can—that when you read a book, you're discovering yourself, and what you discover there is what you need. The only thing that a writer can be glad of, Proust added, is that his work can help somebody else to live his own life. And I agree with this completely.

(1984)

STEVE REICH

ALONG WITH TERRY RILEY AND PHILIP GLASS, Steve Reich and John Adams are two of the most extraordinary of the so-called "repetitive" or "minimalist" composers of the past thirty years. During this period, they have developed and extended their musical boundaries into full-scale masterpieces such as The Desert Music *(Reich) and* Harmonielehre *(Adams). The following two interviews focus on these two compositions.*

All great events, William Blake once stated, start with the pulsation of an artery. It's almost as if one could say: "In the beginning was the Pulse." And in the beginning of The Desert Music, *one immediately enters the realm of pulsation.*

Purely. And without anything else added or subtracted. The opening of the piece is a kind of chorale, only instead of individual chords sounding for a given length of held notes, they're pulsed; instead of a steady tone you get rapid eighth notes repeating over and over again, which sets up a kind of rhythmic energy that you'd never get if the notes were sustained. And that energy is maintained in different ways by the mallet instruments throughout the work. *The Desert Music* begins with this pulsation in order to set up the feeling, structure, and harmony of the entire piece.

The Desert Music *takes its title from a volume of poems by William Carlos Williams, from which you've selected most of the texts for your piece. In fact, however, the Williams poems you've chosen aren't about the desert at all. I was wondering whether the idea of the desert—that terrain that confronts a traveler only with himself and whose silence makes him listen only to the innerness of his being—has anything to do with the title and atmosphere of your piece.*

There were a number of things that went through my mind as I worked on the composition and as the title kept working on me. And they were related to very particular deserts. One of them was the Sinai. When the Jews entered the Sinai 3,500 years ago in their exodus from Egypt, they were going into a land where life was insupportable, where they should have died, and the only thing that kept them alive was divine intervention. It is also important to remember that the divine revelation wasn't given in the land of Israel, but in the *desert*, in a land belonging to no one. Later, in the New Testament, Jesus goes to the desert to confront his visions, to overcome his temptations, to struggle with the devil, to fight madness—and you find this idea in the stories of Paul Bowles in our time. The desert is associated with hallucinations and insanity. It threatens one's normal thinking.

In this regard, I remember taking many trips years ago to and from California, and traveling through the Mojave. Sometimes I'd begin to feel very strange there because I'd get so dehydrated, I'd have to drink enormous amounts of fluids just to keep going and keep my mind functioning normally.

Finally, there is another desert that is central to *The Desert Music*: White Sands and Alamagordo in New Mexico, where weapons of the most intense and sophisticated sort are constantly being developed and tested. Hidden away from the eyes of the rest of the world are these infernal machines that could lead to the destruction of the planet—and it is to this possibility that the words of William Carlos Williams, which I set in the third movement, refer ("Man has survived hitherto because he was too ignorant to know how to realize his wishes. Now that he can realize them, he must either change them or perish."). So it was these images that particularly struck me, though they seem to be ingrained in people's thinking generally when the idea of the desert comes to mind.

How did these associations connect to the music?

Well, there's no portrayal of the desert in my piece as there is in, say, the *Grand Canyon Suite*—no picturesque evocation of sand dunes! I don't think there's any direct correlation between the title and the music, except as regards the setting of the text.

Now that I think of it, though, the last movement has a very long opening orchestral section. And when I first played a taped version of that section to someone, I remember turning to him and saying, "Out on the plain, running like hell." And that's the image—it's as if you're in the desert and you're running as fast as you can. There are these very large clouds of harmony that seem to tilt the entire rhythmic structure in different directions until rehearsal number 318 of the score, when, finally, after about forty minutes, we return to the tonal center of the piece. For me, this is an extremely emotional moment. And the chorus enters and sings, "Inseparable from the fire / its light / takes precedence over it. / Who most shall advance the light— / call it what you may!" That last line is just thrown out, and then you return to the pulse—the pulsation we talked about in the beginning. So, yes, in a sense, at least for me, there is a desert in this piece; and it's in the opening of the last movement, where there are no words at all.

When we're first introduced to the chorus in the first section of The Desert Music, *we hear singing but no words.*

Right. The chorus begins wordlessly. You know, a voice can sing words—but does one hear the voice or the words? At certain points in *The Desert Music* there's no more to be said—there are things that can only be said musically. So the voices continue, without words, as part of the orchestra. The text emerges out of a completely nonverbal, totally abstract sound into something that says, "Begin, my friend . . ." Maybe it's fitting that the piece begins *and* ends with a totally abstract use of the voice, going into a text and then out of it again.

In your previous work for voices and instruments, Tehillim, *you set a psalm from the Bible that reads: "The heavens declare the glory of God, / the sky tells of His handiwork. / Day to day pours forth speech, / night to night reveals knowledge. / Without speech and without words, / nevertheless their voice is heard."*

Yes, that's from the Nineteenth Psalm. The "voice" here refers to the voice of the sun and moon and stars. And what is happening is that the patriarch Abraham is looking up at the sky and thinks, "There's an intelligence behind all of this"—he hears the voice of the perceivable universe. But instead of saying, "Let's worship the sun or moon or stars," Abraham realizes that he's the recipient of a wordless communication, he has an insight into things that is basically nonverbal.

All pieces with texts—operas, cantatas, whatever—have, in my opinion, to work first simply as pieces of music that one listens to with eyes closed, without understanding a word. Otherwise, they're not musically successful, they're dead "settings." To the composer, the text may be a kind of a good, as the Williams poems were to me. *The Desert Music* grew out of the text; I picked out passages by Williams, organized them into a shape, and then the music started coming. So the words were the motor or the driving force, but the listener doesn't have to know that. He or she merely has to listen and hopefully, if moved, will follow the text as well.

"I am wide / awake. The mind / is listening" *is one of the passages by* Williams *that you've set in* The Desert Music.

You know, some critics of my earlier pieces thought I was intending to create some kind of "hypnotic" or "trance" music. And I always thought, "No, no, no, no, I want you to be wide awake and hear details you've never heard before!" People listen to things any way they wish, of course, and I don't have anything to say about it, even if I *have* written the pieces. But I actually prefer the music to be heard by somebody who's totally wide awake, hearing more than he or she usually does, rather than by someone who's just spaced out and receiving a lot of ephemeral impressions.

This suggests that Buddhist idea of the mind that attends.

One has to be in relative stillness to hear things in detail. All meditative practices are based on some sort of silence—inner and outer. Williams says: "We half close / our eyes"—you're closing your eyes to hear more intently. And Williams continues: "We do not / hear it through our eyes. / It is not / a flute note either, it is the relation / of a flute note to a drum." And then, suddenly, the eyes are open, "I am wide / awake." He sort of reaches out and grabs you: "The mind / is listening." At which point the chorus sings, "dee-dee-dee-dee-dee-dee ..." It goes into something completely nonverbal, it leaves language behind.

It becomes pulsation again.

Pulsation and vocalese, pure sound. "I am wide / awake. The mind / is listening." And off you go into pulsation. Words come to an end, and musical communication takes over.

Two of the things that contribute to musical communication in The Desert Music *are the amazing ways you use and develop a kind of rhythmic ambiguity that occurs in a good deal of African music, as well as a kind of simultaneous elaboration of simple musical materials at different speeds—something that is at the heart of Balinese music.*

Listening to *umm*-pah-pah, *umm*-pah-pah over and over again is intolerable and, indeed, a mistake. So if you want to write music that is repetitive in any literal sense, you have to work to keep a lightness and constant ambiguity with regard to where the stresses and where the beginnings and endings are. Very often, I'll find myself working in twelve-beat phrases, which can divide up in very different ways; and that ambiguity as to whether you're in duple or triple time is, in fact, the rhythmic lifeblood of much of my music. In this way, one's listening mind can shift back and forth within the musical fabric, because the fabric *encourages* that. But if you don't build in that flexibility of perspective, then you wind up with something extremely flat-footed and boring.

As far as your second point about combining different musical speeds: Years ago, someone said rather testily to me, "Don't you ever write only *slow* music?" Actually, it was a good question. What I asked that person in response was: "In my *Octet*, are you going to concentrate on listening to the pianos—that's the rhythm section of fast eighth notes that never let up—or to the strings, which are playing much more spaciously?" Sustaining instruments like strings or the electric organ often move at a very slow rate of change in my pieces, while chattering in their midst is a thriving anthill—the metropolis is buzzing, but the clouds overhead are passing calmly over a field. And that gives the listener the possibility of not necessarily listening just to one thing or the other; it allows them to realize that different things are happening *at the same time*. What I'm trying to do is to present a slow movement and a fast movement simultaneously in such a way that they make music together.

It's often been pointed out that a good deal of contemporary painting can be seen as on enlarging-upon of certain particularized textured and ornamental aspects of the works of the old masters. This also seems to be true of your music as well.

Certain musical passages that suggest the kind of music I write have existed in the Western musical tradition for some time. The C major Prelude that begins Book I of *The Well-Tempered Clavier*, for example, is all sequences—it's all the same rhythm over and over, but the notes keep changing. Another example is the Prelude to *Das Rheingold*, where a long E-flat major chord is sustained from the very beginning for several minutes with very small, slow changes. But these passages are done *en passant*, as special cases within a basically different musical language. In Bach's case he is beginning a series of keyboard preludes and fugues in all the twenty-four major and minor keys. He begins in C, the basic key, with a basic prelude written in imitation of lute playing. He then goes on to more complex pieces in other keys. In Wagner's case he sets up the held E-flat tonality as a kind of musical metaphor for the rolling river with rising mists. Some annotators speak of this held E-flat as Wagner's "Nature *Leitmotiv*." In any case, as we all know, Wagner, is basically about extreme chromaticism that eventually led to Schoenberg. It's only now that we've come to focus on this kind of repeating melodic pattern or long-held tonality as the center of compositional interest—as the main dish, so to speak. And this has given birth to a lot of new music.

Ultimately, it seems to me that both the music and the text of The Desert Music *are really about hearing and seeing, sound and light.*

I once had a vision where light became a metaphor for harmony, for tonality. You know, of course, that the notes on the piano keyboard aren't all there are—there's a continuity of vibration from the lowest to the highest sounds we can hear. Slowly, over more than a thousand years, out of this complete continuity of vibration from low to high, musicians in the West have evolved the selection and ordering of notes we find on the keyboard and in all our other instruments. These notes, and the harmonic system we have used to order them, struck me as a light radiating out of the dark infinitude of available vibrations. And when listening in particular to two pieces—Handel's *Water Music* and Stravinsky's *The Rake's Progress*—I used to get a vision of a kind of barge of light, floating down a river in very dark surroundings, in complete darkness.

You see, I understand that human conventions are, in a sense, the *light*—a kind of conveyance in which we ride, in which we live, and without which we die. And the human construct that we call our *music* is merely a convention—something we've all evolved together, and which rests on no final or ultimate laws. And it sails, in my mind, like a ship of light down an endlessly dark corridor, preserving itself as long as it can. And no more and no less.

(1985)

JOHN ADAMS

YOU ONCE STATED that your 1981 composition Harmonium *"began with a simple, totally formed mental image: that of a single tone emerging out of a vast, empty space." But* Harmonielehre *begins in quite a different way—with a series of almost exorcistic-sounding, pounding chords that speed up in rhythmic diminution, suggesting an unsettling and powerful sense of a breaking down of barriers.*

Those seven slamming E-minor triadic chords that open the work are almost like a grinding of gears, and I think that the feeling of this beginning *is* very violent and shocking. And, yes, the chords *are*, in a sense, exorcistic.

You see, *Harmonielehre* was created after a terribly frustrating fallow period, during which I composed every day for a year, and nothing worthwhile came out of it. And I think that what was going on inside of me was a multifaceted crisis with regard to understanding myself as an artist and a human being, and to my relationship to my own music and to contemporary music in general.

And I can remember the day that I just sat down at the piano and hit those opening chords. I'd just had a dream the night before in which I saw myself driving across the San Francisco Bay Bridge, and, looking out, I saw a huge tanker in the bay. It was an image of immense power and gravity and mass. And while I was observing this tanker, it suddenly took off like a rocket ship with an enormous force of levitation. And as it rose, I could see this beautiful brownish-orange oxide on the bottom part of the hull. Now, when I woke up the next morning, the image of these slamming chords came to me, and the piece was off like an explosion. After a year of no progress at all, *Harmonielehre* now came very quickly; and I wrote this forty-minute work in about three months.

It's interesting that these opening chords suggest the ending of a piece as much as they do the beginning of one.

The first movement of *Harmonielehre*, which lasts about seventeen minutes, is really an architectonically monolithic entity—pardon me for that!—and it concludes with the same chords and the same disposition with which it began. But I didn't predetermine that. I'm not the kind of composer who prescribes or previsages the entire structure of a piece in advance. I like to feel that the composition is a voyage of discovery—on a personal, psychological, spiritual, as well as on a technical level. So, in a certain sense, I *feel* the structure as I'm creating it—as if an architect were building on an empty site without a blueprint . . . a rather terrifying notion for the plastic arts, but an exciting one if you're working in sound.

Hindemith once said that a musical work should appear to the composer like an apparition in its completed form and that the act of composition is simply a matter of filling it all in. But to me, it's just the opposite. I find composing to be a journey through the underworld. And the reason I have heroic endings in my pieces—something that is terribly anachronistic in 1985!—is because I'm totally amazed to have emerged from the tunnel out into the light. The act of composing is the *creation* of the light for me—it really is like a biblical trial.

The second movement of Harmonielehre *is, apparently, about such a trial. The movement is titled "The Anfortas Wound," which refers to the medieval grail-questing King Anfortas. And you've stated that Anfortas was wounded "due to pride, to hubris, and the wound caused impotence. 'The Anfortas Wound' is a piece about sickness and infirmity, both physical and spiritual."*

Wagner describes the wound Anfortas received in battle as being in his side; but in the original French version of the story, it's in his testicles. So, to me, it's a *creativity* wound—of re-creation, of pro-creation. Now, there are two climaxes in this movement, and the second of them is almost psychotic—there's a scream in it, after which nothing seems to have been achieved. And, in a sense, the entire movement itself is a kind of musical scenario of the fallow year I spent, unable to create. But when I completed this movement, I felt I'd somehow confronted my darker side, and the darker side of life, too.

To me, the last two movements of *Harmonielehre* are a pair— "The Anfortas Wound" exists under a bad sign, it has to do with an existence that is without grace. And then in the third movement, grace appears for no reason at all . . . that's just the way grace is, the unmerited bestowal of blessing on man.

So the light at the end of the tunnel appears in this third movement, entitled "Meister Eckhardt and Quackie," which refers to the great medieval theologian and to your sobriquet for your daughter, Emily.

The first generating image for *Harmonielehre* was that dream of the tanker taking off, and the second was that of Meister Eckhardt floating through the firmament with a baby on his shoulder, as she whispers the secret of grace into his ear. And the first half of this third movement is an evocation of this latter image.

With regard to the dreams and images you've talked about, I'm reminded of the Virgilian notion of mythical characters descending to and reemerging from the Elysian Fields either through the gate of horn (the passageway of true and prophetic dreams) or the gate of ivory (that of false dreams). And I'm struck by the fact that you often talk about your compositions in terms of "gates" and "slews" and "levels."

A lot of this has to do with my relationship to keys. I'm a tonal composer. And, in my case, a key or mode has a certain psychological and emotional feel to it. It's actually the *relationship* of one key to another—up a major or a minor third, for example—and the immense emotional power that's brought about by a modulation that interest me. So I've used the term "gates"—a term that comes from electronic music to designate a module that passes a certain amount of current on a given command. In my compositions, however, a "gate" is an abrupt transition point in either a mode or a key. And since my music often progresses over long periods in a single key, these moments of transition are very powerful; and I work hard to achieve that sense of emotional change when a modulation occurs. There are certain composers of the past who mean a great deal to me because of their ability to do that so well—Beethoven, of course, and Sibelius in his Fifth and Seventh Symphonies, for example. So there is a sense of using key as a structural and psychological tool in building the structures of my works.

I remember once, while listening to the slow movement of Beethoven's Op. 135 string quartet, I found myself visualizing the amazing modulations in that piece as boats entering and rising to higher levels in canal locks.

Certainly. At the end of *Harmonielehre*, in fact, there's an extended passage in one key; and at that point a tremendous struggle for keys takes place in order to see which one is going to come out the victor. Now, in a more traditionally worked-out tonal piece, there would be a modulatory sequence that would present the outcome in a rather dialectical way. But in this case, I simply placed the keys together, as if in a mixer, and let them battle it out. And finally, E-flat won out through its strength, and it feels like a kind of epiphany. But I must say that in *Harmonielehre*, there is somewhat of a breakdown of these long periods of tonal homogeneity, since I was trying to make my harmonic language more psychologically ambivalent; and in that sense I think I've moved very far away from the standard minimalist canon. There are repetitive elements in the actual interior workings of the piece, but the larger architectural level is much different.

I've listened to Harmonielehre *many times, and each time I experience very different aspects of the music—as if, in a Heisenbergian sense, my position vis-à-vis the piece were continually changing, and so, therefore, my perceptions of it.*

I think that when my compositions are good, that is exactly the effect I intend. This is certainly true in Sibelius, by the way. Often, when I listen to his greatest symphonies, I find that I don't know where I am . . . and that's a nice feeling.

Some people might find it extremely anxiety-producing!

Of course! I'd say that most German composers would be horribly threatened by that, imagining it to be indicative of sloppy musical habits.

I'm reminded of the term Durchführung—to *lead through, to develop.*

Right, it has the word *Führer* in it! Now, I don't develop my material, I don't work with identifiable motifs, but rather with a forward motion that's colored by its harmonic atmosphere; and I use large, powerful blocks . . . perhaps I should say "images," since I think that my music is more pictorial or cinematographic than it is developmental.

Many listeners of Harmonielehre *may occasionally imagine hearing passages that sound like Berg or Sibelius or Debussy or Mahler or Ives. But it's my sense that in fact your harmonic and melodic materials do not "quote" so much as they light up the subconscious history of twentieth-century music ... if that makes any sense to you.*

My music *does* resonate more brightly or candidly with the musical past, probably because I've never truly felt like a vanguard personality. My attitude toward creation is one of incorporating everything I've learned and experienced of the past in my compositions, and I've never received any powerful creative energy from the idea of turning my back on the past. Many artists *have* to do that—it's like the primal scene with the father that Norman O. Brown talks about in *Love's Body*, where the act of patricide is one of self-survival. But I've never found that a necessity.

I like to think of the example of the architect Philip Johnson, especially in his most recent work. Someone like Johnson went to the farthest limits of the fertile territory of modernism with regard to stripping elements down to their most primal configurations, and then went on to develop a new language that resonates with the past—the A.T. and T. building in New York City is an example of sensuousness, reminiscence, and sentiment, but it also feels like a part of our contemporary experience.

Now, I'm not saying that my music has split pedestals and curlicues, but there is a sense of the past in it. What comes through, however, is not, say, "Mahler," but rather John Adams's personal, private experience of Mahler . . . or whomever. And I find that the best art is that way. Certainly, no one takes James Joyce or Thomas Mann or William Gaddis to task for their filtering through of the past.

The opening of Harmonielehre's *third movement seems to exemplify, in brief, the resonant, multitiered aspects of the entire work. What I hear, first of all, is a texture made up of high-pitched string harmonics and bowed crotales, a sustained string melody and a repeated triadic pattern played by piano, harp, and piccolos. Then I hear a sustained, long-breathed melodic string line, supernal glissandi, arpeggiated flute and piccolo undulations, a gamelan-type percussion, and a kind of ground bass and brass line.*

Yes, it's a seven-voice counterpoint, and it's contrapuntally very rich.

What all of it reminds me of is the way Charles Ives used polytonality, polyrhythms, and polytextures to suggest interdimensional worlds. And in this section of Harmonielehre, *I'm especially struck by the "transcendental" quality both of this piece and of your work in general.*

I have to say that my relation to Ives is very ambivalent. I come from New England and grew up in a small town in New Hampshire where I played clarinet in a local band with my father—how can you be more Ivesian than that? And Ives *was* a heroic figure for me when I was young. I think that the greatest thing about American music is its ability to combine the vulgar/demotic with the highest level of spiritual speculation. And Ives is the primary example of the composer who brought these elements together.

But, today, what I don't like about Ives is his unwillingness to yield to the sensual in his music. He had a tremendous desire to negate his own anima. At moments of real tenderness in his works, he will somehow negate them; and when he doesn't, it's often when the music has some specific religious aspect associated with it. But I find this rigidity in Schoenberg's music after *Gurre-Lieder*, too. I don't know what it is—perhaps it's the birth of modernism.

Anyway, I feel it's presumptuous to think of myself in comparison to Ives, because whatever his problematic relationship with his feminine side, there's such a breadth of human experience in his music that I'd be very grateful if I could come close to reflecting even a half of that experience. As I've said many times, I find so much of contemporary art afraid to deal with these transcendental issues. And when people attack my work and say to me, "Oh, you're just writing tonal music," I have to respond, "Well, do you understand how hard it is to write tonal music in 1985?" It's the hardest thing there is because it's already been done. And to do something fresh and meaningful and possibly "transcendental" in this tonal realm is unbelievably difficult.

(1985)

JONATHAN DEMME
On *Konbit: Burning Rhythms of Haiti*

THE FILMMAKER JONATHAN DEMME *exemplifies what William Blake called "Enthusiastic Admiration." In movies like Crazy Mama, Melvin and Howard, Something Wild, and Married to the Mob, he explores, with unflagging and delighted interest an American society and landscape gone both awry and to seed, with its Sleep-in-a-Wigwam motels, Hello Gorgeous beauty parlors, While-U-Wait marriage chapels, kitsch souvenir shops, and 7-Elevens galore. And Demme films this world with a comic astonishment and a stylistic grace that take one back to the works of Preston Sturges, Raoul Walsh, and Sam Fuller.*

Not since Kenneth Anger's Scorpio Rising (1965), moreover— a joyously subversive little film about the Hell's Angels set to rock songs of the early 1960s—has there been a director who has used music in his movies in such an original and exuberant manner. Aside from Stop Making Sense—perhaps the best concert film of a band (Talking Heads) ever made—Demme has consistently conceived of music as an equal partner to his images. Something Wild, for instance, begins with David Byrne singing his song "Loco de Amor" accompanied by salsa queen Celia Cruz; features more than fifty songs on the soundtrack and an on-screen concert appearance by the Feelies; and ends with reggae princess Sister Carol performing her version of "Wild Thing"—the musical/thematic motif of Demme's drama.

Demme is also one of the few masters of the music video, filming his subjects in a variety of styles and moods appropriate to their songs—from the simple, long shots of New Order's musicians' hands, eyes, and instruments ("The Perfect Kiss") to the rapid cutting of UB40 and Chrissie Hynde rehearsing "I Got You, Babe"—in both cases conveying the effect of an entire movie in microcosm.

Demme's most recent enthusiasm—Haitian music—is celebrated in his one-hour 1987 television documentary, Haiti Dreams of Democracy (co-directed with Jo Menell) and in his latest video, "Konbit," featuring an American-Haitian collaboration between the Neville Brothers and Les Frères Parents. This five-minute film looks as if Eisenstein, the late Brazilian cinema nuovo director Glauber Rocha, Fellini, and, of course, Jonathan Demme himself had all come together to create a whirling, passionate, agitprop Creole anthem, where English titles blazon forth the meaning and urgency of its message: that Haitians—and people everywhere—should work side by side to overcome brutality, injustice, and inequality.

"Konbit"—a Haitian word that suggests such a collaborative effort—is the title track of a 1989 album, Konbit: Burning Rhythms of Haiti, conceived by Jonathan Demme with help from a number of his colleagues and Haitian musician friends. Consisting of *twelve songs—social in their concerns and exhilaratingly sociable in their African-influenced dance rhythms—the album brings a heretofore mostly unknown but inspiring music to the awareness of American listeners.*

On the eve of the release of Konbit *I discussed the conception of the album with Demme in his New York City film production office, whose walls are appropriately filled with scores of Haitian paintings depicting wedding and biblical scenes, angels and spirits, city streets and farms, and peasants and villagers rebelling against government troops. At the topmost part of one of the walls hangs a painted wooden plaque, originally installed on a tap-tap (one of Haiti's jazzily colored buses), displaying two black hands—one shaking the other—in a gesture of true* konbit. *It is a gesture that also exemplifies Jonathan Demme's attitude and approach to making movies, as well as to the creation of this path-breaking album.*

Why Haiti?

On my very first trip there, over Christmas of 1986, I fell in love with the people, and the spirit of the people—they're going through an extraordinary struggle down there and they're not giving up. I also fell in love with Haitian culture. Haiti has enriched my life. I've gone back many times since that first trip.

Someone I know who also loves Haiti told me that because of the island's incredible poverty, all that really exists there are the basics: nature, the spirits, and the companionship of fellow human beings.

That's a great distillation of how I feel about it, too. During my first week in Haiti, I remember having the thought: "Haiti is the center of the universe." What I meant was that the problems overwhelming the island aren't really unique to Haiti. Widespread poverty, unemployment, disease, violence, pollution, environmental crisis: these are global problems. But in Haiti the courage, stamina, and imagination with which they're being dealt with should set an example for everyone.

In America we throw old or broken chairs in the trash, whereas Haitians would either fix them up and try to sell them, or they would at least break them up and use them as firewood to boil the water a child has walked four or five hours to bring home from a river in order to cook the small portion of rice they might have been lucky enough to have gotten ahold of that day. So the question isn't so much, What can we *do* for Haiti? as, How can we *learn* from Haiti?

What did you learn about the "spirits" and the world of voodoo?

My knowledge of voodoo is limited to what I've picked up along the way, and in how it seems to manifest in the lives of my Haitian friends. It's a religion that teaches respect for all elements of nature. It doesn't view mankind as outranking other creatures.

I was lucky enough to visit the great *houngan* [voodoo priest] and painter André Pierre in his studio. He pointed through his window and said, "That tree out there is just as important as you are, its spirit is as important as yours." A butterfly, as if on cue, came fluttering into the studio, and André says, "And that butterfly's spirit—just as important as yours." So I pointed to a rock outside. And André threw his forefinger into the air and laughed and said, "Ah! That rock is *more* important than you because it's never been, and *can't* ever be, corrupted."

André says the rainbows have left Haiti because the *loas* [deities] are so sad that the island has become so devastated. The

Valdez oil spill breaks our American hearts. But in Haiti, where the damage has gone on for so long—there are so few birds, so few trees—when you *do* see a tree or a butterfly, one's reverence for nature is all the more powerful. It reinforces the voodoo worldview that all creatures are extraordinary.

Being exposed to the Haitian reality, you get stimulated on many levels. And that makes someone who works in the media want to try to push the upside of Haiti into the global eye, to fight the proliferation of the negative press that exists out there.

Which explains this new album that you conceived.

Exactly. I'm the kind of music freak who likes to tape my favorite songs on cassettes and send them off to friends. So this album is a dream come true—a compilation of music I love that will be in record stores so that I can share the music with everyone.

We decided to emphasize songs of social concerns on the album—songs that are tremendously important in Haiti today because of their consciousness-raising and information-spreading power. I want to emphasize that the album is only a first, not the last, word on Haitian music . . . it's meant as an introduction, by no means a definitive statement. The arena's just too rich for anything like that.

What about the Haitian Creole language of the songs?

It shouldn't be a problem. I mean, who knew what pop songs like "Sukiyaki" or "Volare (Nel Blu Dipinto di Blu)" were about at first? Or the Gipsy Kings? And if the language *is* a problem, you can read the translation in the liner notes, which also include a lot of information on the language, social themes, and the history of voodoo so that those whose curiosity is stimulated can write to the

Creole Institute at the University of Indiana or to the International Alliance for Haiti. We *do* want to get people interested in and concerned about Haiti and to make enough money from the sale of the album to contribute to the creation of new water supplies in Haiti. That would be literally a dream come true. But regardless of that, I think that the music itself is irresistible.

I've always been open to new kinds of music. I was a little kid when rock 'n' roll was invented, and I got swept away by that . . . just as I was by reggae, new wave, country and western, and punk. When I first went to Haiti, songs by Tabou Combo and Les Frères Parent had the same effect on me. It's great music!

Your interest in Carribean and Afro-American culture reveals itself not only in your music videos ("Sun City," "Sister Rosa") but also in your last two feature films. In Something Wild, *Melanie Griffith attempts to appear as a self-styled mambo queen, with her fetish rattle, African jewelry, and icon-decorated car; while in* Married to the Mob, *Michelle Pfeiffer takes her beau to a Third World dance party in New York City's Lower East Side. In both films, moreover, rappers, street people, the reggae princess Sister Carol appear in surprising, comic, and always enlivening ways. What is this all about?*

I was recently taken to task by a critic who took exception to these films' supposedly incongruous elements that acknowledged the African roots of American culture. Yeah, I *do* acknowledge the rich and varied ethnic makeup of our society. I believe that terrible toxicity results from enforced separation of the races; and those of us with European ancestors lose a tremendous positive potential for growth when we keep people of African ancestry at arm's length.

When I was working on the character of the straitlaced stockbroker [played by Jeff Daniels] in *Something Wild,* for example, I tried to discover what this bonehead's good qualities might be. The most important one, I decided, was his ability to be racially color blind; and the more faithful he was to that part of himself, the more he'd be empowered by that.

As the Neville Brothers and Les Frères Parents sing on the song "My Blood" on the Konbit *album:* "Wis se frènouyo ye, kèlkèswa koulè you" *("Yes, they're our brothers, whatever their colors.")*

"Se you sèlla nou ye, ede nou met tèt ansanm / Yon sèl ligla nouye! ("We are all one, help us put our heads together / We are all one family!")

(1989)

LOU REED

Quite often in 1988, when I turned on the radio or television, I would occasionally—and incredulously—take a look at the calendar to make sure it really wasn't 1968. Rock stars like Steve Winwood, Eric Clapton, Paul Simon, Jerry Garcia, and, of course, Michael Jackson were still recording and performing music that, in many cases, was more popular now than it had been twenty years before. This in the rapidly waxing and waning world of rock 'n' roll, where names, faces, voices, and songs often seem as ephemeral as cherry blossoms or the snows of yesteryear.

Now, at the outset of 1989, comes along a new solo album by Lou Reed, one of the most original and influential poetic and musical innovators in the history of rock 'n' roll. Reed was the lead singer and songwriter of the legendary rock band the Velvet Underground, for which he wrote such classic songs as "Sweet Jane," "Sister Ray," "Heroin," "I'm Waiting for the Man," and "Pale Blue Eyes," and whose 1967 debut record was called by critic Stephen Holden "the classic New York rock album of the sixties." Since 1972, Reed has made a score of fascinating, mostly neglected solo albums—the most famous being the David Bowie–produced Transformer which featured "Walk on the Wild Side," Reed's first (and last) Top 20 hit.

From the beginning of his career, Reed entered into, explored, chronicled, dramatized, commented on, criticized, and celebrated the seductive shadow side of the New York City psyche— particularly the demimonde world of street hustlers, teenage runaways, transvestites, drug dealers, princesses and queens for a day, and other Bohemian, hipster, and punk denizens of the wild side of New York.

A true poète maudit, Reed followed Rimbaud's program of "deranging" all the senses, and in so doing found a vital language for the poisons and inanities and ecstasies of urban life. Reed communicated his vision of the body and city politic in tight, intense rock 'n' roll music and a poetry of sardonic and often surprising beauty.

Except for the absence of the characteristic black sunglasses that one usually sees him wearing in most of his photographs, I couldn't help observing that Reed's curly dark hair and thin, intense good looks; his casual gray Italian leather jacket and black T-shirt; his jeans, boots, and Rolex watch ("one of life's little pleasures," he says with a laugh, adding, "it'll last forever!"); and his rapid, mordant, acerbic sense of humor, with its echoes and cadences of Lenny Bruce, all belie the passing of decades. In fact, the passion and enthusiasm with which he discusses his latest work—his twentieth solo album—suggest an ebullient kid who has just released his first record.

Simply entitled New York, *Reed's controversial new album, which has the explosive tone and force of biblical prophecy and street-preacher anger, conveys the amazingly direct, spare, elemental rock 'n' roll quality that has spawned hundreds of acknowledged and unacknowledged musical imitators through the years (among them, Patti Smith, David Bowie, and Bryan Ferry). With Mike Rathke and Reed on Pensa-Suhr custom guitars, Rob Wasserman on upright six-string bass, co-producer Fred Maher on drums, and Maureen "Moe" Tucker on percussion, this record provides the perfect musical medium for Reed's highly charged depiction of and verbal onslaught against an AIDS-stricken New York in which friends are continually "disappearing"—a city of abused children and battered wives; of child police-killers, teenage bigots, and racist preachers; and of thousands of homeless people panhandling, rummaging for food in trash baskets, and sleeping in streets, alleys, and doorways. It is a world of hypocrisy, greed, ugliness, selfishness, and degradation—in comparison to which a song like Bob Dylan's "Desolation Row" is like a weekend outing to the Hamptons.*

Lou Reed discussed his new album in New York's Warner Bros. Offices in 1989.

What's interesting about my situation is that unlike musicians like Clapton, Winwood, and so on, I've never gotten popular. I'm what they call a cult figure, and that's about where it is. Except for "Wild Side," which was a fluke, I'm certainly not a household word. Also, I don't sell that many records, so there can't be so many people out there with an image of me. And I've been around so long that an image must be kind of boring by now. I mean, what possible use could it be?

I'm reminded of a journalist who called me up and asked me all about my supposed "shocking" image. And I said to him, "You're so parochial! Why don't you give us all a break?" I mean, there's nothing shocking about "Wild Side" or any of my music. If you compare them with the writings of Hubert Selby Jr., William Burroughs, or Allen Ginsberg, none of my songs would be considered shocking. It's just that this material is in rock 'n' roll—so it's that rock journalist's problem, not mine. I'm forty-six years old now and I can't be bothered with that kind of stuff. And if I'm less concerned right now with "deranging all the senses," as you were calling it, let's just say that *I* might call it just growing up.

With most of my albums I've felt that I was behind myself, that the albums didn't represent where I really was when they came out. But on this one I'm not behind myself—this is where I am. We had all the time we needed to record it, and when the sessions ended, we all knew it was over. I gave it my best shot.

On New York *you seem to be saying that the city is hopelessly sick.*

In my song "Endless Cycle" I say: "The bias of the father runs on through the son / and leaves him bothered and bewildered. . . . The sickness of the mother runs on through the girl / leaving her small and helpless." There are such terrible images running through the album, like in "Xmas in February," the song about the abandoned, unemployed Vietnam vet "on the street with the sign that reads / 'Please help send this vet home'/ But he is home." *But he is home!* I listen to that and think, What have I done? The images just come at you. And some of them were hard for *me* to deal with.

I spent almost three months writing those words, and I tried to find a way to surround them properly, to get the rhythm of the words working in the right way against the beat, and then get the nuances in the vocal so that listeners could hear the words—that was the raison d'être of this record. This is my vision of what a rock 'n' roll album can be—it doesn't have to be a twenty-four-hour, below-the-belt type of experience all the time. And I suppose I should say that I'm kind of disappointed in rock 'n' roll today. Put it this way: I'm writing for an educated or self-educated person who has reached a certain level. I'm not aiming *New York* at fourteen-year-olds. The album has fourteen songs on it and, as I say in the liner notes, it's meant to be listened to in one fifty-eight-minute sitting as though it were a book or a movie.

You know, just about 100 years ago, another New York poet, Walt Whitman, had something quite different to say about the city. He wrote: "Mannahatta! How fit a name for America's great democratic island city! The word itself, how beautiful! how aboriginal! how it seems to rise with tall spires, glistening in sunshine, with such New World atmosphere, vista and action!"

He should really see it now! That's what this album is all about. Every day when I go outside I see the result of the emptying of the mental hospitals, of not having enough halfway houses, of having all kinds of services cut, of backing off on funding for schools and for food for kids, of holding out on just about anything, and here we are. You read me Walt Whitman, so let me read you a few lines from my song "Romeo Had Juliette": "I'll take Manhattan in a garbage bag with Latin writ on it that says / 'It's hard to give a shit these days'/ Manhattan's sinking like a rock, into the filthy Hudson what a shock / they wrote a book about it, they said it was like ancient Rome." And I don't think I'm the only one who feels this way. You've got to give to people, you can't just sit there saying that things are good for me. And I'm trying to make you feel the situation we're in—feel what it's like.

It's interesting that in 1929 the Spanish poet Federico García Lorca came to live in New York for a year, and in his book A Poet in New York, *he also tried to make people feel the monstrousness he experienced in the city: "I denounce everyone / who ignores the other half / the half that can't be redeemed / who lift their mountains of cement / where the hearts beat / inside forgotten little animals / and where all of us will fall / in the last feast of pneumatic drills / I spit in all your faces."*

That's wonderful! Lorca, of course, was writing during the first years of the Depression, and I think that today we're headed toward another one. I also feel that the people who run things have knowledgeably and intentionally messed up the lives of people who can't possibly defend themselves—the aged, the poor, the young, the old. Lorca was livid about the situation, and so am I.

In your beautiful thirteen-year-old song "Coney Island Baby," you say that though the city is "something like a circus or a sewer," one can look up to see the "princess on the hill" and that the "glory of love just might come through." But on New York *you seem to offer no possibility of salvation. And some people might take it to be extremely nihilistic. For one thing, there doesn't seem to be any love song on the album.*

But there certainly is! If you look at the last song, "Dime Store Mystery," which is dedicated to Andy Warhol—whom I really miss and was privileged to have known—you'll find the lines: "I wish I hadn't thrown away my time / On so much Human / and so much less Divine / The end of the Last Temptation / The end of a Dime Store Mystery." There are all kinds of references to the film *The Last Temptation of Christ* in that song. But those are some of the most stunning lines I've ever written in my life; I'm enormously proud of them. It's not the moon-spoon kind of love song, but I think it's a supreme love song.

But coming back to people thinking of *New York* as nihilistic: it would be a shame if that's all they got out of the album. I think that people should get together and do something about the situation I'm describing. That's the salvation. Look at what's going on, then do something about it.

Besides, don't people realize that the album's also funny, "leavened with humor"? Some of the worst comments on it are hilariously funny at the same time. I mean, we're so dulled by all of this. You just don't have to make anything up anymore. In "Sick of You" I say: "I was up in the morning with the TV blarin'/ brush my teeth sittin' watchin' the news / All the beaches were closed the ocean was a Red Sea / but there was no one there to part in two / There was no fresh salad because / there's hypos in the cabbage / Staten Island disappeared at noon / And they say the Midwest is in great distress / and NASA blew up the moon / The ozone layer has no ozone anymore / and you're gonna leave me for the guy next door."

I've heard it explained that one cannot possibly eliminate pain through aggression, that it's like eating oneself from the inside out, and that when you eat yourself, the eater remains unsatisfied. Yet on "There Is No Time," you sing: "This is no time to swallow anger / This is no time to ignore hate."

Look, I'm not unaware of other points of view. I'm *doomed* to see the other person's point of view continually. I can see why he or she is right, I can see why I could be seen as being wrong. And then there's a third, a fourth, a fifth point of view, and on and on. Until you end up davening. But there are certain points of view I have now, and I think that *New York* is a legitimate channel for them.

In the title song of your 1984 album New Sensations, *you say: "I want the principles of a timeless muse / I want to eradicate my negative views / And get rid of those people who are always on a down."*

Ah! You probably want to know if those lines trumpet a new

mellow Lou? But there's no reason to get into autobiographical things with me, because I'm a writer and musician.

Actually, I was going to ask you about the "timeless muse." Who is that muse?

There was a time in my life when the ability to write wouldn't be there anymore, and I'd be panicked, thinking: It's gone forever, it'll never be back. I was confused about where the talent came from, how it functioned, what it could do, what it didn't want to do. And I thought of the poet Delmore Schwartz's wonderful essay on *Hamlet* in which he points out that Hamlet came from an old upper-class family and began saying very disturbing things to his friend Horatio and to others. And as Delmore put it, the real secret about Hamlet is that he was a manic-depressive, and a manic-depressive just *is*—like being right-handed or having brown hair.

So in my particular case, I finally realized that my talent just *was*—I didn't have to worry about it going away, all I had to do was sit there and go about my business, or hang upside down in gravity boots, and it would always be there. In "New Sensations" I said that I wanted it—I wasn't in touch with it at that point. But since then, I am, which is just a blessing. I had a little dream and I got it.

I want to be in touch with the "timeless muse" and I have to follow it because I get enormous satisfaction out of it. And that's what my life is all about. I did Honda and American Express commercials so that I could continue doing albums like *New York*, so that I could take the time off to write the way I really wanted to. But I don't have to be a big shot or rich. All I want to do is *more*.

In *New York*, the Lou Reed image doesn't exist, as far as I'm concerned. This is me speaking as directly as I possibly can to whoever wants to listen to it. If someone accuses me of attacking my former image, by saying: "Oh, but you *once* said . . .," All I can now say is: "And what did you once say? And what did we all once say? And what might I say tomorrow?"

(1989)

LEONARD BERNSTEIN

LEONARD BERNSTEIN WAS NOT ONE FOR CELEBRITY INTERVIEWS. "I don't have favorite orchestras, favorite composers, favorite symphonies, favorite kinds of food, favorite forms of sex," he warned me with a smile when I arrived at his New England country home in Fairfield, Connecticut, one windy, late-autumn afternoon in mid-November of 1989. "So don't ask me those 'favorite' journalist questions."

"I won't. I won't," I promised.

"Okay, Okay." The white-haired but boyishly ebullient maestro, wearing a sweater and linen slacks, beamed. He led me out of the cozy, white-clapboard, 1750s farmhouse, filled with early American furniture and antiques and with books on almost every subject, across the grounds of gingko, mulberry, Japanese maple, and half-weeping cherry trees to his nearby music studio (formerly a spacious groom's quarters). Inside, the walls were covered with scores of photos (mostly signed) of teachers, friends, and heroes, including Aaron Copland, Igor Stravinsky, Fritz Reiner, Arturo Toscanini, Glenn Gould, Jennie Tourel, Nadia Boulanger, Abraham Lincoln, John Kennedy, and Bernstein and his late wife (the actress Felicia Montealegre) seated together at a piano.

Having turned seventy-one on August 25, Bernstein was, as always, America's most famous and most awarded musician (fifteen honorary degrees, eleven Emmys, thirteen Grammys), one of its most popular composers (On the Town, Kaddish, West Side Story), a charismatic teacher (acclaimed for his remarkable fifty-three Young Peoples' Concerts, his Omnibus, and other television presentations), and one of this century's greatest conductors (with about 400 recordings to his credit).

Born in 1918 in Lawrence, Massachusetts, Leonard Bernstein was educated at Harvard University, the Curtis Institute of Music, and the Tanglewood Summer School, making his legendary debut with the New York Philharmonic on November 14, 1943, by substituting, on only a few hours notice, for an ailing Bruno Walter. The first work on that historic program was Schumann's "Manfred" Overture, based on the poem by Lord Byron. And indeed Leonard Bernstein truly led a life of Byronic intensity—passionate, risk-taking, convention-breaking, continually productive, universally inspiring.

From the start, he conducted with a flamboyance and obvious rapture that led some critics to accuse the young maestro of being exhibitionistic and overemotional on the podium. But as Bernstein once asserted: "Life without music is unthinkable. Music without life is academic. That is why my contact with music is a total embrace." Unlike almost any other classical performer of recent times, Leonard Bernstein continually, and controversially, refused to separate emotional, intellectual, erotic, and spiritual longing from the musical experience, describing it as a "marriage of form and passion" with its occasional "bliss of ambiguities." And in defining what he saw as the "dualistic energy source" of the music of Gustav Mahler—with which he always had an uncanny affinity—Bernstein might well have been suggesting a sense of his own complex, multifaceted musical and personal self: "subtle and blatant, refined, raw, objective, maudlin, brash, shy, grandiose, self-annihilating, confident, insecure, adjective, opposite, adjective, opposite."

As we entered Bernstein's music studio, he said, "Do you mind listening to a recording I made about twenty years ago of Sibelius's First Symphony?" And without waiting for an answer, he gently pushed me into a chair and offered me a glass of vodka—particularly appropriate for the wintry Finnish music to come. "I'm supposed to perform the work in a few months with the Vienna Philharmonic and I haven't listened to this old performance for years."

Glass in hand and dragging, amidst fits of coughing, on a cigarette dangling from his mouth ("When you're a Jet, you're a Jet all the way / From your first cigarette to your last dying day"), Bernstein rummaged through a collection of ancient LPs, dug out a still-pristine copy of the Columbia Records album featuring the New York Philharmonic ("a much-underrated orchestra," the maestro announced), and placed it on a turntable. Balancing his vodka glass in one hand or another, he then proceeded to sing, dance, and conduct to the first movement, while adding recitative-like interpolations, explanations, words of approval and disapproval, and comments concerning the music for my benefit:

*"Listen, child! Here's the Jewish rabbi theme . . . There's Beethoven . . .
There's Tchaikovsky (just wait for some Borodin and Mussorgsky later on)
. . . Some Grieg (but better than Grieg) . . . And now comes Sibelius—
Just listen, that's unmistakably Sibelius. [L.B. quickly writes out for me on
an old envelope the distinctively Sibelian rhythmic cell we've just heard.]
Now, a wind . . . sighing . . . And now a pop song [singing]: 'What-
did-we-do-till-we-loved?' . . . Yeah, that's completely Carousel . . . And
now a breeze comes along . . ."* And the now-motionless maestro, glass
upraised, bent his head and closed his eyes.

"There sure are a lot of borrowings in this movement," I said,
breaking the spell.

"But it's so marvelous how all music is tied up together!"
Bernstein replied enthusiastically. "I mean, I could go through
Stravinsky's Rite of Spring with you and point out what comes from
Mussorgsky and Ravel—note-for-note passages from Ravel—
outright, out-fucking-rageous steals! I could show you what
Beethoven took from Haydn and Mozart. But what's the point of
doing that? Everyone comes from somewhere."

"I was thinking of Carl Orff," I said.

"Orff took nine-tenths of his style from Stravinsky's Les Noces
and the other tenth from Israeli horas. [L.B. is off and away singing
and dancing a hora, pounding the table as he goes along.] *And
Orff was such a Nazi. Of course, the Israelis stole from the
Romanians. So? If you're a good composer, you steal good steals!
Because a composer is the sum total of his listening experience . .
. plus the voice and jism that belong specifically to him and that*

make him instantly identifiable: ' I am Wolfgang Amadeus!' ' I am Ludwig!' 'Me, me, Sibelius!' "

Leonard Bernstein removed the Sibelius record from the phonograph. "What a symphony!" he exclaimed. "It's amazing to think it was originally denounced as trash." Then he walked over to the large table where I was sitting consuming my second vodka, raised his right hand, gave an upbeat with his glass, and said: "And now . . . to begin!"

You once said: "I am a fanatic music lover. I can't live one day without hearing music, playing it, studying it, or thinking about it." When did this obsession begin?

The day in 1928 that my aunt Clara, who was in the process of moving, dumped a sofa on my family—I was ten years old at the time—along with an old upright piano, which, I still remember, had a mandolin pedal (the middle pedal turned the instrument into a kind of wrinkly-sounding mandolin). And I just put my hands on the keyboard, and I was hooked . . . for life. You *know* what it's like to fall in love: you touch someone and that's it. From that day to this, that's what my life's been about.

At first, I started teaching myself the piano, and invented my own system of harmony. But then I *demanded*, and got, piano lessons—at a buck a lesson—from one of our neighbor's daughters—a Miss Karp. Frieda Karp. I adored her, I was madly in love with her. She taught me beginner's pieces like "The Mountain Belle." And everything went along fine until I began to play— probably very badly—compositions that she couldn't. Miss Karp couldn't keep up with my Chopin *ballades*, so she told my father that I should be sent to the New England Conservatory of Music. And there I was taught by a Miss Susan Williams, who charged three dollars an hour. And now my father started to complain: "A klezmer you want to be?" To him, a klezmer [*an itinerant musician in Eastern Europe who, for a few kopeks, played at weddings and bar mitzvahs*] was little more than a beggar.

You see, until that time, neither my father (who was in the beauty supply business) nor I really knew that there was a real "world of music." I remember his taking me when I was fourteen years old to a Boston Pops concert—a benefit for our synagogue—where I fell in love with Ravel's *Bolero*, and, several months later, to a piano recital by Sergei Rachmaninoff—both at Symphony Hall; and my father was just as astonished as I was to see thousands of people *paying* to hear one person play the piano! But still he balked at three-dollar lessons for me. One dollar for lessons and a quarter-a-week allowance—that's all he allotted for my music. So I started to play in a little jazz group, and we performed at . . . weddings and bar mitzvahs! [*Laughing*] Klezmers! The sax player in our group had access to stock arrangements for "St. Louis Blues," "Deep Night," and lots of Irving Berlin songs; and I'd come home at night with bleeding fingers and two bucks, maybe, which went toward my piano lessons.

Now, my new teacher, Miss Williams, didn't work out—she had some kind of system, based on *never* showing your knuckles. Can you imagine playing a Liszt *Hungarian Rhapsody* like that? So I found another teacher . . . at *six* dollars an hour . . . and therefore I had to play *more* jazz, and I also started to give piano lessons to the neighborhood kids.

Meanwhile, I was going to Hebrew school after regular school; and the temple we belonged to [Congregation Mishkan Tefilah] also introduced me to live music. There was an organ, a sweet-voiced cantor, and a choir led by a fantastic man named Professor Solomon Braslavsky from Vienna, who composed liturgical compositions that were so grand and oratorio-like—very much influenced by Mendelssohn's *Elijah*, Beethoven's *Missa Solemnis*, and even Mahler. And I used to weep just listening to the choir, cantor, and organ thundering out—it was a big influence on me. On hindsight, I realized, many years later, that the "gang call"—the way the Jets signal to each other—in *West Side Story* was really like the call of the shofar that I used to hear blown in temple on Rosh Hashanah.

West Side Story is your most famous and successful work. Did you have a sense that it would be so popular when you composed it in 1957?

Not at all. In fact, everybody told us that the show was an impossible project. Steve Sondheim [who wrote the lyrics] and I auditioned it like crazy, playing piano four-hands in order to convey a quintet or the twelve-tone "Cool" fugue. But no one, we were told, was going to be able to sing augmented fourths—as with "Ma-ri-a" (C to F sharp). Also, they said the score was too "rangy" for pop music—"Tonight, Tonight"—it went all over the place. Besides, who wanted to see a show in which the first-act curtain comes down on two dead bodies lying on the stage? "That's not a Broadway musical comedy." And then we had the really tough problem of casting it, because the characters had to be able not only to sing but dance *and* act *and* be taken for teenagers. Ultimately, some of the cast *were* teenagers, some were twenty-one, some were thirty but *looked* sixteen. Some were wonderful singers but couldn't dance very well, or vice versa . . . and if they could do both, they couldn't act.

Somehow it worked out. And it even saved Columbia Records—which at the outset didn't want to invest in or record it—from bankruptcy. Remember: it was a bad time for popular music. Bebop's appeal was limited and was practically over, and there was mostly a lot of smarmy ballads sung by people like Johnny Mathis.

Also, Columbia Records didn't get into rock 'n' roll in the late fifties, even though the birth of rock 'n' roll was several years old by then.

Honey child, there was rock 'n' roll in the late *1930s*—before you were born—so don't tell me *that!* I first heard the phrase "rock 'n' roll" in a song that Ella Fitzgerald recorded with the jazz drummer Chick Webb for Decca—it was called "Rock It for Me." You don't know it? Do you want to hear some of it?

You remember it after half a century?

[*Undaunted, the maestro sings, snaps his fingers, growls the horn riffs, and bangs the table in a memorable performance:*] "Now it's true that once u-pon-a-time / The opera was the thing [*bahm bam*] / But today the rage is rhythm and rhyme / So won't you satisfy my soul with a rock an' roll. / You *can't* be tame while the band is playin' / It ain't no shame to keep your *bod*-y *sway*-in' / So be-*heat* it out in a mi-hi-nor key / Oooh! *Rock* it [*baf!*] / *Rock* it [*baf!*] / Oh, won't you ro-*hock* it for me (*WAH!*)."

That was the first time I heard about "satisfyin' my soul with rock 'n' roll," and I used to go wild when I heard Ella (my angel!) sing that song . . . So, here am I giving you an education!

Through your Young People's Concerts, television specials, books, lectures, and preconcert chats you've been giving people an education for more than forty years. You yourself once called teaching probably the "noblest," "most unselfish," "most honorable" profession in the world. And you once referred to "this old quasi-rabbinical instinct" you had for "teaching and explaining." It's said that in traditional Jewish society, a child, when he was six or seven years old, was carried to the schoolroom for the first time by a rabbi, where he received a clean slate on which the letters of the Hebrew alphabet had been written in honey. Licking off the slate while reciting the name of each letter, the child was thus made to think of his studies as sweet and desirable.

Though I can't prove it, deep in my heart I *know* that every person is born with the love of learning. Without exception. Every infant studies its toes and fingers; and a child's discovery of his or her voice is one of the most extraordinary of life's moments. I've suggested that there must be proto-syllables existing at the beginnings of all languages—like *ma* (or some variant of it), which, in almost every tongue, means *mother*—*mater, madre, mutter, mat, Ima, shi-ma, mama.* Imagine an infant lying in its cradle, purring and murmuring *MMM* to itself . . . and suddenly it gets hungry. So it opens its mouth for the nipple—every kid does it—and out comes *MMA-AA!* . . . and thus it learns to associate that syllable with the breast and the pleasure of being fed. *Madre/mare* (mother/sea) are almost the same word in Spanish; and in French, *mère/mer* are homonyms. The amniotic sea is where you spend your first nine months—that great ocean in which you don't have to breathe or do anything . . . it all *comes* to you. Even after the trauma of being born—which we never get over—there's still that delight with which children first *learn* to say "MA!"

Then, one day, the kid says "MA!" and the nipple does not arrive. This can happen on day five or month five of the child's life; but whenever it happens, it's an unimaginable shock. I know great big grown-up guys who have jumped—literally *jumped*—into the arms of their lady therapists and *wept*, hoping to be cradled at their breasts!

Like MAH-ler?

[*Laughing*] Why not? You know, Mahler made four appointments with Sigmund Freud, and three times he broke them because he was so scared to find out why he was impotent. His wife Alma—who at various times carried on with Gropius, Kokoshka, Werfel, and Bruno Walter, among others—sent him to see Freud. He was twenty years older then she, and she was the prettiest girl in Vienna—rich, cultured, seductive . . .

Didn't you yourself once meet her?

Certainly. Many years ago she was staying at the Hotel Pierre in New York, and she invited me for "tea"—which turned out to be "aquavit"—then suggested we go to look at some "memorabilia" of her composer husband in her bedroom. (I spent a half hour in the living room, a minute or two less in the bedroom.) She was really like a wonderful Viennese operetta.

Anyway, Mahler didn't pay enough attention to her; he was busy writing his Sixth Symphony up in his little wood hut all night, and she was tossing around in bed. Mahler was terribly guilty about it all—when he gets to the "Alma" theme in the scherzo of the Sixth Symphony, the margins of the score are filled with exclamations like "Almschi, Almschi, please don't hate me, I'm dancing with the devil!" [*L.B. sings the "Alma" theme.*]

Mahler finally met up with Freud at the University of Utrecht in Holland, where they sat on a campus bench for a couple of hours. And Freud later commented in a letter to one of his pupils, writing something to the effect of: "I have analyzed the musician Mahler"—a two-hour analysis, mind you! Freud was as crazy as his patient—". . . and as you will notice, Mahler's mother was named Maria, all his sisters had Maria for their middle names, and his wife is named Alma Maria Schindler."

[Singing] *"I've just kissed a mom named Maria!"*

Indeed. Freud thought that Mahler was in love with the Madonna image and was suffering from the Latin-lover dilemma—the mother versus the whore: you worship the former and fuck the latter. Anyway, Freud considered Mahler to have had this problem in spades. . . .

But back to my point about infants who are all born with the craving to learn: having experienced the birth trauma, the denial traumas, and the series of other traumas—I almost forgot about gender discovery!—that cause tantrums (the terrible threes, the fearsome fours, the frightful fives) . . . My own granddaughter, according to *her* mother (who is *my* daughter Jamie—the first fruit of my loins) made a great confession when she was two and a half years old. Until then, everything had revolved around her—she was the goddess and queen, and now a new baby was expected: Enter Evan! And she went into *tantrums*! Jamie stroked and caressed and calmed her down until she finally admitted: "You know what, Mommy? I don't like the new baby." And just to have come out and *said* that will probably save her a good ten years on the couch! For each time a kid learns a new trick of manipulating a parent—"I'll scream, I won't pay attention, I won't speak when spoken to"—he or she becomes more cynical, and turns off. And each manipulation and each trauma *impairs* the love of learning with which the infant is born.

Moreover, anybody who grows up—as those of my generation did *not*—taking the possibility of the immediate destruction of the planet for granted is going to gravitate all the more toward instant gratification. You don't get the nipple so you *push* the TV button, you *drop* the acid, you *snort* the coke, you *do* the needle: "*Right* away, *right* away, yeah, man!" It doesn't matter that it makes you impotent. You've gotten so high and then you pass out in the bed . . . and you wake up, cynical and unsatisfied and guilty and ashamed and full of manic fears and anxiety . . . and one thing reinforces the other.

Then, if you happen to born into a black, single-parent family in the inner city—impoverished, disadvantaged, along with all the shocks and traumas that man is heir to—by the time you go to school, if you're not a Hasidic or Sikh child who's learned to lick the honey-coated letters (wherever the written tradition is important), you're already completely resistant to learning. And the more poverty and greed of the Reagan-Bush kind around you, the greater the attraction of the streets—the instant gratification of crack, television, fast food. Anything of a serious nature isn't "instant"—you can't "do" the Sistine Chapel in one hour. And who has time to listen to a Mahler symphony, for God's sake?

In the sixties, many kids could be seen wearing MAHLER GROOVES *buttons.*

That was nice. That was very nice. I was around then. And I'll bet you didn't know that I made up the slogan MAHLER GROOVES? To this day, I've got a MAHLER GROOVES bumper sticker pasted onto the first page of my score of the Sixth Symphony. But you can't say MAHLER GROOVES to kids in Harlem . . . or, for that matter, to the musicians in the Vienna Philharmonic Orchestra. Those are *my* kids, but they don't really care about a "groovy" Mahler.

You know, in 1988 I took the orchestra to Israel, and one of the works we played in Jerusalem was, in fact, Mahler's Sixth. *That* was an experience! Imagine . . . this all-Catholic orchestra whose players, before I conducted them, didn't know what a Jew was— musicians growing up in the birthplace of Freud, Schoenberg, Wittgenstein, Karl Kraus . . . not to mention Mahler—a Vienna that had become a city with almost no Jews!

Once, when the players were rehearsing my work *Kaddish* for the first time, they stopped the rehearsal of their own accord to ask me what *kaddish* meant. I said that it was related to the word *sanctus,* "*kadosh.*" Later, one of the musicians said, in astonishment, to me: "Are you telling us that Jesus was Jewish?" I couldn't believe it. Another player then explained: "We were brought up from the age of two not to ask questions. And if you did, you got no answers. We learned a couple of things in magazines and from TV, but that's all." I mean, those guys didn't know that Jesus spoke a language called Aramaic or that there was a connection between the Old and New Testaments. They were all church-going kids, brought up in the traditions of their Nazi grandfathers. And yet I think of them as my dear children and brothers. People sometimes ask me how I can go to Vienna and conduct the Vienna Philharmonic. Simply, it's because I love the way they love music. And love does a *lot* of things.

You know, we've already lost a whole generation of kids who are blind to anything constructive or beautiful, who are blind to love, love, LOVE—that battered, old, dirty four-letter word that few people understand anymore.

You often talk about faith, hope, belief. Obviously, you're a believer not just in love but also in the idea of continuity.

We must get back to faith and hope and belief—things we're all born with. Unfortunately, we're also born thinking we're the center of the universe. And of all traumas, that one is the biggest and most difficult to get rid of. And the hardest principle to absorb is the Copernican one: we're just specks on this planet, which is just a speck in our solar system, in our galaxy.

The hardest thing in the world is to enter adolescence and have to come to terms with mortality. I once did a Young People's Concert on this theme, in which I talked about Nietzsche and concluded with a performance of Strauss's *Also Sprach Zarathustra*. No subject is too difficult to talk about. You just have to know where the pain is, what the kids are suffering from, why they fold their programs into airplanes and shoot them around. Their attention span isn't too great, so you have to anticipate and invent some tricks when you feel them slipping away—especially the younger ones.

It was Nietzsche who asserted that "in any true person hides a child who wants to play."

We *play* Tchaikovsky's Sixth Symphony. We go to see a Shakespeare *play*. Hamlet is a *player*. Stravinsky said that music is the "*play* of notes"—twelve notes . . . less than half of an alphabet. I'm a compulsive anagrammatist: *beard* and *bread* have the same letters but mean different things. *Play* technique. And that's all music really is.

My first Young People's concert [January 18, 1958] was called "What Does Music Mean?" I talked real hard stuff to those kids—no paper airplanes sailed around Carnegie Hall—and they loved it. We started off by playing the beginning of the *William Tell Overture*. Then I turned around and asked the kids, "What's that?" "*The Lone Ranger!*" they shouted. "Wrong! It's a Rossini overture. How about that?" "Boooo!" "I'm sorry, they use it on the *Lone Ranger* show, but what's the difference? Music doesn't *mean William Tell* or *The Lone Ranger*." And by the end of the program they realized that music doesn't have to mean anything except itself.

You're an amazingly "playful" teacher; but if an adult doesn't have a child within him that wants to play, kids probably aren't going to respond to that person at all.

I don't think that that's the secret, because *everyone* has a child within him. Nietzsche speaks of a "true" person. But what is a *not-true* person? If you've lost your sense of playfulness, you can find it again. I and a musician friend named Aaron Stern have conceived of an institution called the Academy for the Love of Learning (A.L.L.). We haven't done too much with the idea yet, but it's registered as a nonprofit corporation, and besides the obvious attempt to get music and kids together, there will be the overriding goal of teaching *teachers* to discover their own love of learning. Then the infectious process begins. These ideas are now being tested, particularly in Nashville. I think the timing is right: it should be fairly soon because I'm old—even if playful!—and don't have all the time in the world. Being with young people has kept me alive, and I would do anything for them.

Since 1951, you've regularly taught young musicians at Tanglewood, where you yourself first studied conducting with Koussevitzky in 1940. In 1986 you began working with young conductors and created a training orchestra at the Schleswig-Holstein Music Festival in northern Germany. And now you're continuing your teaching journey on the other side of the world with the Pacific Music Festival that begins this June. What is that?

Originally, Michael Tilson Thomas and I were supposed to tour China this coming summer with the London Symphony Orchestra, and also start a summer school in that country with young musicians from both China and Japan. But then came Tiananmen Square. And the phones went dead. And then, as if from heaven, Nomura Securities Co., Ltd., got in touch with my manager, Harry Kraut, to say they'd be happy to pick up the project and let us bring it to Art Park, a large wooded area outside of Sapporo—the capital of Hokkaido, which is the second-largest and northernmost island of Japan.

The idea is to create a Tanglewood Festival for the Pacific Rim. Aside from the LSO, we'll be creating an orchestra of young musicians from countries bordering the Pacific—which will mean not only Japan and South Korea but also Chile and New Zealand. I'll be conducting and teaching . . . as I do at Tanglewood and Schleswig-Holstein; and while the LSO will perform works by Beethoven and Benjamin Britten, we also plan to present performances by Ecuadorian and Aboriginal musicians, for example. It's all part of teaching *and* learning. I'm an eternal student, and maybe that explains why I'm a pretty good teacher. . . .

When did you first get interested in "the music of the world's peoples" (to use Henry Cowell's phrase)?

When I was nineteen, I particularly remember the Uday Shankar Dance Company performing for a week at Symphony Hall. The beauty of the music and the dancing—the subtle movements of the fingers, hands, and eyes—*completely* freaked me out. I can't tell you how enraptured I was; and I went back to see them every night—no matter that that was the week of my midyear exams!

I was fortunate enough to meet the musical director of the troupe, a man named Vishnudass Shirali, who explained the ragas and had the musicians demonstrate the sitar and tabla to me. To reciprocate, I invited him to Symphony Hall on a Friday afternoon to hear Koussevitzky conduct Mozart's G Minor Symphony. And at some point in the first movement, I realized that Shirali was asleep. I poked him and said, "This is the great G Minor Symphony of Mozart." The slow movement began, and he nodded off again. So during the intermission I asked, "What's the matter? No reaction at all?" "No," he replied, "no reaction at all. It's baby music—it's for little children. Deh-de-*dah* deh-de-*dah* deh-de *dah*-dah / Dah-de-*deh* dah-de-*deh* dah-de-*deh-deh*. What's that? It's uninteresting." I said: "But what about all those chords? You don't have chords. What about those harmonic changes? What about that crazy sequence in the development section? Those odd phrases and deletions?" Nothing. I couldn't talk him into it. So I added: "You're just getting even because many Americans fall asleep during those forty-five-minute ragas. The interest there is in the line and in the microtones of the monodic, lineal music . . . and, of course, in the rhythms and the drone bass, which never gives up, never gets off that dime. At least Mozart gets into a subdominant and modulates." "That's for babies," Shirali assured me. "The melodies are dumb, the rhythms are ordinary and square."

So I thought: Is it possible that human beings on the same planet, subject to the same laws of the harmonic series and to two-leggedness, etc., can really not talk to each other musically? And I realized that it was just a matter of time, of exposing oneself and being exposed to a new music—like being exposed to a foreign language or foreign customs—and treating it not as the "alien" but as a friendly cohabitant of the planet. And isn't it wonderful to get to know someone who's a little different from yourself?

All kids are born with a language and a musical competence. Otherwise you wouldn't be able to account for a two-year-old child's saying "I like the green ice cream better." That's the pentecostal alphabet—the letters of fire—that God gave us: His *greatest* gift, the ability to talk and communicate. And a big part of communication is music. Every kid is born with a sense of rhythm, and has the ability to tune in on the overtone series. It's part of the air we breathe, part of our bodies. The harmonic series is in everybody—the octave, the fifth, the fourth, the third, the major and minor seconds. An infant knows the interval of an octave because his or her mother sings a note or a melody one octave higher than the father does. In every country of the world, kids tease each other with the same tune: Nya nya, nya nya—the first two different overtones of the harmonic series. And every child is born with the knowledge of 1–2, 1–2—he has two hands, two feet, two eyes, he breathes in and out, he knows up and down, left and right, and he can march: toddle-toddle, toddle-toddle!

So when we wreck this ability by giving our children inhibitions, teaching them to be cynical, manipulative, and all the rest—this in addition to the usual childhood traumas—we are robbing kids of the natural rights to sing and dance and understand speech and music. Until we realize this, young people are never going to like listening to any kind of music except that which goes with a drum machine and doesn't make any impositions on their time or attention. It's like masturbating—*"Ba-by!"* (chuk-a-chuk) *"I-need-ya!"* (chuk-a-chuk).

In the introduction to your book The Infinite Variety of Music *(1966), you wrote: "At this moment, as of this writing, God forgive me, I have far more pleasure in following the musical adventures of Simon & Garfunkel or of The Association singing 'Along Comes Mary' than I have in most of what is being written now by the whole community of 'avant-garde' composers. . . . Pop music seems to be the only area where there is to be found unabashed vitality, the fun of invention, the feeling of fresh air." What do you think of rock music today?*

Boo, hiss! I've become very disappointed with most of it. In the sixties and seventies there were many wonderful musicians I liked.

And to me, the Beatles were the best songwriters since Gershwin. Recently, though, I was at a party where there were a lot of kids in their twenties, and most of them didn't even know songs like "Can't Buy Me Love," "She's Leaving Home," "She Said She Said," or any one of ten other Beatles masterpieces. What is *that*? And if I hear one more metallic screech or one more horrible imitation of James Brown, I'm going to scream.

When I was in Spain several years ago, I remember watching huge rings of people in the square of a Catalonian village, joining arms and dancing *sardanas* to a type of band called a *cobla*—dances with twenty-seven counts, dances of such complexity that I couldn't learn them. Talk about innate dance and musical competence! Those people just *did* it. Like those drunken Greek sailors who come into a *taverna* and start dancing in fives or sevens—and the band doesn't *know* that it's playing in 5's or 7's. *That* is extraordinary music—much more exciting than almost anything the current rock world has to offer.

What do you think of today's widespread use of synthesizers?

In 1988 I let myself be talked into getting the biggest synthesizer you've ever seen. New England Digital sent me its *latest* and *greatest* synclavier, which had originally been designated for MIT. It took ten days to install it in my studio. Looking like the dashboard of the Concorde, it was placed next to my modified piano. A Mac 14–36-B-Jaguar (or something like that) was then brought in, and a printout machine was set up in the adjoining room. All this took *another* week. Then an "expert" arrived to teach me how run the synclavier. He came every day for a week, followed soon after by a kid from Oberlin; and he, *too*, had to be instructed. "Just leave me alone with the expert," he told me; "it's a piece of cake." They left everything on all the time, and I was told

I could improvise to my heart's content all night, and that in the morning they'd come to interpret the printout, which was filled with fifteen tied thirty-second notes in no significant metrical context (and other such notations).

The whole thing turned out to be a wrestling match with the click track (which gives you the bar lines on the printer). Now, *nobody* can beat the click track except with the use of a drum machine . . . and I *cannot* have a drum machine, I'm just not the type! To prove my contention, I played the slow movement of Beethoven's *Pathétique* Sonata—with no rubato, no *anything*—against the click track. And after just *a bar and a half*, we were already not together. Because in the millisecond it takes to press the key to produce a singing tone, the printer is showing something that looks more like Charles Ives than Beethoven—an amorphous blob of sixty-fourth notes, two sixteenth notes, and so on. "*You* sit down," I said to my two assistants, "and *you* do it." They couldn't either. Moreover, when I tried to compose, I felt totally inhibited, sitting all alone being watched by that Argus-eyed monster. Finally, after six weeks of torture, I had the system removed . . . which took *another* week.

So in answer to your question: How do I like synthesizers? Great in the theater pit and on discs. But for composition? Fuck 'em!

How do you like fortepianos [early forms of the piano] and the period instruments that are so popular now in performances of seventeenth-, eighteenth-, and early nineteenth-century music?

Sometimes, sometimes. I've played Mozart's piano in his Salzburg home, and boy, what a noise it made! I played Chopin's piano in *his* house in Warsaw, and Beethoven's pianos in Bonn and Vienna. I also have a double harpsichord in my own home—an absolute copy of a Couperin harpsichord from the French Baroque period. And I tell you that if the instrument can bring you closer to the intention of the composer, fine. But you have to have *seykhl* [common sense], too. Ultimately, it all depends on who's playing the instrument. In my opinion, the conductor Trevor Pinnock's work in this area is particularly exciting—his performances of Bach and Handel make me jump out of my seat!

How do you like CDs?

The greatest thing that's ever happened to recorded music. You don't have to turn them over, there's no hiss, no surface noise. Perhaps I miss the *floor* a little bit—the sound seems to be *hanging* there. But, of course, it also *comes* to you. It really is a marvel. I was listening to my own remastered 1966 version of Verdi's *Falstaff* (with Fischer-Dieskau and the Vienna Philharmonic) the other day on my car's CD system, and the sound was so extraordinary that when I arrived home, I couldn't turn off the engine, I just sat there till the end of the work. And this was an almost twenty-five-year-old recording!

Do you think it's really possible to listen to (or perform) the century- or two-century-old symphonic warhorses of Beethoven, Brahms, and Tchaikovsky as if "for the very first time"—like a virgin, so to speak?

I had that experience with Beethoven's Seventh Symphony when I recently conducted the work with the Vienna Philharmonic in Bonn—Beethoven's birthplace—at (are you ready for this?) a Beethoven/Bernstein festival! Dennis Russell Davies presented about ten works of mine with the Beethovenhalle Orchestra; and I was asked, at the last minute, to conduct Beethoven's Seventh—a piece I hadn't done in a couple of decades. So I stayed up all night restudying the symphony from bar 1, as if I'd never seen it in my life. And I made an enormous number of red marks for accents and diminuendi and rebowings in the score. Now, the orchestra had played the piece a thousand times—at *least*—and here we were, with one rehearsal, flying with it, discovering and creating a really surprising version of this true Surprise Symphony . . . since that is what the work is all about— shocks and surprises. Because when something is repeated in the score, the accent occurs in exactly the other place from where it appeared the first time—a *left* to the jaw, a *right* to the body!

Was that performance in Bonn recorded?

No, and I wish it had been. But how many Beethoven Sevenths can you listen to? I mean, there must be 500 recorded versions of that piece. Toscanini alone did it three or four times.

And Von Karajan?

Von Karajan never stopped! Yet another "perfect," shiny Beethoven Seventh made in the studio. At least my recent recordings are taken from live concerts.

In order to avoid the predictable, boring 501st version?

Well, why else? Not so that you can hear the audience coughing! There's nothing like a live event compared to an immaculate studio performance that you put together like a jigsaw puzzle. What I do is to take a live concert and use that as the matrix of a record. Of course we have to do retakes to cover coughs, noises, and wrong notes; but my new albums are basically live performances.

People are always going to go to concerts. Laser discs and film aren't going to replace congregating and being together and touching. But the nature of the events will undoubtedly change. You can't remain locked into the tradition of handing down subscription tickets from grandfather to son to grandson—Series B, Series C, Series D. And the functions of an orchestra are going to have to be multiplied, such that there will be chamber orchestras and string quartets within it, and associate members—like out-of-work Julliard musicians, say—to enlarge it. Every orchestra must also develop ways of educating older concert-goers and those young people we talked about before who usually listen only to rock music. Of course an orchestra should continue to perform Beethoven's Seventh and Tchaikovsky's *Pathétique*: Wouldn't it be awful if the "museum" dies? But it will have to change if it *itself* isn't going to fade away.

Do you think that any of the world's great orchestras are greater or more distinctive-sounding than another?

When a conductor talks about *my* orchestra's "sound," forget it. I have yet to hear a conductor talk about Haydn's or Ravel's sound. Eugene Ormandy used to refer to "the Philadelphia sound"; and he even said something to the effect that, really, there *was* no Philadelphia sound, there was only an "Ormandy sound," and that he could make any orchestra sound like the Philadelphia Orchestra. And he probably could. But what good is that?

Under him, that orchestra advertised its supposed "velvet string sound." But then someone once asked: "Who wants strings to sound like velvet?"

But sometimes you *do* want the strings to sound *exactly* like velvet—in Brahms, say. But who wants that in Haydn or in the scherzo of a Mahler symphony?

Velvet freaks.

Right. And then they can relax to Gene Ormandy and His Velvet Strings!

So you wouldn't say whether, in your opinion, there's a "greatest" orchestra in the world today?

NO! I don't have *favorite* orchestras. There *is*, however, such a thing as a particular orchestral tradition and a certain identifiable "sound" resulting from the instruments that musicians have inherited from their grand- or great-grandfathers . . . and there is a difference between French and German bassoons and trumpets. There are also "schools" of teaching. But even taking all of these things into consideration, any orchestra can and should be made to sound like the *composer* it's playing, and not like itself—Haydn in Haydn's style, Ravel in Ravel's style . . . and not in the "Philadelphia" or the "Berlin Philharmonic" style.

In your new recorded traversal of Mahler's symphonies, you're using three different orchestras—the New York Philharmonic, the Vienna Philharmonic, and the Amsterdam Concertgebouw. Why?

Because those were the three orchestras that Mahler himself conducted in performances of his symphonies during his lifetime. And they don't sound alike, by any means. But they all sound like *Mahler*—they cry and bite and caress and pray.

Mahler once made the provocative suggestion that "the artist represents the feminine element opposing the genius that fertilizes him"—as if the composer himself were making love to himself.

No: as if the composer were being made love to by a *divine essence.* Mahler meant exactly what Jesus meant. There's the father/son idea, then the eat me/drink me phenomenon—*his* body/*his* blood. He is impregnating his believers. Think of the Song of Songs, in which Christians see Jesus as the Bridegroom and the Church as the Bride. Think of the sun god who makes of his worshipers the receivers of his benefits—*his* light, *his* heat—the vessels through which the god speaks. And in a similar manner, the god comes to impregnate Mahler with the divine message, who writes it down like a good secretary—just as Mozart did.

Mozart once stated that he got many of his musical ideas while traveling in a carriage or while strolling after a particularly satisfying meal.

A lot of musicians compose while walking. Beethoven, Brahms, and Benjamin Britten composed like that. Someone like Stravinsky, on the other hand, worked from ten o'clock till midday every day . . . then had lunch, read his mail, had a nap, looked over what he'd done that morning . . . and in the evening, either went out or thought about how to orchestrate the piece. The next morning— *bam!* Back to composing at the piano.

It's said that Wagner had to be in a kind of psychotic frenzy in order to compose.

Wagner was *always* in a psychotic frenzy, so he was *always* writing music.

What's amazing about Mozart, though, is that he claimed to be able to hear a complete (or nearly complete) piece in his mind. "Nor do I hear in my imagination the parts successively," he wrote, "but I hear them, as it were, all at once."

But it's *true*. I've always been on my knees to Mozart. He didn't mean, however, that he heard the whole piece at one moment. But he could hear, let's say, a bar of music and see, in his mind's eye, the entire structure of the piece—he could see exactly where it was all going. Though don't forget that Mozart was composing at a time of formulas—sonata formulae, cadential formulae, rondos, minuets, etc. Just imagine how many times Mozart wrote [*Bernstein sings a characteristic Mozartian cadence and rhythmic figure*]. What is *really* to genuflect about is that he could foresee the developmental structure—in a moment of inspiration he knew what the transposition was going to be from theme one to theme two; which cells or parts of the themes were going to be concentrated on; how he would go about returning to his recapitulation—sneak back to it or crescendo into it or surprise you by bursting out of it. *All* of this is what's amazing. And, remember, I've only been talking now about one movement!

You once wrote that "a conductor is automatically a narcissist, like any other performing artist; he is an exhibitionist by profession." But you suggested that there was a difference between the conductor "who is vain on his own behalf" and the conductor "whose ego glories in the reflected radiance of musical creativity."

I've often been said to be an exhibitionist on the podium, but everything I do is *to* the orchestra—what the audience sees from *their* side is their business . . . I can't be responsible for that. I don't plan any gestures, I've never rehearsed with a mirror. And when my students ask me what they should do to get the orchestra to play a phrase the way I did it, I can't tell *them*—I have to ask them what I did. I can't say: "You put your third finger here and flex your wrist and keep your elbow in." I don't have any recipes or methods. I don't beat time, and I don't allow my students to "beat" music. In fact, I teach them not to make a diagonal downward sweep on the third beat the way so-called conducting teachers do—it's like flogging a dead horse. I just advise students to look at the score and make it come alive. If you can, you're a conductor; and if you can't, you're not. I've asked members of the Vienna Philharmonic and the New York Philharmonic, "How did you follow that, how did you know what I meant when I was barely moving?" And they'd say, "We don't know, we just looked at your left eyebrow."

If I don't *become* Brahms or Tchaikovsky or Mahler when I'm conducting their works, then it won't be a great performance. The only way that can happen is when I feel I'm making the piece up as I go along. Inventing it: "Oooh, yeah! That would be a *great* idea . . . bring in the English horn here . . . a bass pizzicato . . . now a trombone chord." And the other way I have of knowing it's been a good performance is when it's all been over for a long time— because it sometimes takes me one, two, or even up to three minutes to know where I am or who I am or what's all that noise behind me. Sometimes I've been so far away . . . so far away.

It sounds like being lost in the middle of the ocean or a desert.

No, it's not *lost* at all. It's *found* . . . but *away*. And the orchestra is away, too. We're all there. And the longer it takes for me to get back—to turn around and bow—is a sign of how far we've all been.

To come back to a more constricting realm, I wanted to ask you about your refusal last November to accept an arts award from President Bush and to attend a dinner given by John Frohnmayer, the new chairman of the National Endowment for the Arts, in response to the latter's decision to withdraw the agency's sponsorship of an exhibition about AIDS—a result of congressional legislation against government financing of supposed "obscene" and overtly political art.

The last time I went to the White House was during Jimmy

Carter's administration, when I was honored along with Agnes de Mille, James Cagney, Lynn Fontanne, and Leontyne Price, among others—a good bunch. I love the White House more than any house in the world—after all, I'm a musician *and* a citizen of my country—but since 1980 I haven't gone there because it's had such sloppy housekeepers and caretakers.

With regard to the Jesse Helms–inspired restrictions on federal funding, the worst thing concerns the removal of "politics" as an acceptable subject of artistic works. Because then you'd have to forget Goya, Picasso's *Guernica*, Hemingway's *A Farewell to Arms*. Forget everything. And as for "obscenity": almost the entire Metropolitan Museum of Art would have to come down—Mars fucking Venus, the Rubens collection of large, fleshy ladies with wet thighs, and the naked ephebes from ancient Greece, Hermes with his cock up innumerable inches! . . . And the picture of *little* Jesse Helms running around the Senate, as if it were the boys' lavatory of a high school, showing dirty pictures to the other senators is so disgraceful that I cannot ever forgive him.

We had eight lovely, passive, status quo, don't-make-noise years with Ronald Reagan. The *fights* I had with my mother! "Don't you dare say a word against our president!" she'd say to me. She's now ninety-one years old—God bless her!—and she's still bright and witty. She doesn't like the family name being dragged in the mud; and when she saw my name in the newspaper every day regarding my refusal to attend the White House luncheon awards ceremony given by Bush (or the Frohnmayer dinner), she'd call me up to say, "You're on the front page of the *New York Times*." And I'd say, "Hold your water, baby: I was also on the front page of the *Washington Post*." And she'd exclaim, "Well, that's horrible!" So I informed her that some of my most conservative midwestern friends sent me congratulatory messages . . . people who voted for Reagan!

We now have a black governor in Virginia, the right governor in New Jersey, and Dinkins in New York City. That's terrific! In the past, I've met and argued, in pessimistic fashion, with Helmut Schmidt, Ted Heath, and François Mitterand about the mindlessness, carelessness, and heedlessness of the Reagans of the world. But I think there's a turnaround coming—look at what's happening around the world from Central Europe to South Africa to Haiti. And I'm looking forward to Jesse Helms being routed in the near future.

People like William Buckley, Jr., William Safire, and George Will think of me as a kind of "liberal" fool. Basically, a liberal is a progressive who wants to see the world change and not just remain stuck in the status quo. So, yes, I'm a liberal; but one who believes in people, not in some "thing." And I've never felt more strength and confidence.

What you call "liberal" was once termed "radical chic" by Tom Wolfe in his infamous article/book about the party you gave in 1970 to raise money for the Black Panthers.

Wrong on all counts! What happened is that my wife [*the late Chilean actress Felicia Montealegre*] hosted a meeting in our New York City apartment for the American Civil Liberties Union in connection with its defense of thirteen Black Panthers who, at that time, were imprisoned in the Tombs without the rights of due process. At our reception were one Black Panther and two pregnant Black Panther wives and Felicia gave the reception in order to raise contributions for the ACLU defense fund and to allow invited friends of ours to ask questions. My wife had requested that the press *not* cover this event; and Charlotte Curtis—then the editor of the Woman's Page of the *New York Times*—arrived (simply as an individual, we thought), accompanied by a young friend of hers in a white suit. He turned out to be Tom Wolfe. So what am I to do? You can't beat the legends. Fortunately, legends eventually die. And maybe I can help this one on its way.

For many years, musical lore has had it that "tonal" music was dispensable—merely culturally and ideologically conditioned. Yet in the six lectures you gave at Harvard in 1973, you asked the question: "Whither music?" And among things, you answered it by pointing to and defending the significant innateness of tonality—a system rooted in a preordained and inborn musical grammar known as the harmonic series. It is interesting that almost twenty years later, an increasing number of composers—old and young—are increasingly writing music with obvious tonal implications, or even unabashedly "tonal" music itself. How would you answer your question—"Whither music?"—today?

The return to tonality seems to be coming true. But of course there's no law against *any* kind of music, and there shouldn't be. For a long time, many composers stated that tonality was dead, that serial works were the only thing that could and should be written. Serialism, twelve-tone music, wild chromaticism, neoclassicism, neoromanticism, Dadaism—all kinds of music can be great, but not to the exclusion of tonality, which, as I said in my lectures, constitutes the roots of music. I think that will *always* be true.

In Wagner's Die Meistersinger, *Hans Sachs sings: "Your closing key is not the same, / This gives the Masters pain; / But Hans Sachs draws a rule from this: / In Spring, it must be so! 'Tis plain!" And regarding these lines, the atonal, twelve-tone composer Arnold Schoenberg wrote: "In the development of art, it must always be as it is in spring!" You yourself still seem to believe in the springtime-ness of music.*

And how! I feel the meaning of it very deeply.

You know, you caught me on a good "springtime" day. Maybe because I wrote a little piece this morning for my granddaughter Francisca (known as Frankie). It's called *Dancisca*—to dance to. At the moment it's just one page, but eventually it will turn into something bigger. It's the first piece I've written all year, I'm sad to say. I just haven't had any solitude until the past couple of weeks, and then only for a few days . . . in the midst of conducting all-Copland and all-Tchaikovsky programs with the New York Philharmonic, and of preparing for a performance and recording of my *Candide* in London. (It's the first time that I've actually conducted the work.)

But when I was brushing my teeth at four o'clock this morning, I heard something like my new little piece—the rhythm first and then the melody—but I got immersed in a crossword puzzle and forgot to write it down. When I woke up, I heard the piece again in the shower, but this time, before going down to breakfast, I wrote almost all of it down   . . . then came over to the studio a few hours ago, finished the piece, and drew the double bar on it.

And that, my interlocutorial friend, is The End! Till the next one.

(1989)

[This was Leonard Bernstein's last full-length interview.]

MICHAEL
TILSON THOMAS

WHEN MICHAEL TILSON THOMAS was attending nursery school in Los Angeles, he remembers, a woman came two times a week to play piano for the kids. "We all had an assortment of sticks and noisemakers," Tilson Thomas says. "One time she was doing some sort of Spanish piece. I was filling in with my drumsticks all kinds of complicated rhythmical riffs, à la castanet parts. Most everybody else was going click-click-click. And I remember thinking, Wow, that is so boring! Here I was, five years old, thinking, What's going on? Why don't they fill in what's in between the beats?" It was at this moment that Michael Tilson Thomas manifested the conductor's mentality.

Twenty years later, in 1969, when he was appointed assistant conductor of the Boston Symphony Orchestra, Tilson Thomas used to attend after-hours shows of the James Brown Band, at places like Boston's Sugar Shack, in order to listen to and learn from a rhythmic journey quite more sophisticated than the ones Tilson Thomas took as a five-year-old: "I just wanted to see and learn. I was so excited about his show. You know, it was music, singing, dancing, but on the other hand, more than anything else, it was a personal rap between him and you. That's what was so incredible about it. You never felt he was onstage doing a number. I saw him with the rhythm section playing and him talking in rhythmical cadences. I mean, he would say, 'And-so-that's-the-way-it's-gonna-be'—it was all in the length of the phrase and how he pitched his voice. It was all worked out with the rhythm."

After years of international guest conducting, Tilson Thomas began his tenure as musical director of the San Francisco Symphony Orchestra in 1995. In that city, he is as well known as a rock star. When he took over the symphony, San Francisco welcomed him by displaying his visage on more than ninety billboards around town. In return, MTT, as he is called, quickly turned a conservative and slightly fusty orchestra into the most adventurous, inspiring musical organization in this country. Who besides Tilson Thomas, critics have asked, is as at home with music ranging from Gustav Mahler's orchestral songs and Josquin des Pres's Missa Pange Lingua to early Brazilian and island music and Erykah Badu? Says MTT of his musical passions and proclivities, "I'm always snooping."

One of his most unusual journeys into other musical realms came in 1996, when the remaining members of the Grateful Dead—in their first gig after Jerry Garcia's death—performed classical music with Tilson Thomas at San Francisco's Davies Symphony Hall. "It was a huge event that was beyond categorization," Tilson Thomas says. "People from the classical world didn't know what to think, and people from the rock 'n' roll world didn't know what to think—it was a fusion of so many things."And one should not overlook his work and projects with the New World Symphony—a wonderful training orchestra in Miami Beach for young musicians, of which MTT is artistic director; concerts with the London Symphony, of which MTT is principal guest conductor; his programs for young people, titled Music for Families (only Leonard Bernstein was such an acclaimed teacher); compelling compositions by MTT himself (when he has the time to work on them); and the many more CDs that he and his two orchestras will be releasing in the next few years (MTT has made more than 100 CDs, with many national and international orchestras).

"I think it is life-filled, what I do," he says. "And a very big part of my mission is this incredible musical tradition, a very big part of which is involved with caring for it in any way that I can. We are all in this together, and we have to fight for it and keep it on course. It's not about conductors conducting their conducting wars—of who's going to conduct Strauss's Elektra next week in Salzburg. That doesn't matter to me at all. What matters to me is having music a part of our lives."

I visited San Francisco in early October 1999 to attend two morning rehearsals, two evening concerts, and an afternoon Families concert, and talked to MTT at his Davies Symphony Hall dressing room and also at his refurbished 1906 Victorian townhouse in San Francisco's Pacific Heights, overlooking San Francisco Bay. On one of the walls hangs a portrait of his grandmother Bessie Thomashefsky, who, along with her husband, Boris, co-founded the Yiddish Theater in New York City. (MTT has called them the Elizabeth Taylor and Richard Burton of their time.)

"She would say that although she was often called a bohemian, she never gave anything less than a passionate performance," MTT says. *"The truth is that there is no such thing as an unimpassioned performance. After many years, I know more about what she meant, because as a performer you have to keep vulnerability and openness to a whole range of experiences. It's not just the fun-and-games part of it; it depends on what you put into it. Most people seal away parts of their lives that were painful to them. But with music, you can have the ability to get to that raw material and really use it to animate and to power what it is you're doing."*

What do you think of all the classical music—a 200-CD set of Mozart, 180 CDs of the complete Bach—that one can find in the CD megastores these days?

That it's available is, of course, fantastic; that it's potentially overwhelming is frightening, possibly alienating. For me, any serious discussion about music and what music is in people's lives has to start with what they experienced as children. And I personally consider that I am what I am because I had extraordinary teaching, starting at around ten or eleven years old. But even before that, there were hours in school when we sang songs and played recorders and had eurythmics. Also, in our homes, we had 78-rpm records of Bach, Brahms, Schoenberg, Billie Holiday, and Broadway shows. So it was a whole range of things: the different possibilities of what music can be, not to mention a lot of Yiddish tunes, which were being performed by the old-timers who came around and sang to us.

Most of all, I was participating, I was singing along, I was dancing or clapping out rhythms. And through these participatory game experiences you have with an art, you really make it your own and take it past the place where you are only being a consumer. One of the things that we're doing today is developing into the kind of society that is impatient and selfish and, dare I say, manufacturing soulless change surfers, where there are so many possibilities that at the slightest whim someone will flip off to another channel. Change the channel. Change the format, change the prospect, change the medium. And then the attention span gets shorter and shorter, and people lose the qualitative sense of what art is supposed to do for them.

How does participating help to change this situation?

At some point, through participation, you can feel at home and inside of it. Even if you want to be a listener, the fact that you may have played and sung something, that you've had this experience of harmony, of being in an ensemble, in concord with other people, gives you an appreciation of what it's about. In sports, people are thrilled to watch these amazing heroes, because at one time or the other they have tried to shoot hoops or score a goal, and we all know how hard it is to get past the technique and the strategies of the game. So if more people have a sense of what an extraordinary thing it is to invent a new and beauteous melody or play an amazing virtuoso passage, they'd be clued into music in a much more meaningful way than they are.

What do you think of all the mergings of present-day musicians, groups, and symphonies, like the sixty-piece orchestra that performs "rock" classics by people like the Beatles, the Rolling Stones, Alice Cooper, and Roger Daltrey?

I can't stand those pieces where a rock musician comes in and plays his usual number while the orchestra plays an A-flat in the background—it's like another Mamas and Papas date, except realized live onstage with orchestra. It's so uninteresting. But I now think that both sides who love all these kinds of music will get together and make something special. And that's why I enjoy seeing what Mickey Hart, for example, is doing with his group Planet Drum, by combining Indian and rock traditions.

What do classical and rock have to learn from each other?

I've found generally when I've talked to rock performers that I've known a good deal more about rock than they've known about classical music. When I talked to Clyde [Stubblefield] or Bootsy Collins in James Brown's band about certain things that were going on in Messaien, it blew their minds. But on the other hand, even if most rock musicians have fairly stereotyped ideas about classical music, I think it's the ultimate condescension on the part of the symphony orchestra to criticize. Because if a rock group is really good, it's totally together in what it is, and the orchestra can only make it less tight.

You've talked about the "tightness" of the Rolling Stones. What do you mean by that?

The kind of thing I like is the way the Stones produce their records, the way they do this slight delay, reverb, on their double tracking. I love how imprecise it is—so that instead of hearing a voice that is absolutely synced with its echo, it's a certain precise fraction of a second behind. It's almost like a vague general melodic line that's being drawn, which has all kinds of little peaks and points on all sides—"*This* time Jagger decided to delay a little bit where the *L* goes, that time the *K* comes a little sooner"—so that the relationships within the lines are changing all the time.

What about the Beatles?

The reason I like them so much is that to me they really were an Elizabethan music group. Their melodies, their harmonies—so much of it was 500 years of music coming home, but this time with echoes of the blues and rock 'n' roll with which they grew up. They couldn't escape the expressive modalities of their own traditions, and whether they knew it or not, it's all there in the Lennon-McCartney songs. But when I listen to those tunes today, what I am constantly hearing is Shakespearean music and songs—music that comes from the Elizabethan court.

What do you think music can do for us?

In every society, everything goes back to the primal music: lullabies to put the baby to sleep, songs to praise the gods, laments for the dead, serenades for one's beloved, work songs to get the job done, marches to invigorate you. And from these primal musics come these different repertoires: folk music, dance music, religious music . . . all those flavors of all those kinds of music.

Then there are certain moves that music makes—harmonically, melodically, rhythmically. And then you have classical music, which is based on those basic forms. You can hear that in Beethoven and Schubert, all over the place. Those composers are like cinematographers who are using every bit that is available to make this fantastic vision of moves and ideas, expressing the totality of human thought, the whole voyage that the human spirit makes.

What's scary is that this basic stuff, this primal music—the folk and dance and hymn tunes—I believe we are losing. When I was a small boy, there were summer camps and temple and church groups, and we sang folk songs and did square dances. We knew what an "amen" cadence sounded like. But now, in the New World

Symphony, which I conduct in Miami, I see young musicians who don't know the hymn and folk tunes that Charles Ives used. They don't know songs like "The Erie Canal." And that, to me, is cultural disenfranchisement. They've lost a whole sense of consciousness about what it means to be an American.

What role did rock 'n' roll play in your life as a musician?

I remember when I was young in L.A. and driving to see the cellist Gregor Piatigorsky in the morning and composer Pierre Boulez in the afternoon, and I was driving in my little Volvo from place to place, listening to Wolfman Jack on the XERB radio— "The Mighty 1090"—and hearing all those James Brown songs and the Chi-Lites. I loved all that music.

But as we know, even within its brief history, rock has already come to a point where it is basically repeating most of the moves that it made in the first thirty or forty years of its creativity, and is more and more linked to production values and hooks, and one somehow suspects that there's a cynical, controlled obsolescence behind it. It's not meant that the pieces should hang around and last forever. It's meant to kind of exist, grab people's ears for a week or two, and then it's gone and has to be replaced with something else.

Never before has an art form been so hyped, sold, merchandised as pop music has. Just to imagine that someone can hum or stumble over a few notes, even a few intelligible words, and there is machinery that can take this over and make it so important and essential, when nearly all of it is dross.

Now there's a tremendous push for Latin music. But there's a real difference between the earlier Latin stars and today's stars, who are much more well produced and so much further away from a sense of real urgency. I mean, compare the recent popular dance tracks to the kind of energy and focus that Gloria Estefan's earlier tracks had when she was the same age as today's groups. Listen to the way she pronounces her words, the way she pops the syllables so that they really interact with everything that's happening with the rhythm sections, or the way she could hear so clearly what the drummer's doing as it goes back and forth between backbeat, rock, salsa, and the way those grooves go, masterfully blended one into another.

I am a huge Dylan fan. The rebellion that's in Dylan and in the more chaotic moments of the Rolling Stones—I can, as a musician with a long sense of history, accept that. Whereas I cannot in any way accept groups like, say, Nirvana. It's in no way focused enough or good enough. It's just not happening. The "classics," whatever they are—the last song of Schubert's *Winterreise*, "Sophisticated Lady," Laura Nyro's "Captain for Dark Mornings"—have something about them so that you are drawn back to them again and again, and then each time you hear something else in them. They still reflect their time, place, and era, but something more than that seems to go across time.

Take Monteverdi's *Vespers*, which were written in 1610. For 400 years, people have been obsessed by the beauty of this work. Or take Beethoven's compositions, written more than 150 years ago, when you're talking about some piece that's been admired with no hype, no advertising, just because people wanted to hear it and devote their lives to learning how to play it. There's a message here, a power encoded as an essential guide to the human soul, and it is profound and, I believe, necessary in people's lives.

What do you think of CDs with titles like Mozart in the Morning *or* Vivaldi for Valentines?

There are a lot of different ways of doing things and being constructive. A record like *Mozart for Meditation* could be a very good thing, because it puts that music into people's lives. But that's different from inflated, schlocky, popularized versions of music to make it seem relevant or "with it" to the adoring hordes. Nutritionally, it's like empty calories; you get a quick, sweet taste. But you don't remember the haunted mood of, say, a Schubert *Ländler*. I remember the driving, sexual energy of Stravinsky from *The Rite of Spring* or the dazzling highjinks of the last movements of Mozart's piano sonatas. Whatever: this is long-lasting.

What do you think of the rock 'n' roll of the nineties?

I'm not so much following current rock—and when I do it's mostly on the car radio again—but when I do, it seems repetitive. Most of the music that exists now is not real music, it's just "indicative" music—you understand that it's supposed to be exciting or lyrical or loving or defiant. But it's just posing as music.

What do you mean by "indicative"?

I mean that this music is just indicative of people displaying the length of their breath, the power of their amplifiers, the deluxe qualities of their equipment, or arrangements, or whatever it is. And that's very disappointing to hear these albums that combine highly famous performers doing exactly the same thing—the same little break in the voice here, the same sigh there—all these same manipulative, utterly false devices that have been slapped onto whatever tune it is. And we're supposed to be diverted and convinced by that?

What American popular music has stayed with you for a while?

From the sheer spinning of a phrase, from the musical stand-point, there's no question that Sarah Vaughan, Ella Fitzgerald, Smokey Robinson, James Brown were inspiring. Also, there was Laura Nyro and Joni Mitchell—colossally important.

Do you like Joni Mitchell's words or her music?

Everything. I just think it's altogether fabulous. I know those songs. When you talk about music that really stays with you, that is important for most of your life when you need to hang on to something, all that music is in my heart, along with Schubert and Monteverdi. It's all there.

Does anything special ever appear for you in this musical morass?

A song that broke through was "Nothing Compares 2 U"—a song written by Prince and sung later by Sinéad O'Connor. That, to me, took things in a different direction, because to me it was an extension of the gesture that's made by the blues. And what's interesting about the blues is that it's a music of ruins, the way in which the singer doesn't manage to sing the phrase. It falls off where words are supposed to be, the way in which it gets through its emotion that falls to pieces, and that is what makes it so profound. But I think that "Nothing Compares 2 U" is a step even beyond that, because it's a kind of distillation of a primal scream or wail that just hangs there and then comes back like a keening, mournful child. And it was arresting, it was saying something different. It wasn't just trying to push those same old buttons.

It's been thrilling for me to hear Cher's recent album and hear her new song "Believe" and to hear that message in the song and realize that in Elizabethan England there were many songs that say the same thing, and even use similar note patterns; this music walks across the centuries, and there are places in our heart that are the same as they were five centuries ago.

Think of the astonishing ways James Brown, Smokey Robinson, and Ike and Tina Turner rediscovered sonata form, rondo forms, all of these forms that had been discovered by eighteenth-century composers. Just think how many years it took for Johnny Otis to work out the groove of "Willie and the Hand Jive." It's this very special, finessed kind of thing, which we can all appreciate. Probably we can say that after sex, drugs, and rock 'n' roll, what will be left? And the answer is going to be classical music, with its enormous legacy of great notes, great grooves, great harmonies.

Now we're in a moment when the total possibility of musical language is there before us. We don't need any more experiments. What we need now is for people to use what is available in the most effective way to say what they have to say. That, for me, is what life is like. Aaron Copland said he wanted to write music so that people would know how he felt as a child walking the streets of Brooklyn. And that's the same thing that Charles Ives was asking for and I'm sure that Beethoven was asking for as well.

How do you feel now as musical director of this orchestra?

As a musician, I'm here to connect the past, the present and the future, to care for it in any way I can, and I hope to make it as inclusive as possible without sacrificing any of its quality. It's like I'm up to bat now, and I'm trying to hit the ball out of the park so that, in the accelerated cyberfuture, some of what we are doing will still resonate. And I feel so lucky to be here because of this partnership I have with everybody who's performing with me.

Let me give an example of the way the orchestra and I work together. Take a passage for the strings in Berlioz's *Symphonie fantastique*. Who can we say is leading, who's following? Who knows? The strings come in and linger a bit on the first note, gently falling on their way down to the rest of the phrase with such vulnerability and such magic. And the only way to do that is to have everyone look up from his or her music and have their ears open and find one another in that psychoacoustical space. It's this tracery and vulnerability that is so extraordinary—that sixteen or so string players can do that together with that kind of very personal tenderness.

Certain orchestras are thought of as athletic teams. But I like to think about my orchestra as a kind of loving, loyal wolf pack: When we see one another, we growl. Our musicians happily growl at one another, because things are good. When the orchestra plays well, I just lower my head and look at and growl at them. I'm so proud of them. Many people start out with the idea of establishing the greatest orchestra in the world, but as far as I know, not many people start out with the idea of establishing the happiest orchestra. And that is the dream of myself and our players, who are utterly for the music and for one another.

What advice would you give to young musicians today?

Being a musician is a life of study and practicing. It's like staying in training until the end, physically, mentally, and spiritually. You have to feel the necessity to do it, that the process itself is necessary; to make music must be as essential to you as breathing and eating. If that's so, you should be a musician. It's like a musical Hippocratic oath.

People have CD players, record players, video players; we don't need any more players. What we need is performers. They're the whole future of classical music.

(1999)

ARTICLES
AND
PROFILES

VIRGIL FOX
AT THE FILLMORE

ORGANIST VIRGIL FOX PLAYED an all J. S. Bach program on his portable electric organ to the accompaniment of Joe's Lights and a cheering, sold-out audience at Fillmore East on December 1, 1970. Fox was encircled by 144 speakers which hummed during whispering chorale preludes and roared with fortissimo effects during the "Passacaglia and Fugue in C," as if couplers, swells, pistons, and crescendo pedals were overpowering the theater. "Do you begin to see the secret of this man Bach?" Fox asked exultantly when he was near the end of the concert. The crowd gave the organist the kind of standing ovation usually reserved for Eric Clapton, calling out for more, and Fox happily played six encores. Both this concert and the again-sold-out repeat December 14 performance have been recorded by Decca, and are being released as a "Heavy Organ" album through its rock division.

According to publicity handouts and radio ads, fifty-eight-year-old Fox was supposed to bring Bach's genius to youth-culture heads at the "East Village rock mecca" dressed in a billowy white crepe shirt, silver-brocaded vest, crushed-velvet bell bottoms, and rhinestone-studded pumps. In fact, he appeared wearing a modest light brown suit and interspersed his performances with short, excited, hand-punctuated quasiministerial remarks about the "genius of this man Sebastian Bach" and the "perfection of the human soul manifested in you and me."

Fox, who plays seventy concerts a year ("Have organ, will travel, that's my motto") in places like Cody, Wyoming, or New York's Philharmonic Hall and who claims to have learned to play the organ in a previous incarnation, talks with a raved-up gusto and the expressive American nuances reminiscent both of Little Richard and James Purdy's amazing midwestern characters.

"I got down on my knees behind Joe's Lights just before I went onstage," Fox says, "and asked the great power to pass *through* me the message of the greatest composer of all time. And when I came down those steps, baby, my physique was completely exhausted. I'd only had a few hours' sleep, but it was that *power*, sonny boy, that took over. You've got to come the whole way. And those kids know. To have a composer of Bach's depth walk into the Fillmore and get over to those kids is amazing. They're honest people who are trying to get through when the rest of the world is going blotto. The Aquarian Age is coming on, and everything is finished—concert halls, the *New York Times*, everything. It's the jet stream, it goes twice as fast.

"You've got to illumine the greatness of Bach on this dumb mechanical instrument called the organ. The Scotch call it the kist of whistles. I don't like Bach performances that sound like a typewriter. The professional organists are so green-eyed to think that an organist like me is in the mainstream. Every concert management and all those big festivals say we're so sorry, there's no audience for the organ as a concert instrument. Listen, I face two thousand people every three nights. That proves to me that the way the average concert organist plays is a crock of shit—no nuance, no gradation, no expressiveness.

"The people I address live in the twentieth century. They listen to the accelerated action of the Steinway, for instance. There's no such thing as 'authentic' Bach or Beethoven. What if Bach said, 'I can only do what was done two hundred years ago'? That music was infantile."

"Mr. Fox," I said, "do you think the music of Dufay and Josquin is infantile?"

"Of course, my child, you're a creature of the creator," Fox said sweetly, "and you're entitled to your opinion. But the important thing is that we had something absolutely fantastic the other night at the Fillmore. That gives us common ground, brother. So just tell them what happened, sweet child."

"Mr. Fox," I said, "you were far out the other night, and it's terrific to have an informal setting where you can hear great music, but like maybe one can play Bach not just with highly contrasted and sharply alternating loud-soft volumes of sound, but by clarifying the structure and the textures and not using so many rubatos and retards and twisting the phrases, you know?"

"Listen, Johnny," Fox replied, "we had a few problems getting all the equipment set up right at the Fillmore. I need three days and only had half the time, so there was an artificial ring of sound around the hall, and the backstage fans and air conditioning added to the hum of the speakers. But I was aware that kids at the Fillmore wanted to be reached at the same volume scale that they're used to.

"As far as what you call the overuse of rubato, I like it. I'm not concerned with a cerebral approach to music. If you have ice cubes laid on a windless plain, you have no reach to humanity. If you don't have living, breathing, honest, musical, emotional, warm, expressive playing, it ain't music. Mountain peaks of power is what I aim for.

"I was the pupil of Wilhelm Middelschulte, who, along with Max Reger, was the greatest organ contrapuntalist between Bach and our time. I had a psychic happening with him in church, brother. We touched the mountaintops, and he branded me when I was sixteen with an illumined thing across my brow. My mission was to go beyond the organ's mechanical limitations and create true music and do what few organists ever do.

"I played in Cody, Wyoming, where Buffalo Bill is sitting on the plains and you run all over the sagebrush, and I played Bach, just as I did for kids in Nashville and Hollywood High, where I quieted everybody down by playing the lowest C pedal note and pointed to a girl sitting up front and said, 'That girl and me can fit in that pipe.' That got them. And the kids got the music sight unseen."

"Mr. Fox," I said, "your publicity and program notes say you're the 'greatest living interpreter of Bach's organ music.' What about Lionel Rogg and Helmut Walcha? Do you think you might be immodest?"

"I think I'm terribly immodest," Fox said. "I'm the only non-German organist ever to have played at Bach's last church in Leipzig, and a critic there said that, and I quote, 'This youth proved to us that he has an understanding of the innermost secret of the art of Bach.' Nobody plays it like me. Lillian Russell, who was Diamond Jim Brady's girlfriend, once said: "It would be absurd for me to pretend I'm not beautiful. I look in the mirror and can see that I am.' That's right. And I think she would have added, as I do about myself, that 'to be beautiful is another story, and I wish to be a beautiful character.' I've been called the greatest performing organist, and any publicity firm that doesn't use that recognized opinion is just plain foolish.

"The composer of *Hair* is going to write a piece for me and orchestra, and I'm going down to the White House to play for a reception for Prime Minister Heath soon. And then there's the repeat Fillmore concert. Just tell them what happened, baby!"

(1970)

IGOR STRAVINSKY
(1882-1971): An Appreciation

IGOR STRAVINSKY TELLS OF A DREAM in which he wanders outside a house, trying to enter. In his parable "Before the Law," Kafka writes about a man begging admittance to the Law. At the conclusion, the doorkeeper, seeing that the man is at the end of his strength and that his hearing is failing, bellows in his ear: "No one but you could gain admittance through this door, since this door was intended only for you. I am now going to shut it."

Kafka saw a freedom which could exist for him only when it became unobtainable. Just the opposite of that is the vision Stravinsky expresses in his music. "You are free and that is why you are lost," as one character in Kafka's *Fragments* says to another, and this thought is duplicated many times in *Amerika* and *The Castle*. Stravinsky's music, conversely, conveys the sense of breaking down the obstacles to that freedom which Kafka never attained.

Here is the key to Stravinsky's musical personality: the composer wants to and succeeds in breaking into the house—a house which can be seen as a metaphor for Stravinsky's self-determined musical choices—right away. His employment of staccato, marcato, and sharp ostinato—his musical attack, in other words—all suggest the typical Stravinskian sound. The conflict between metrical and rhythmic materials, the unresolved appoggiaturas, the superimpositions of conflicting modalities, the juxtaposition of rhythmic cells, all create an enormous musical tension and exhilaration. And it is this unique violent sound that unifies all of his music from *Fireworks* (1908) to the building-of-the-ark section in *The Flood* (1961).

Masterpieces such as *Renard* (1916), the Piano Concerto (1950), *Movements for Piano and Orchestra* (1959), and the *Variations for Orchestra* (1965) reveal the same musical power and kinetic energy, transcending annalistic periodization. "The true purpose of linear historicism," Stravinsky writes, "is simply to open up more midwestern territories of the mind to Ph.D. candidates." And Stravinsky's striking and recognizable musical inflection is always the same. As he writes in *Dialogues and a Diary*: "I do not understand the composer who says we must analyze and determine the evolutionary tendency of the whole musical situation and proceed from there. I have never consciously analyzed any musical situation, and I can follow only where my musical appetites lead me."

When Stravinsky uses Pergolesi, Tchaikovsky, Weber, Wolf, or Gesualdo, he employs the old in order to renew his already strong musical personality. Milhaud's adaptations of Lully or Richard Strauss's borrowings from Couperin reveal to us more about the originals than about the adapters. But Stravinsky's *Pulcinella*, *The Fairy's Kiss*, *Monumentum pro Gesualdo*, or the harmonization and arrangement of "The Star-Spangled Banner" (which, when it was first performed in 1944, got the composer into trouble with Boston officials who accused him of "tampering with national property") are pure Stravinsky, who takes from his musical forebears in order to renovate and enrich his own singular vision. Everything is there: the unique inflection and stylization, the freezing of the leading tones, the stricken gestures, the rhythmic attack.

Pleasure, delight, and play infuse his music. Building and acting are at the base of composition. "My knowledge is activity," Stravinsky says. "I discover it as I work, and I know it while I am discovering it, but only in a very different way before and after." As in the building-of-the-ark scene in *The Flood*, the act of building, as of composing, is as exuberant as child's play. It is a music of intense activity, an aural manifestation of motion and locomotion—a music of true liberation: "*Chaque geste te dégage*" (Each gesture frees you).

From the *Ebony Concerto* to *Dumbarton Oaks*, from the *Symphonies for Winds* to *Agon*, Stravinsky's music conveys a joy in being. "I myself having been created," he writes, "I cannot help having the desire to create." Like Grandgousier, who said to his wife, pregnant with Gargantua, "Bring this boy into the world, and we'll soon make another," Stravinsky kept (one wants to say "keeps") on composing one powerful work after another. And these works include not only the close to 100 pieces of music available on recording, but his *Poetics of Music* lectures and, the five books co-authored with his friend and assistant Robert Craft, which are rich, moving, and beautifully written, reminding one of the novels of Vladimir Nabokov:

"How does a man grow old? I don't know; or why *I* am old, if I must be (I don't want to be), or if "I" am "he." All my life I have thought of myself as the "youngest one," and now, suddenly, I read and hear about myself as "the oldest one." And then I wonder at these distant images of myself. I wonder if memory is true, and I know that it cannot be, but that one lives by memory nevertheless and not by truth. But through the crack of light in my bedroom door, time dissolves, and I again see the images of my lost world. Mama has gone to her room, my brother is asleep in the other bed, and all is still in the house. The lamp from the street reflects in the room, and by it I recognize the simulacrum as myself. Stravinsky recalls how Augustine, having grown old, appointed the priest Eraclius as his successor. "Eraclius stood forward to preach, while the old Augustine sat behind him: 'The cricket chirps,' Eraclius said, 'the swan is silent.' "

(1971)

THE MUSICAL MYSTERIES OF THE GREGORIAN CHANT

IF CHANTING THE NAME OF THE LORD can set you free—as George Harrison once sang—then we should remember that the Lord has many forms and that "chanting" is a universal phenomenon, occurring as it does in Tibetan and in Japanese Zen monasteries, in the Russian and Byzantine churches, in American Indian rituals, in Jewish liturgy, in Muslim prayer, and, of course, in Catholic monasteries all over the world.

No matter who composed these chants originally—whether religious novitiates, tribal shamans, "inspired" worshipers (think of the songs of the American Shaker tradition, for example), or someone like Queen Mara, who, giving up her court and all her possessions, journeyed throughout India as a beggar, singing the songs she "received" from Krishna—these chants all reveal themselves similarly as totally transparent mediums, egoless like crystals, through which the power of the divine can be comprehended and communicated.

Today we are witnessing the latest and most comprehensive resurgence of an unorganized ecumenical spirit on the part of psychologists like Robert Ornstein, writers like William Irwin Thompson, religious devotees like those at New York's Still Point community (where yogic techniques are combined with the Jesus Prayer), and composers like La Monte Young, Charles Morrow, Terry Riley, and Karlheinz Stockhausen (especially in *Stimmung*). Their principal aim is the reformulation of a tradition that combines (among other things) Pythagorean, Tantric, and Sufic ideas in terms negotiable for the construction of a new cultural synthesis. And as part of this synthesis, Gregorian chant—the liturgical chant of the Roman Catholic Church—might well reassume its role as a relevant and significant model of meditative and musical importance.

Gregorian chant was, in fact, only one of four "local dialects" of the music of the early Christian church (the others being the Ambrosian of northern Italy, the Gallican of France, and the Mozarabic of Spain). Pope Gregory I (540–604) collected, codified, and standardized the use of various pagan, Gnostic, Syrian, and Jewish liturgical chants for the Catholic service. But it was only in the eleventh and twelfth centuries, when the Roman rite had become "fixed" through more or less precise notation, that the basic outline of plainsong—*cantus planus*, as Gregorian chant came to be called in the thirteenth century—attained its most characteristic shape.

The present-day Gregorian chant repertory consists of almost 3,000 melodies—all monophonic, sung with measured but rhythmically free lines, and performed without instrumental accompaniment (with several exceptions) partly by the cantors (the two to six leaders of the chorus) and partly by the entire choir—in unison, and often antiphonally or responsorially.

Used as the material for the Mass and for the daily offices of the Roman Catholic Church (Matins, Lauds, Vespers, etc.), plainsong melodies and formulas are used as the simplest of intonations or as the richest and most expansive of melodic patterns.

It should of course be remembered that from the early Church fathers to the sixteenth-century Council of Trent, all establishment religious authorities attempted to harness "music" to the reins of the "holy words"; for, like Plato, they believed that "rhythm and harmony were to be regulated by the words and not the words by them."

But music, following its own sonic and dialectical laws, always resists such bridles. Alleluias, sequences, and tropes—with their melismas, flourishes, and added texts—entered the fabric of plainsong, eventually giving rise to medieval motet writing and Renaissance polyphony—only to be "restrained" anew by Monteverdi and his colleagues.

There is no question that Gregorian chant represents a perfect confluence of words and music, revealing in the heightened declamation of the word an utterance of spiritual rapture. But today, with the general secularization and neutralization of liturgical traditions and practices, we are able, more than ever before, to focus specifically upon the music itself and to perceive in plainsong the ideal norm of Western melodic technique.

As has often been pointed out, many of the chants, with their subtle intervallic symmetries and formal repetitions, actually formulate the entire structures of major symphonic forms. But it seems mistaken to see these chants simply as embryos of fully developed structures, since, in their intense plainness, they convey a lucidity and beauty of expression that an additional "accompaniment" would destroy. Like those haunting Swedish herding tunes played by shepherds in Lapland (one thinks, too, of the unaccompanied shepherd tune in Wagner's *Tristan*) or like the single-voiced lullabies sung all over the world, the diaphanous quality of plainsong suggests the silence by which the mind becomes the mirror of the universe. As a French philosopher once wrote: "The sound of music is not, like the sound of words, opposed, but rather parallel to silence. Music is silence, which in dreaming begins to sound."

Like Indian religious songs, Gregorian chant demands from its performers a musically and spiritually disciplined communal life. Yet the critic and poet Kenneth Rexroth has pointed out that while Roman Catholicism claims that its very lifeblood flows in holy communion, it is ironical that its entire structure is fundamentally anti-communitarian.

There are many persons who have refused to listen to this music because of what they feel is its association with the hypocrisy and formalism of organized, authoritarian religion. But it is moreover true that most people—inured to and satiated by Western harmony—find it disconcerting to listen comfortably to long stretches of monophonic singing. In its deepest expression, plainsong ineluctably insists on one's attuning oneself to one's self. And in order to resurface into this meditative world, the most effective musical decompression chamber would certainly be a quiet retreat to a Benedictine monastery or next best, a contemplative listening to plainsong recordings.

Many of the best of these recordings were made in the monophonic era and are now out-of-print. But stereo albums are still released occasionally by both small and larger American and European companies. Archive Productions, for example, has recently issued three of a projected six-record series, offering different monastic scholae in performances of the Roman, Ambrosian, and Mozarabic repertoire.

The most disputatious issue concerning the realization of Gregorian chant has always been the problem of rhythmic interpretation. No one knows definitely whether the notes of the chant were meant to be of equal duration or whether and how they were originally accented. Members of the accentualist and the mensuralist schools have been debating these problems for years.

The schola of the Benedictine monks from the Abbey of Saint Pierre at Solesmes (a village near Le Mans, France) is justifiably famous for its interpretation of Gregorian chant. And its solution to the rhythmic performance of plainsong (using notes of equal time value, but with a de facto accentual emphasis and with groups of two and three taken as units of pulse) has been officially accepted by the Roman Church.

Today, there is new evidence to support a theory that distinguishes between long and short notes. But whatever the "ideal" solution—and, to me, the Solesmes approach seems successful in practice—there is little question as to the vocal mastery of the Solesmes monks' performances. With regard to all aspects of phrasing, intonation, and timbre, their recordings are surcharged with an unequaled lambency and radiance. One of the most extraordinary of these features Funeral Music and a Mass for the Dead. You might not expect a album dedicated to funeral music to be quite as ingratiating as it is here, but perhaps it is exactly in this kind of music that we can experience the real secret of plainsong. The "Dies Irae" of the Mass, which we usually associate with vertiginous musical stress and disquiet, is here simply presented with the gentlest of voices and a tone of transcendent amiability and rapturous calmness. Like all the music on this recording, its melodic invention has its origin in a perfect repose: it is a music that can attune you to the unheard harmonies and to all that which has been harmonized by the immaterial Breath.

(1971)

YOKO ONO AND HER SIXTEEN-TRACK VOICE

*I'm the fish and you're the sea ... I'm
the apple and you're the tree ... I'm
the door and you're the key.*
—John Lennon "One Day (at a Time)"

IN DECEMBER 1970 John Lennon and Yoko Ono came to New York City for the first time as a couple. They visited some of Yoko's old friends; went out, as they rarely did in London, to films like *Diary of a Mad Housewife* and *Lovers and Other Strangers* and to the Muhammad Ali fight; made two new films of their own—*Up Your Legs Forever* and *Fly*—for inclusion in a three-night minifestival of John and Yoko films at the Elgin Theater; and did some publicity for their extraordinary twin albums, *John Lennon/Plastic Ono Band* and *Yoko Ono/Plastic Ono Band*.

The following scene takes place in a hotel room one Sunday evening: John is turning on the radio to hear Alex Bennett's WMCA phone-in program on which, tonight, he's playing tracks from Yoko's album—the first time her music has been featured on AM radio.

"There are people who are going to love it and people who are going to hate it," Bennett says enthusiastically. "I think that in 1980 music will probably sound like this. Here's a track called 'Why Not,' so phone in and tell us what you think of it."

"*It's today's 'Tutti-Frutti,'* " John writes on a notepad, so as not to interrupt the music.

"I'm forty-nine years old," a listener calls in to say, "forty-nine, and I dig it. I heard trains going through a tunnel, then rain—I'm just using my imagination—then what sounded like a bunch of Indians. I dig it, but I really like songs with a melody."

"It was truly disastrous," a nasal-voiced listener comments.

"It's music, you idiot!" John exclaims to the radio. "Because it's not got *da-da-da*, there's nothing for him to hook onto."

"You don't mind hearing the program?" Yoko asks.

"I want to," John says. "You see, with Yoko's and my album, we're both looking at the same thing from different sides of the table. Mine is literate, hers is revolutionary. She's got a sixteen-track voice!"

The radio program ends, and John and Yoko are relaxing on their bed, John half watching the soundless television screen and reading an essay called "Concept Art" by violinist and composer Henry Flynt, whom John and Yoko have just visited.

"Before I met John," Yoko begins saying, "and when I had become sort of famous because of my film *Bottoms* [*the 1967 film of 365 backsides for eighty minutes, a film John described as Many Happy Endings*], that was the loneliest time in my life. Some people resented me because of my fame and made me feel isolated. Now, when my record is played on the radio, I've got someone who's pleased.

"And, concerning my notion of music, when I met John originally, he said it was okay for me to listen to the Beatles' sessions."

John: "I had to get permission!"

"And after one of the sessions I asked John, 'Why don't you use different rhythms instead of just going *ba-ba-ba-ba*?' It was a kind of avant-garde snobbery on my part, because my voice was going [*vibrating; uhghh . . . ghuhhh*], but there was no beat. So I thought to myself [*simpering tone*], 'Well, simple music!' You see, I was doing music of the mind—no sound at all, everybody sitting around, just imagining sounds. At my earlier New York City concerts I was throwing peas from a bag at the people and I had long hair and I was circling my hair and the movement was a sound. Even then, some people were saying that maybe it was too dramatic. Then there was my *Wall Piece*, which instructed you to hit the wall with your head, and that was called too dramatic as well. But I felt stifled even with that, I was dying to scream, to go back to my voice. And I came to a point where I believed that the idea of avant-garde purity was just as stifling as just doing a rock beat over and over."

"Dear," John interrupts, "one thing that's going to throw you. Henry Flynt is talking about 'Sweets for My Sweet' by the Drifters—he's been rocking for a long time. You know, he played us some fantastic stuff the other night when we saw him. 'Sweets for My Sweet' was a big rock 'n' roll hit, so he's been aware of that for a long time. I don't think he got to that sound pissing about with mathematics. I had to interrupt since I was just reading something he wrote about concept art and it's bloody hard, but he gets to 'Sweets for My Sweet' and I understood him."

"Probably I was the only one who didn't," Yoko says.

"Right," responds John, singing: "Dun de dun dun! I'm not putting you down, I'm just very surprised to read this."

"I know you mean well," Yoko replies, "but I get sort of lost."

"You were talking about the 4/4 beat."

"I realized," Yoko continues, "that modern classical composers, when they went from 4/4 to 4/3, lost the heartbeat. It's as if they left the ground and lived on the fortieth floor. Schoenberg and

Webern—Webern's on the top of the Empire State Building. But that's all right. Our conceptual rhythm got complex, but we still have the body and the beat. Conceptual rhythm I carry on with my voice, which has a very complicated rhythm even in 'Why,' but the bass and the drum is the heartbeat. So the body and the conceptual rhythms go together. These days I'm putting a beat under everything I do."

"Yoko and I have clashed artistically," John laughs. "Our egos have smashed once or twice. But if I know what I'm doing as an artist, then I can see if I'm being hypocritical in my reactions. I sometimes am overawed by her talent. I think, fuck, I better watch out, she is taking over, I better get meself in here. And I say, are you taking over? And then say all right, all right, and I relax again. I mean, she's going to haul three hundred and sixty-five legs and make a bloody film about a fly crawling over some woman's body, what is it? But it's all right, I know her."

"An artist couple is the most difficult thing," Yoko continues. "On the David Frost program, some guy was saying, 'I like to write music and my fiancée likes to write poetry.' The fact is that we both paint, compose, and write poetry, and on that basis I think we're doing pretty well."

"If you do two LPs there might be a little change!" John laughs. "But until then I don't mind. When she wants the A side, that's when we start fighting. The reason the covers of our albums are similar is that I wanted us to be separate and to be together, too, not to have it appear that old John-and-Yoko is over, because they're dying for us to fall apart, for God knows what reason. It's just that everybody doesn't want anybody else to be happy, because nobody's happy."

"I think it's a miracle that we're doing all right. But we are doing all right, don't you think, John?"

"It's just handy to fuck your best friend. That's what it is. And once I resolved the fact that it was a woman as well, it's all right. We go through the trauma of life and death every day, so it's not so much of a worry about what sex we are anymore. I'm living with an artist who's inspiring me to work. And, you know, Yoko is the most famous unknown artist. Everybody knows her name, but nobody knows what she does."

Yoko stands five feet two and weighs ninety-five pounds, more or less. "It is nice to keep oneself small," she once wrote, "like a grain of rice, instead of expanding. Make yourself dispensable, like paper. See little, hear little, and think little."

An autobiography she once wrote states:
born: Bird Year
early childhood: collected skies
adolescence: collected sea-weeds

late adolescence: gave birth to a
grapefruit, collected snails,
clouds, garbage cans etc.
Have graduated many schools
specializing in these subjects.

"I dropped out in my third year at Sarah Lawrence," Yoko explains, "and I started living in New York around Eighty-sixth and Amsterdam, where all the trucks go all the time. My new life was very exciting for me because I was living next to a meat market and I felt as if I had a house with a delicatessen in it. The only thing was that I couldn't figure out how to present my work because I didn't know how to communicate with people. And I didn't know how to explain to people how shy I was. When people visited I wanted to be in a big sort of box with little holes where nobody could see me but I could see through the holes. So, later, that developed into my *Bag Piece*, where you can be inside and see outside, but they can't see you.

"When I was going to Sarah Lawrence, I was mainly staying in the music library and listening to Schoenberg and Webern; they thrilled me, really. And I was writing some serial works at that time. But I was lazy writing out a whole score. And, further, I was doing the *Match Piece* in those days, just lighting a match and watching until it disappeared. And I even thought that maybe there was something in me that was going to go crazy, like a pyromaniac. See, I was writing poetry and music and painting, and none of that satisfied me. I knew that the medium was wrong. Whenever I wrote a poem, they said it was too long, it was like a short story; a novel was like a short story and a short story was like a poem. I felt that I was like a misfit in every medium.

"I just stayed in Scarsdale at my parents' home, and I was going crazy because I couldn't communicate with them very well. I was lighting matches, afraid of becoming a pyromaniac. But then I thought that there might be some people who needed something more than painting, poetry, and music, something I called an 'additional act' that you needed in life. And I was doing all that just to prevent myself from going mad, really. And when I had this apartment in New York, what happened was that instead of drying my face with a towel, I used my best cocktail dress. And then I was imagining myself all the time as a kite, holding on to a kite, and when I was sleeping, I'd lose my string, go off floating. That's the time I thought: I'll go crazy. So I just imagined myself holding on to a kite, and the kite was me.

"People asked me what I was doing. I didn't know how to explain that actually I was just holding the string, making sure that

I wouldn't let go. This was a trait I had when I was a little girl, too, when my mother asked me what I was doing all by myself, and I would say: 'I'm breathing,' and I was really counting my breathings, and thinking: 'My God, if I don't count them, would I not breathe?' That later became my *Breathing Piece*. And those events that I was doing in New York were very much connected with necessity."

This sense of disappearing, flying away, flames going out, suggests what the psychologist David Cooper writes about in *The Death of the Family*: the effort not to see oneself anymore, "to see through oneself as a person limited to relative being . . . . Few people can sustain this nonrelative self-regard for more than a minute or two without feeling that they are going mad, in the sense of disappearing. That is why people use mirrors in order not to see their selves with the possibility of seeing through, but to see fragmentary manifestations like their hair, eye make-up . . . and so on. If one did not effect this evasive fragmentation of the mirror image, one would be left with the experience of knowing that seeing oneself means seeing through oneself. There can be nothing more terrifying than that.

"Draw a line with yourself," Yoko writes in her *Line Piece*. "Go on drawing until you disappear." Many of these "pieces" are printed in *Grapefruit*—compositions of "music, painting, event, poetry and object"—in which the idea of dismembering and disrobing is seminal. Thus, in one of her events, Yoko asks each participant to cut off a piece of her dress until she is naked. And one remembers John and Yoko naked on the cover of *Two Virgins* and in their two *Self Portrait* films. Yoko once wrote: "People went on cutting the parts they do not like of me; finally there was only the stone remained of me that was in me but they were still not satisfied and wanted to know what it's like in the stone." The point is that the act of taking off one's clothes is merely a metaphor for the uncovering of the self.

Yoko's "Music of the Mind"—e.g., "Peel. Peek. Take off." (*Pieces for Orchestra*, 1962)—came to fruition in the winter of 1960. She rented a loft on Chambers Street in New York. "All the windows were smoked glass so that you couldn't really see outside, but there was the skylight, and when you were in the loft you almost felt more connected to the sky than to the city outside. It was a cold-water flat, $50.50 a month, and it was great. I didn't have chairs or beds, and so people downstairs gave me orange crates and I put all the crates together to make a large table, crates for the chairs, and at night I just collected them and made a bed out of them. And I started to live there.

"A friend of mine told me that there was a group of artists who were thinking of putting on their works and would I mind if they joined me and did things together. And I said, no, I wouldn't mind, and perhaps they wouldn't mind painting my loft for free. Everyone was lazy and didn't get around to painting it white, but I got used to the gray."

The famous Chambers Street loft concerts featured artists, musicians, dancers, and poets, a list of whose names reads like a roster of the avant-garde hall of fame: Walter De Maria, Joseph Byrd, La Monte Young, Jackson Mac Low, George Maciunas, Phillip Corner, George Brecht, Diane Wakoski, Yvonne Rainer, Henry Flynt, David Tudor, and Richard Maxfield. "But there was no mention that I should have a concert there, and I wasn't going to be the one to mention it," Yoko says. "Somehow my work was still suffering. The idea had been to stop my suffering by getting a place to present my work and at last letting everybody know what I was doing. But it just went on like that. Many people thought that I was a very rich girl who was just 'playing avant-garde.' And some others thought that I was a mistress of some very rich man, which wasn't true either. I think that the reason that some people thought the whole thing was organized by some Chinese man was because La Monte's name is Young. And meanwhile I was just surviving by teaching Japanese folk art."

Within the next couple of years, Yoko had concerts featuring her own work at the Village Gate, the Bridge Theater, and Carnegie Recital Hall. Her first art exhibition took place at the Agnus Gallery, owned by Fluxus originator George Maciunas. (Fluxus was the name of a group of Zen- and John Cage–influenced avant-garde artists who often worked in mixed media.) And among the instruction paintings there were: *Painting for the Wind*, which featured a bag full of seeds hanging in front of a blank canvas, and when the wind blew, seeds would fall out through the bag's small holes; *Smoke Painting*, where you lit a match and watched the smoke against the canvas; and *Painting to Be Stepped On*, where you stepped on the canvas and made a mark until many marks made up the painting. It was this element of participation, of adding things, of watching things grow and change, that enabled you to see Yoko's instructions as a way of "getting together, as in a chain letter." And, following this exhibition, Yoko presented a lecture-concert at Wesleyan College, events in Japan; and exhibitions in London, such as the one in 1966 at the Indica Gallery, where she met John, all of which created a growing interest in her work and an equal amount of incomprehension.

And it was Yoko's and John's extensions of the idea of participating—the "additional act" that would suggest to others how reciprocally to involve themselves—that led to the famous peace events, filmed and reported on many times—the bed-ins, the "War Is Over" poster, which appeared in hundreds of newspapers around the world, and the sending of acorns to world leaders, who were invited by John and Yoko to plant them and watch them grow.

Yoko's first important concert took place at the end of 1961 at Carnegie Recital Hall. "It was a big moment for me," Yoko recalls.

"George Brecht, Jonas Mekas, La Monte Young, Jackson Mac Low, just about everyone performed in it. And Richard Maxfield helped me on the electronic side. I set up everything and then made the stage very dim, so you had to strain your eyes—because life is like that. You always have to strain to read other people's minds. And then it went into complete darkness. The week before I had given instructions to everyone as to what they should do, so that there would be a feeling of togetherness based on alienation, since no one knew the other person's instructions.

"So everybody was moving without making any sounds onstage. There was a point where two men were tied up together with lots of empty cans and bottles around them, and they had to move from one end of the stage to the other very quietly and slowly without making any sounds. What I was trying to attain was a sound that almost doesn't come out. Before I speak I stutter in my mind, and then my cultured self tries to correct that stutter into a clean sentence. And then it comes out like 'Oh, and how are you today?' instead of 'O-O-Oh-h-how are you?' But before it comes out like that you have this stuttering in you. And I wanted to deal with those sounds of people's fears and stutterings.

"So I thought that if everything was set up in a lighted room and suddenly the light was turned off, you might start to see things beyond the shapes. Or hear the kind of sounds that you hear in silence. You would start to feel the environment and tension and people's vibrations. Those were the sounds that I wanted to deal with, the sound of fear and of darkness, like a child's fear that someone is behind him, but he can't speak and communicate this. And so I asked one guy to stand behind the audience for the duration of the concert.

"I wanted the sound of people perspiring to be in it, too, so I had all the dancers wear contact microphones, and the instructions were to bring out very heavy boxes and take them back across the stage, and while they were doing that they were perspiring a little. There was one guy who was asthmatic, and it was fantastic. And in the toilet there was somebody standing throughout the evening. Whenever I go to a toilet in a film theater, I always feel very scared. If nobody's there I'm scared, but if somebody is there it's even more scary. So I wanted people to have this experience of fear. There are unknown areas of sound and experience that people can't really mention in words. Like the stuttering in your mind. I was interested not in the noise you make but the noise that happens when you try not to make it, just that tension going back and forth.

"I think I would never want to go back again to where I was, doing things like that, even though few people have touched this area. Where I'd be so lonely and miserable that nobody understood. And the kind of thing I'm doing now is more understandable. I'm not saying it's better or worse. But now I just want to feel sort of playful sometimes. And when I feel playful, to do something. That's when people seem to understand more, or at least accept more."

She once wrote: "After unblocking one's mind, by dispensing with visual, auditory, and kinetic perceptions, what will come out of us? Would there be anything? I wonder. And my events are mostly spent in wonderment." Before they are anything else, Yoko's poems, events, films, and music exemplify a wonderment that suggests childlike awe, a way of seeing things as if you were entering a strange street, invisible until now, for the first time; or as if, for example, you were watching a western—the sheriff, rustlers, corral fights—through the eyes of one of the horses. More than that, wonderment implies intensity of perception resulting in one's identification with what is seen, not as the "utterly other," but as the utterly same. Thus the everyday becomes the numinous. And eventually the perceived object or person disintegrates, for when you see something at this level of clarity, it disappears, and you find yourself asking, what really is there?

David Cooper writes: "To commence the unuse of the word 'neurosis,' let us regard it as a way of being that is made to seem childish by one's fear of the fear of others about one's becoming childlike. . . . The fear is the fear of madness, of being childlike or even being before one's origins, so that any act may cohere others against oneself to suppress any spontaneous gesture that has socially disruptive, archaic resonances." The childlike gestures and awarenesses reveal themselves in Yoko's ways of seeing everything: "An intensity of a wink is: two cars smashed head on. / A storm turned into a breeze. / A water drop from a loose faucet" ("Wink Talk"). And in her "Touch Poem," Yoko writes: "Give birth to a child/See the world through its eye / Let it touch everything possible / and leave its fingermark there / in place of a signature."

"Sometimes," Yoko says, "I think that some of the things I've done could have been done by John, and vice versa." John, in fact, used Yoko's *Imagine* instructions (e.g., "Imagine the clouds dripping. Dig a hole in your garden to put them in") as the seminal idea for his song "Imagine." And together they collaborated on a number of films that, among other things, seem to be about seeing things as if for the first time—the "love that has no past."

Fly, John and Yoko's most recent film, made in New York in two days, shows a naked woman lying motionless on her back as one fly at a time settles on different parts of her body to go about its business—mainly leg-tasting-and-feeling. Some of the flies were stunned with CO_2, having failed to follow a trail of sugar water over the woman's body. The woman's catatonia remains a mystery.

Watching *Fly*, one might almost imagine that Walt Disney and the minimalist director Jean-Marie Straub had collaborated, for the film's magnified focus on what a fly does if you don't brush it away is shot in long takes, with the camera obliquely observing the transformed landscape of a mountainous breast, a hillock nipple, or a desert of fingers on which the fly stands, legs investigating the scene. And at the film's conclusion, you see a long shot of the entire body with six flies standing here and there as if on a dead Christ—an amazing Buñuelian moment that makes the fly a metaphor for pain. The flies finally fly away, and we're left with a shot through the window of a New York Bowery roof, veiled in a diaphanous blue light like Saint Elmo's fire, suggesting the beauty of seeing things anew.

"The idea of the film came to me," Yoko says, "when I thought about that joke where someone says to a man: 'Did you notice that woman's hat?' and he's looking at her bosom instead. I wondered how many people would look at the fly or at the body. I tried, when filming, to accept all the things that showed up, but at the same time tried not to make the film too dramatic. It would have been very easy for me to have made it become pornographic, and I didn't want that. Each shot had to project more than a pretty image of a body, so it was used more as an abstract line."

Yoko's voice on *Fly*'s soundtrack is a subtle rhythmic embodiment of the fly's excursions—intersected by John's forward and backward guitar track. And these amazing sounds reveal again those childlike gestures and archaic resonances. For it is most obviously in what John calls her "sixteen-track voice" that Yoko displays her extraordinary art. It is the true distillation of her *sens plus pur*, a kind of psychophysical instrument of amazing disparateness, richness, and range. Yoko's voice is a kind of vocal tachistoscope (the shuttered magic lantern that projects images for a thousandth of a second), immediately and almost subliminally communicating glittering movements of the smallest elements of sound, reminding you of the screams, wails, laughter, groans, caterwauls of both a primordial, prebirth, premammalian past, as well as of the fogged-over, pained immediacy of childhood.

Musically, what happens is that pitch inflections interpolate, and permute to convey the impression of anything from a Japanese *shakuhachi* to bantams in pine woods to swamp animals' madrigals to the feeling of being inside of one's own body cavities. Yoko's voice enters sound to reveal its most basic frequential characteristics and proposes to the listener that if he wants to hear, he might as well stop trying. "She becomes her voice," John says, "and you get touched." This vocal quality can be heard most powerfully on "Don't Worry Kyoko"; the soundtrack for *Fly*; and *Yoko Ono/Plastic Ono Band* (with John on guitar, Klaus Voormann on bass, Ringo on drums, and, on "AOS," by Charles Haden, David Izenzon, Ed Blackwell, and Ornette Coleman).

"When I say things," Yoko comments, "I stutter a little bit. Most of us kill off our real emotions, and on top of them you have your smooth self. It's like the guy in the film *Diary of a Mad Housewife* with his singsong voice. There's that unreal tone. But when I want to say 'I'm sorry' in a song—because music to me is something so honest and so real—I don't feel like saying [*singsong*] 'I'm sorry, mother,' but rather as an emotion should be [*groaning, stuttering*] 'I'm so-or-orrrry.' A stutterer is someone who's feeling something genuine. So in 'Paper Shoes' I say: 'Pa-pa-pa-a-a-per sh-shooooes!'

"The older you get, the more frustrated you feel. And it gets to a point where you don't have time to utter a lot of intellectual bullshit. If you were drowning you wouldn't say: 'I'd like to be helped because I have just a moment to live.' You'd say, 'Help!' but if you were more desperate you'd say, '*Eioughhhh*,' or something like that. And the desperation of life is really life itself, the core of life, what's really driving us forth. When you're really desperate, it's phony to use descriptive and decorative adjectives to express yourself."

But isn't there another side, such as the seeming gentleness of "Who Has Seen the Wind?"—the quiet little song Yoko presented on the B side of John's "Instant Karma!"? "On that song," Yoko says, "the voice is wavering a little, there are shrills and cracks, it's not professional pop singing; the background is going off a little. There was something of a lost little girl about it. What I was aiming at was the effect you get in Alban Berg's *Wozzeck*, where the drunkard sings—a slightly crazed voice, a bit of a broken toy. In that sense, it was a quiet desperation."

Religion, a philosopher once said, is what you do with your aloneness . . . or, one might add, with your pain and desperation. Yoko's music pushes pain into a kind of invigorating and liberated energy, just as a stutterer finally gives birth to a difficult word, since it existed originally at the fine edge between inaudibility and the sound waves of dreams. About her music for *Fly*, she comments: "It's nice to go into that very very fine, intricate mixture of sounds and rhythm. It's almost like going into a dream, getting something that doesn't exist in the physical world, unutterable sounds—a kind of metaphysical rhythm."

What Yoko calls "metaphysical sound" seems at first to be the true opposition to her unblocked music. Yet it is less an opposition than the idea of the dream of sound from which her new art emerges, a music which, the philosopher Max Picard tells us, is "silence, which in dreaming begins to sound . . ." and, as Picard—in a very Ono-esque manner—continues: "In silence the lines of the mouth are like the closed wings of a butterfly. When the word starts moving, the wings open, and the butterfly flies away."

"Around the time that I met John," Yoko tells me at the conclusion of our conversation, "I went to a palmist—John would probably laugh at this—and he said: 'You're like a very, very fast wind that goes speeding around the world.' And I had a line that signified astral projection. The only thing I didn't have was a root. But, the palmist said, you've met a person who's fixed like a mountain, and if you get connected with that mountain you might get materialized. And John is like a frail wind, too, so he understands all these aspects .... I'm starting to think that maybe I can live. Before, it seemed impossible; I was just about at the vanishing point, and all my things were too conceptual. But John came in and said, 'All right, I understand you.' And just by saying that, all those things that were supposed to vanish stayed."

(1971)

HARRY PARTCH
Sound-Magic and Passionate Speech

IN 1930, THE THEN-TWENTY-NINE-YEAR-OLD composer Harry Partch was living in a small room on Charles Street in New Orleans. Sometime earlier or later, sleeping in one of the many California arbors where he picked grapes and prunes as a hobo during the Depression, Partch woke up one morning and realized that he and Western European music were through.

In that luminescent hour, it seemed as if the concert hall ("where inhibited strangers sit stiffly in flank, before and after"), the restricting twelve-note scale with its faithful and obsequious servant (the piano), and the entire corpus of symphonic "classics" were a claustrophobic cultural mirage receding into the Western night.

"Out of such abysses," Nietzsche once wrote—as if to describe the moment—"also out of the abyss of great suspicion, one returns newborn, having shed one's skin, more ticklish and sarcastic, with a more delicate taste for joy, with a more tender tongue for all good things, with gayer senses, with a second dangerous innocence in joy, more childlike and yet a hundred times more subtle than one has ever seen before."

"*Pure* music, *pure* drama, *pure* telephone poles in the virgin grazz," Partch later wrote, nose-thumbing the cultural establishment; "*pure* black-and-white tails, *pure* orchids on a *pure* bosom (I *love* music!),″ as he pulled away the veils covering the traditional notions of what music should be: "Whistle softly, and as each loving muscle snuggles under, and each tiny cilia wiggles free, you will see—shimmering before you—the curves of x million perceptible changes in pitch, at least 127 varieties of female giggles, and no less than 17 kinds of falsetto wails in each cubic foot of free vibrating air."

Back in that room in New Orleans, cilia struggling to wiggle free, Harry Partch gathered up sixteen years' worth of his youthful compositions, placed them in a potbellied stove and burned them all in what must have been a ravishing auto-da-fé. "Not free *from* what, but free *for* what" might have been Partch's motto for the next four decades, during which the now-seventy-three-year-old composer [1973] revealed himself to be one of the great originals in the history of American music. Jacques Barzun has called Partch's work "the most original and powerful contribution to dramatic music on this continent." And his admirers have included composers as diverse in style as Howard Hanson, Otto Luening, Douglas Moore, and Lou Harrison—as well as jazz musicians like Scott LaFaro, Chet Baker, Gerry Mulligan, Gil Evans, and Bob Brookmeyer.

But because Partch's instruments are one of a kind, requiring specially trained musicians to perform them and master the composer's forty-three-tones-to-the-octave scale, and because works like *The Bewitched* are enormous ritualistic music dramas demanding at least six months of rehearsals, there have been few opportunities to experience directly Partch's extraordinary art.

"The work that I have been doing these many years," Partch has said, "parallels much in the attitudes and actions of primitive man. He found sound-magic in the common materials around him. He then proceeded to make the vehicle, the instrument, as visually beautiful as he could. Finally, he involved the sound-magic and the visual beauty in his everyday words and experiences, his ritual and drama, in order to lend greater meaning to his life. This is my trinity: sound-magic, visual beauty, experience-ritual."

In order to realize his new conceptions of sound-magic, Partch, over a period of forty years, has designed and built close to thirty beautiful-looking and -sounding instruments. These include:

The Zymo-Xyl, an "exercise in hither and thither aesthesia" constructed out of hubcaps and a kettletop, oak blocks placed above a triangular resonator, and wine and liquor bottles turned upside down in two banks—starting with Old Heaven Hill and gently lurching up a scale consisting of Vat 69 and Gordon's Gin (among others), finally ending up with Harvey's Bristol Cream Sherry.

The Gourd Tree and Cone Gong, an instrument made up of twelve temple bells attached "like exotic fruit" to a bar of eucalyptus—each bell bolted to a gourd resonator—and two nose-cone gongs salvaged from a reject Douglas Aircraft bomber.

The Mazda Marimba, an instrument named after Ahura Mazda—the Persian god of light—consisting of banks of tuned lightbulbs, severed at the sockets and with their entrails removed, and sounding like "the percolations of a coffee pot."

The Spoils of War, an instrument made of seven artillery shell casings, Pyrex chemical-solution jars, a woodblock and marimba bar, a gourd *guiro*, and spring steel flexitones (known as Whang Guns): "How much better to have them here than shredding young boys' skin in the battlefield," Partch once remarked.

The Cloud-Chamber Bowls, an instrument created out of the tops and bottoms of Pyrex chemical-solution jars (Partch found them in the glass shop of the University of California radiation lab) which are suspended on a rack and hit on their sides and tops with soft mallets.

"I am not an instrument builder," Partch once said of his musical and sculptural wonders, "only a philosophic music man seduced into carpentry." The result of "an acoustical ardor and a conceptual fervor," Partch's instruments are specifically designed to perform his forty-three-tones-to-the-octave music. Early in his life, the composer decided that the twelve-note scale represented an unacceptable structural rigidity and conceptual imprecision. Certainly, Partch was hardly the first person to turn to the principles of *just intonation*—a system of tuning in which all the musical intervals are derived from the perfect fifth and perfect third and their multiples. (Our twelve-tone scale is acoustically "distorted" for the sake of modulatory simplicity. Play an F-sharp on a guitar or violin and compare these results with the one note on our equal-tempered—or, as Partch likes to say, "ill-tempered"—piano. Or listen to a perfectly sung blues seventh note and contrast it with the piano equivalent.)

The twelve-tone scale, in other words, is not a God-given construct. A fifty-three-tone system was proposed by both the Chinese Ching Fang in the first century B.C. and the seventeenth-century Danish mathematician Nicolas Mercator. Chinese, Indian, and Arab systems of tuning, of course, are based on microtonal proportions. Scores of musicians and theorists used these intervals during the Renaissance as well. In 1555, for example, the Italian composer Vicentino made a harpsichord in which the octave was divided into thirty intervals spread over six manuals, each being tuned to one of the six Greek modes. And in this century, composers like Ives, Haba, Bloch, Bartók, Lou Harrison, Alan Hovhaness, and John Cage, among others, have employed microtonal elements in their work. (It goes without saying that jazz musicians have been the most natural practitioners in this area.)

But Harry Partch is undoubtedly the only Western composer to use successfully a specific just-intonational scale as the basis for all his music. With this scale—forty-three tones to the octave, whose basic tone is 392 cycles per second, our tempered G—Partch dispenses with key harmony and conventional modulations, thereby allowing for an "expanded" harmony and overtone enrichment and offering what the composer claims to be twenty-eight possible tonalities. As the critic Peter Yates has described it, this scale creates "a continuous field of melodic and harmonic relationship among the degrees of spoken, intoned, chanted, sung, melismatic, and shouted vocal utterance—a tonal spectrum filling in the gap between the vocal coloration of opera and the spoken drama. Spoken melody may be taken over by the instruments and translated back again to chant and song."

As performed on his predominantly plectral-percussive instruments, Partch's works certainly reveal affinities with Indonesian, Polynesian, Japanese, and African musical practices (as well as with Yaqui, Zuni, and Cahuilla American Indian chants which, in fact, Partch uses in several of his works)—existing in that region where, as James Joyce once wrote, "that earopean end meets Ind." But rather than suggesting and languishing in an easily imitated and modish kind of atmospheric musical chinoiserie, Partch's compositions instinctively reflect and operate as counterparts to the specific structural and expressive qualities—timbral, articulative, vibratory, and rhythmic—of much non-Western music.

It is interesting, too, to recall a statement that Arnold Schoenberg once made, and one which he never really applied seriously in his own music: "I cannot unreservedly agree," Schoenberg wrote, "with the distinction between color and pitch. I find that a note is perceived by its color, one of whose dimensions is pitch. Color, then, is the great realm, pitch one of its provinces. . . . If the ear could discriminate between differences of color, it might be feasible to invent melodies that are built of colors. But who dares to develop such theories?" And it is exactly this theory (though he dislikes "theory") that Partch put into practice in his shimmering, vibrant music, exhibiting an enormous variety of articulative shadings, fluctuating tremolos, rotating rhythmic patterns, with the steam engine whistles of the Chromelodeon and moaning Crychord sounding like trains passing through the New Mexico and Arizona deserts that Partch remembers from his youth.

Concomitant with Partch's discovery of the world of music within himself came his insight that "spontaneity of execution is the essence of music, vitally connected to the human body through the mouth, the ears, and the emotions. . . . This thing began with truth, and truth *does* exist. For some hundreds of years, the truth of just intonation has been hidden—one could say *maliciously,* because truth always threatens the ruling hierarchy . . . or they so *think.* Nor does the spiritual-corporeal nature of man fare any better. We are reduced to specialties—a theater of dialogue without music, for example, or a concert of music without drama—basic mutilations of ancient concept. My music is visual; it is corporeal, aural, *and* visual."

Partch continually talks about how his musicians "must always present pictures of athletic grace" when they're performing. He speaks of caressing, embracing, and even raping the instruments. And the instruments themselves seem to embody male and female sexual characteristics—resonating tongues in bamboo, nose cones—while their tones and timbres often cause a powerful physical excitation. About his Marimba Eroica—an instrument made of four spruce timbers and large boxlike resonators that can produce an almost inaudible twenty-two-cycles-per-second sound—Partch says: "In the right room, acoustically, the Eroica is felt through the feet against the belly, and if one sits on the floor, it ripples through his bottom. . . . I've dreamed of an Eroica with reinforced concrete resonators going down into the ground and boxes mounted above them like a stairway. One could therefore trip barefoot up the scale to bed and box down to breakfast. Or trip both ways at once to a musical apotheosis."

In 1923 Partch began to develop the two seminal ideas that would fertilize all his later work—those of the One Voice (Monophony) and the Corporeal. The composer saw in ancient Greek drama, whose spirit he thought originated in epic chant, a one-voice/one-instrument idea that has kept itself alive from Homer to the Balkan minstrels. Between 1930 and 1947, in fact, Partch himself performed on only one instrument—his Adapted Viola, built with an elongated neck and played between the knees—with which he accompanied himself singing biblical passages, Li Po poems, and the hitchhiker inscriptions that he included in his hobo epic *The Wayward* (1943), consisting of *Barstow*, *The Letter*, *San Francisco*, and *U.S. Highball*. These four works use on-the-road conversation fragments, boxcar graffiti, signs from derelict havens, newsboy cries, hitchhiker inscriptions, names of railroad towns, and fleeting thoughts—all recited, sung, intoned, and chanted against microtonal moans, instrumental imitations of railway noises, snatches of bar tunes, pentatonic shouts, and seventh- and ninth-chord guitar riffs.

Partch's criticism of the "classical" operatic and lieder tradition was that it avoided the natural spoken rhythms and tonal glides of everyday speech, insisting instead of artificial devices such as rolled r's, precise attacks and releases, the affected stylization of "refined" English, and a choral technique that gloried in the singing of meaningless syllables, short reiterated phrases, and highly dramatic but unbelievable "unison" passages. (Needless to say, Robert Johnson and Chuck Berry had pretty much the same idea. So did W. B. Yeats and William Carlos Williams, the latter of whom, when writing about Lelia Zukofsky's *Music to Shakespeare's Pericles*, talked about the "shouting and spouting, distortion and clouding of words and phrasing that is opera.")

In his book *Genesis of a Music*, first published in 1949 and revised and reissued in 1974, Partch took his notion of the necessary relationship between speech and music—a notion subscribed to by philosophers and composers from Plato to Carl Orff—and followed it through Western history in order to point out how this relationship broke down in the "word distortion of florid secular polyphony and restrictive liturgical polyphony." Partch sees the "musical phoenix rising from the ashes of ancient Rome" in some of the early operatic works of Peri, Caccini, and Monteverdi (the seventeenth-century Italian composers who brought the *word* back into importance after the musically delirious styles of Nenna and Gesualdo). To Partch, Bach and Beethoven represented an unacceptable abstractional approach to art, and he gives approval to only a small number of European compositions, among them pieces by Berlioz, Mussorgsky (a personal favorite of Partch's—"word-loving, sensitive, subtle and natural Mussorgsky," Partch says of him), Wagner (who wrote: "We have to recognize Speech itself as the indispensable basis of a perfect Artistic Expression"), Hugo Wolf, Mahler (*The Song of the Earth*), Debussy (*Pelléas and Mélisande*), Satie (*Socrate*), and Schoenberg (*Pierrot Lunaire*, and *only* that work by Schoenberg). To Partch, the works of these composers are the small lights in the abstract darkness of Western music.

The idea of a music that becomes a "language in itself" seems, to Partch, to deny the human body. But by unequivocally pressing his antagonism to such an idea, he does away with extraordinarily vital music by composers such as Machaut, Dufay, Bach, Beethoven, and Stravinsky. Partch himself, in a new preface to *Genesis of a Music*, admits now that "this survey was not adequate to the facts." Still, his attacks on the concert-hall "star" system, and the mathematical orientation of establishment musical life are at the service of a life-enhancing artistic vision: "One's beginning is a decent and honorable mistake, and long before life has run its course, one is obliged to contemplate—both dazed and undazed—the endless reaches of one's innocence. . . . Rules and standards become meaningless once the simple truth is faced. Let us give to nuts and bolts the standardization of thread that we have come to expect, but let us give to music, magic; to man, magic. . . . My peaks of wrath and nadirs of depression, through some four decades, were akin to the fulminations and despair of the Hebrew prophets, and for exactly the same reasons: the endowed priests of the temple sanctifying form without content, ritual without value. Hollow magic."

Drawing on his idea of Corporeal music and the principles of Greek, Japanese Kabuki, and No and mummers' plays, Partch has created a number of music dramas containing music, dance, mime, shouting, whistling, and slapstick—in all of which the instruments are part of the stage set, their performers in costume, both singing and acting.

Revelation in the Courthouse Park (1960) presents a psychological parallel to Euripides' *The Bacchae*. Shifting between ancient Thebes and a modern park in which Dionysus becomes Dion, the Hollywood king of Ishbu Kubu, Partch's work features—in addition to the actors, musicians, and dancers—a marching brass band, acrobats, gymnasts, and a filmed fireworks display.

Water! Water! (1961) takes place in Santa Mystiana, a large American city whose inhabitants include a disc jockey, an alderman, a lady mayor, and a baseball radio commentator. The city calls on a black jazz band to invoke rain in a voodoo ritual, and when the rains fall, the baseball game is washed out and civilization collapses. After the flood, Arthur, the jazz musician, and Wanda the Witch are sued for millions of dollars and stand trial. But at this moment, the dam begins to overflow, and the citizens accept their fate to the tune of "Santa Mystiana the Beautiful." The producer drives the traveling instruments into the pit of the stage, for "the highest goodness is like water. It seeks the low place, that all men dislike" (after Lao-tzu).

Delusion of the Fury (1963–69), Partch's most recent and most powerful music-drama, is based on a No-drama theme about a murdered man who, in death, must exorcise the moment of his dying in his past existence, as well as on an African folk tale about a deaf man, a deaf judge, a judgment, and the intercession of pagan deities. In *Delusion* and the ravishing instrumental composition *And on the Seventh Day Petals Fell in Petaluma*, which served as the "musical sinews" for *Delusion*, Partch has fully realized his idea of Corporeal music. And the composer's longstanding attraction to No drama gives the key to his understanding of "sound-magic, visual beauty, and experience-ritual." Early on in his career, Partch had spoken of No as a "drama of accomplished grace," and one is sure he meant to suggest both the idea of the highly charged "gesture" as well as of the state of immanence. In his notes for his composition *Oedipus* (1952), Partch spoke of the music as being "conceived as emotional saturation." And like the No drama, where subsisting tensions and longings are resolved in the form of a final dance, all of Partch's later music-dramas are at once rituals of enormous emotional charge and allegories presenting the force of the unrepressed body and spirit in its progress through the abstract world.

Partch's *The Bewitched* (1957) reveals this most clearly. A tribe of Lost Musicians, representing instinctual life, unmaliciously destroys the fake products of twentieth-century European civilization. Titles for the scenes of the drama suggest the amazing humor of the work: "Three Undergraduates Become Transfigured in a Hong Kong Music Hall"; "A Soul Tortured by Contemporary Music Finds a Humanizing Alchemy"; "Visions Fill the Eyes of a Defeated Basketball Team in the Shower Room." Partch's seven-page program notes for *The Bewitched*—filled with discussions about matriarchal society, sexual evolution, and adolescent love, and written with his characteristic verbal brilliance—not only suggest the tone of the work but reflect the composer's larger ideas and feelings about his artistic endeavor. Here is Partch's description of the work's Prologue, entitled "The Lost Musicians Mix Magic":

"The forms of strange instruments are seen onstage. How did they get here? They came on in a dark celestial silence, doing tumbles and handsprings, and for no other purpose than to be discovered by *these* musicians in *this* theater before *this* audience.

"One of the musicians gives a low beat, and others swing in, one at a time. They are neolithic primitives in their unspoken acceptance of magic as real, unconsciously reclaiming an all-but-lost value for the exploitation of their perception in an age of scientific hierarchs—a value lost only about a minute ago in relation to that ancient time when the first single cell moved itself in such autoerotic agitation that it split in two. The first animate magic.

"In the enveloping ensemble the lost musicians have momentarily found a direction, a long-arm extension of first magic. Their direction becomes a power, and their power a vision: an ancient witch, a prehistoric seer untouched by either gossip or popular malevolence, and with that wonderful power to make others see also. The perceptive witch corresponds to the Greek oracle, while the chorus [*the orchestra*]—like the choruses of ancient tragedy—is a moral instrument under the power of perceptive suggestion.

"The lost musicians are quite without malice. On wings of love they demolish three undergraduate egos temporarily away from their jukeboxes. It is the kind thing to do. On wings of love they turn an incorrigibly pursuing young wooer into a retreating misogynist. It is the kind thing to do. On wings of love they catapult the cultural know-it-alls into limbo, because limbo will be so congenial. It is certainly the kind thing to do.

"The witch surveys the world and immediately becomes sad and moody, then takes command: "Everybody wants background music!" the witch-like sounds seem to murmur, and the conspiratorial tone is clear even in gibberish. Let us dance."

In April 1973, I wrote to Harry Partch in San Diego to ask him if I could fly over to visit him and, since I wouldn't have a car, if he could recommend a motel near his home. A week later I received this note:

Dear Jonathan Cott—

The Alamo Motel, 4567 Texas St., San Diego. It is the closest, $10–$12 a day, kitchenette, swimming pool—$35 a week. I think I'll move there—it sounds better than this wretched place. It is close to the No. 11 bus, on Adams Ave. Take that east to Felton, then walk north. . . .

I will be 72 in June, and I've been interviewed for over 40 years. The interviewers are generally nice guys and gals, but very frankly I am sick to death of my "career."

However, you will be welcomed. It is an old habit.

> Yours,
>
> Harry Partch

The Alamo Motel is one of an enormous number of those culturally rootless Southern California apartment-motel dwellings bearing names like Rampart Manor, the Telstar, Lee Tiki, Il Pompeii, and Fountain Bleu which the architect Robert Venturi has classified as "the ugly and the ordinary." By that, Venturi doesn't mean that these places lack charm or interest—Venturi's recent architecture, in fact, uses exactly this quintessential American style to construct things like a firehouse along the lines of an expanded Lionel toy train station.

And the Alamo is certainly a "cheerful" place: the friendly couple who run it chat with the guests right through the day, invite you in for coffee—and when you're not watching TV, you can contemplate the tiny swimming pool stuck in the courtyard alongside a row of rubber plants, banana, and kumquat trees, flag lilac, geraniums, and swamp grass. (It's the place W. C. Fields might have retired to in *It's a Gift*).

Harry Partch lives a mile or so up the road in a small, nondescript suburban home on a street like any other, with TV aerials five times the height of the houses rising out of every roof. Partch, who lived as a hobo for twelve years, has since the forties moved his lodgings every few years—from a chick hatchery in Petaluma where he composed *Petals*, to a laundromat in Venice, L.A., to several homes in the San Diego area where his devoted friend and musical associate Danlee Mitchell works with and assists the composer. (Mitchell, who has been training musicians and performing all of Partch's recent works, stores the Partch instruments in a special studio at San Diego State College, where he teaches.)

The first thing that distinguishes Partch's home from any other on the block is a strange sign hanging on the door:

OCCUPANT IS A HEATHEN CHINEE
MISSIONARIES AT THIS DOOR WILL
FACE THE DOWAGER EMPRESS
AND ANOTHER BOXER REBELLION
PLEASE DO NOT DISTURB
11 AM–2 PM
MISSIONARIES NEVER

"I'm always being bothered by the Jehovah's Witnesses," Partch says as he greets me one morning, dressed in pajamas and bathrobe. He's just gotten over a minor illness, and his living room looks a bit untogether, but comfortably so: a Chinese coolie hat and a Balinese shadow puppet on the wall and a table filled with sharpened colored pencils, black pepper containers, postcards, jumbo Gem clips, a package of Tums, and several books (including *Japan's Imperial Conspiracy* and *Maximum Security: Letters from Prison*, edited by Eve Pell—both of which Partch has recently been reading avidly).

He sits down in the driftwood-supported hammock-type couch and lights up his pipe. "My parents were missionaries in China," Partch says, "and they went *through* the Boxer Rebellion, but I don't think anyone around here has ever heard of it."

"They probably imagine it has something to do with Joe Louis," I suggest.

"Joe Louis!" Partch laughs heartily. "Probably do . . . I'm making some chicken soup and milk. Please have some."

"I know you were born in Oakland in 1901," I say.

"We left when I was two, so I don't remember that part. But later I lived there, and in fact I wrote *Oedipus* there. Hell, man, I don't care where I am. If I were in the North Pole I'd go on writing. I don't care if I'm in euphoria or in despair—I go on producing. It doesn't make any difference. I went to Hawaii when I was twenty, and everyone said: 'You won't do a *thing* in Hawaii.' Well, I never wrote so many fugues in my life."

Partch comes back with soup and milk and tells me a bit about his life. In the 1880s, his parents received the "call" and were sent to China as missionaries. When they resigned their posts, they moved to Oakland and then homesteaded in a number of towns in southeastern Arizona, where Partch grew up.

"I remember that once when I was hitchhiking during my hobo days," Partch says, "I happened in 1940 to be on the road near Big Sur. Well, I was picked up by this painter named Varda—who became well known later on in Sausalito—and I told him about my music and he said: 'You *must* spend the winter with me.' Varda was living in a place called Anason Creek—fifteen dollars a month—and when the wood ran out, he used to tear down a shack. I remember he once described Arizona to me, saying how it seemed to him to be just like Christianity. '*Touch me not*, say the ants, the cactus, and the hot sand,' Varda exclaimed. 'But the purple hills say: *Come, come, come.*' "

Partch's apostate father became involved with agnosticism, secularism, and atheism, while his mother read a lot of Mary Baker Eddy and the New Thought writers. But, as Partch has written, his parents' reading materials—whether Robert Ingersoll or Mary Baker Eddy—"simply did not stack up, in excitement, beside the wild immoralities of Greek mythology, or, in adventure, with the *Anabasis* of Xenophon. In our library there were more books in Chinese, accordion-folded with ivory thongs, illustrated with gory colored lithographs of the beheading of missionaries, than there were books in English."

At one point during his childhood, Partch lived just outside a tiny Arizona railroad town called Benson, which had a population of three hundred and eleven saloons for transient railroaders along its boardwalk. Partch began ordering instruments through the Sears, Roebuck catalog and learned one at a time—cello, violin, harmonica, mandolin, guitar, and cornet. "I was already devouring the *idea* of music," he says.

In Albuquerque, when he was fourteen, Partch began to write music seriously, played "Hearts and Flowers" in the local movie houses, and worked parttime delivering pharmaceutical drugs on his bicycle to the red-light district. (Partch remembers one lady there offering him his first cigar, which he smoked all the way through without getting sick.)

Self-taught, the composer picked up and devoured an enormous range of nontraditional musical possibilities that obviously influenced his later work: Christian hymns like "Nearer My God to Thee," Mandarin Chinese lullabies (sung by his mother), Yaqui Indian and Congo puberty rituals, Hebrew chants for the dead (heard on Edison cylinder records played for him by a store owner in Arizona), and, later, Okie songs in California vineyards and those of the Cantonese music hall. Partch remembers experiencing these musical worlds—"certain small shafts of intense light"—with a "kind of intimate passion."

For a number of years he worked as a fruitpicker, schoolteacher, and proofreader. Then in 1934 he received a Carnegie grant to study the history of intonation in England. On a trip to Ireland at that time, he took the first instrument he had designed and built— the Adapted Viola—and went to meet and play for William Butler Yeats. "I had read his prefaces—I love prefaces, incidentally—and Yeats had written some wonderful things about music and passionate speech."

In *Ah, Sweet Dancer,* a collection of Yeats's letters to Margot Ruddock, we find the following entry: "A Californian musician called a few days ago and is coming again tomorrow. He is working on the relation between words and music. He has made and is making other musical instruments which do not go beyond the range of the speaking voice but within that range make a music possible which employs very minute intervals. He speaks to this instrument. He only introduces melody when he sings vowels without any relation to words."

"The minute I brought out my viola and sang," Partch recalls, "Yeats just loved it. He's not one for theory. I played and sang 'By the Rivers of Babylon.' 'Marthe, Marthe!' he shouted, 'come here.' Later I met the poet Æ at a party in London and told him about my having played for Yeats. 'Yeats has a tin ear,' Æ said. I told him I disagreed, and we had a discussion. 'He can't tell one tone from another,' Æ insisted. 'That *proves* he has a good ear,' I replied, and Æ was a little taken aback by that. You see, I *contend* this: we hear so *much*, and it's hard to stick with only the twelve tones of the octave. . . .

"Anyway, I had no chance of making a living over in Europe, so I went from English salons to the San Joaquin Valley, where I worked as a dishwasher and flunky and picked fruit and cotton all through the Depression. They were really terrible, terrible times. But I slept out in the fields, and the hobos were my friends. (I kept my music in my hobo bundle wherever I went.) Most of the hobos were reform-school boys or orphans. One of my most beautiful pals was farmed out at the age of five, ran away at eight, and was raped before he was twelve. He was so kindly, I loved the guy. Of course I lost him after six weeks. . . . But I don't worry about these people because any good hobo can take care of himself."

With a little help from his friends, Partch has been taking care of himself for many decades, yet it is unfortunate that, though he has a small number of enthusiastic admirers, his work is generally unknown in this country.

Today, on some Middle American street in San Diego, Harry Partch is talking about the Greek musician Timotheus (446–357 B.C.), who dared to expand the scale on the kithara (an instrument Partch has rebuilt after 2,000 years) by adding four strings to the eight approved of by Pythagoras. Partch picks up a copy of *Genesis of a Music* and reads—as well as dramatically elaborates on—a passage he once wrote describing a scene by the comic poet Pherecrates in which the personification of Music bemoans her outrage at the hands of Timotheus' twelve strings:

"But now comes Timotheus," Partch speak-sings, "who has most shamelessly ruined and massacred me. Who is this Timotheus? asks Justice, one of the other persons in the play. A red-haired Milesian, is the answer. He has exceeded all the others in wickedness. He has introduced weird music like the crawlings of an antheap, unharmonic with most unholy high notes and pipings. He has filled me full of maggots like a cabbage. And once, when by chance, he met me walking alone, he disrobed me and tied me up in pieces with twelve strings.

"The Spartans drove away the immoral Timotheus," Partch dramatically concludes. "He was catapulted onto a Spartan hillside by a Spartan bouncer. To dream of undesirable changes is one thing, to act upon these dreams quite another."

There is a scene in a film about Partch entitled *The Dreamer That Remains* (directed by Stephen Pouliot and produced by one of Partch's devoted admirers, Betty Freeman) in which the composer recalls the words he once saw on the wall of an L. A. screening room belonging to a company specializing in children's films. Along with various appreciative, graffiti-type comments written by children was the following tiny poem: "Once upon a time / There was a little boy / And he went outside."

Harry Partch himself has put it quietly and beautifully: "The small child feels that he is the center of the world, in both his joys and his disasters. It is redundant to say, *the world he knows*. There is no other. And every lonely child builds worlds of his own, both with objects and in fantasy, a dozen a year, or even a dozen a day:

Can this world
From of old
Always have been so sad,
Or did it become so for the sake
Of me alone?
—Anonymous Japanese poem, trans. by Arthur Waley

"And this quality would be unchanged if other words were substituted: *Always have been so happy for the sake of me alone*."

(1973)

OUR MUSICAL PAST
REDISCOVERED
From Fuging Tunes to Sousa

NINETEENTH-CENTURY AMERICAN MUSICAL LIFE—a mixture of carnival exhibitionism, parlor recitals, and tepid academicism—presented an unlikely environment for the conception and development of any kind of important compositional practice. And it certainly seems as if the idiosyncratic twentieth-century traditions represented by composers like Charles Ives, Carl Ruggles, Henry Cowell, Ruth Crawford Seeger, Harry Partch, John Cage, and Elliott Carter were spontaneously generated. Yet it was the early American composer William Billings (1746–1800) who, when asked about the rules of composition, wrote: "Nature is the best Dictator, for all the hard, dry, studied rules that ever were prescribed will not enable any person to form an air. . . . I think it best for every composer to be his own Carver"—words which suggest the later attitudes of both Ives and Ruggles.

Of course, Billings's anthems and fuging tunes (psalms or hymn tunes) were products of a Jeffersonian way of thinking by which composers considered music a "craft" like any other (Billings himself was a tanner as well as a musician). In the nineteenth century, however, musical life was often seen simply as a form of entertainment. The pianist Anton Rubinstein, for example, was advised to blacken his face in time for his "show" in Memphis, Tennessee. A pianist named Hatton would appear on stage with a string of sleigh bells attached to his right leg and would proceed to shake it at some moment during the piece, thus earning him "a storm of applause which had no end" until the act was repeated several times da capo. The widely loved orchestral composition entitled *The Fireman's Quadrille* included the clanging of fire bells, the simulation of a stage fire, and the trooping onstage of a fully attired fire brigade that extinguished the blaze forthwith. Is it any wonder that Jenny Lind was managed in this country by P. T. Barnum?

The aesthetic alternative to these antics—antics which might, in fact, be seen as correlatives to the financial chicaneries of magnates like Oakes Ames and Jay Gould—was usually either a heavy-handed and stultifying acceptance of Teutonic musical models imitated by composers like George Chadwick and Arthur Foote or the cultivation of those sentimental songs performed by traveling "singing family" troupes which featured young "lady" pianists playing on instruments covered with brocade and lace in "rooms stifling with fashionable scent" (Walt Whitman).

John Philip Sousa—whose boyhood ambition was to become a circus performer—represented this era perfectly, writing over a hundred marches, many of which were enthusiastically played during America's many popular military actions in Cuba, the Philippines, and even Peking during the Boxer Rebellion. Robert Offergeld has written that Sousa "became the nearest thing to a real *Kapellmeister* that the White House has ever had (he knew eight or nine Presidents personally)." And "Stars and Stripes Forever" and "Semper Fidelis" are probably the best-known works ever written by an American. Technically brilliant, Sousa's marches are today appreciated as either uplifting patriotic masterpieces, exemplars of authoritarian inebriation, or as "camp" perversities—sometimes as all three, as witness the legendary Vladimir Horowitz transcription of "Stars and Stripes." For something rather more authentic try the extraordinary performances by the Czechoslovak Brass Orchestra, conducted by Rudolf Urbanec, a recording which features eleven marches, including Sousa's portentous contribution to the Masonic order entitled "Nobles of the Mystic Shrine." By clarifying the instrumental textures à la Boulez and thereby revealing all of Sousa's cranking and syncopating musical gears, Urbanec and the Czech Brass Orchestra have given us what is at once the most razor-edged, yet subtly delineated and delicately balanced presentation of these uproarious and elephantine works by the man who once said that a "march should make a man with a wooden leg step out."

As Europeans like Berlioz have shown us, elephantiasis is hardly endemic to America. The "monster concert" is back in the news—exactly 100 years after Boston bandmaster Patrick Gilmore organized an orchestra of 2,000 and a chorus of 20,000 for the 1872 Mammoth Festival in Boston. Last year [1972], members of the Eastman School of Music piano faculty, graduate piano students, and soloists Eugene List, Frank Glazer, Barry Snyder, and Maria Luisa Faini (all conducted by Samuel Adler) gave a triumphant ten-piano sixteen-pianist concert at Philharmonic Hall; and now some of the music presented that evening can be heard on a recording entitled *Monster Concert.* "Stars and Stripes" starts it all off (I still think that the two-handed Horowitz outdoes all twenty-two hands playing here—aside from the density of the sound, who can tell the textural difference between four and fourteen pianos?), with hundreds and hundreds of piano keys contributing to other versions of the *William Tell* Overture, "Thunder and Lightning" polka, "Maple Leaf Rag," "Blue Danube" waltzes, *Semiramide* Overture, "La Gallina," and "Ojos Crillos." These last two pieces—"The Hen" and "Creole Eyes" in translation—are by the American avatar of monstrous musical imaginings, Louis Moreau Gottschalk—America's first great "rock star"-type pianist and composer. About his Havana Festival Concert of 1860, Gottschalk wrote: "My orchestra consisted of six hundred and fifty performers, eighty-seven choristers, fifteen solo singers, fifty drums, and eighty trumpets . . . nearly nine hundred persons bellowing and blowing to see who could scream the loudest."

Born in 1829 in New Orleans to a Jewish-English father of German descent and an aristocratic French Creole mother, Gottschalk went to Paris as a teenager, where he studied piano and was praised by Chopin, Berlioz, and Liszt. At twenty-four, he returned to the States and proceeded to give hundreds of piano recitals in cities and mining towns around the country, drawing enormous and excited crowds, hangers-on, and all types of groupies (his affairs were notorious, and he was often forced to skip town). Indulging in what he himself called "the full force of chromatic grapeshot and deadly octaves," Gottschalk was one of the first American musicians to adopt the stance—now highly cultivated by rock musicians—of Phallic Aggressor at the keyboard. His own music—Latin and French Creole in flavor, veering from the sentimental to the bombastic and full of flashy arabesques and Lisztian embellishments—exhausts as it exploits its treacherous romantic emotions. Gottschalk's best pieces are those like the two Cuban dances featured on *Monster Concert*—both of which are airy, kinetic, and based on an unpretentious cultural tradition that fostered neither an academic lassitude nor a self-consuming egomania.

After the exhibitionism of Sousa's and Gottschalk's vertiginous musical styles, it is a calming experience to turn to a recording of the *Songs of Stephen Foster*. Aside from the familiar "Jeanie with the Light Brown Hair" and "Beautiful Dreamer," the album presents infrequently heard songs like the lovely "Ah! May the Red Rose Live Always," the ebullient "If You've Only Got a Moustache," as well as two wonderful mini-operatic dialogues: "Wilt Thou Be Gone, Love?" (with a text adapted from *Romeo and Juliet*) and a comic duet between "Mr. and Mrs. Brown."

This album forces us to reevaluate Foster's heretofore easily dismissed role in nineteenth-century American music. For the first time, Foster's songs have been presented with an integrity, clarity, and the kind of musicianship usually reserved for works like Brahms's "Liebeslieder" waltzes. Using the composer's original sheet music and featuring straightforward and sympathetic instrumental arrangements by composer and ragtime pianist Bill Bolcolm, the songs are recorded with the historical instruments at the Smithsonian Institute (an 1850 Chickering piano, an 1864 melodeon, a one-keyed flute, and a keyed bugle) and are sung with simplicity and grace by baritone Leslie Guinn and mezzo-soprano Jan De Gaetani. The transparency of the performances reveal the ways in which Foster distilled and transformed the clichés of minstrel-show songs, Sunday-school hymns, and parlor melodies and unconsciously created a distinctly American folk art tradition.

But beneath the nostalgia of "Gentle Annie" and the existential gaiety of the marvelous "Some Folks"—both heard on this album—lies the story of not only nineteenth-century American music but also of the by now easily identifiable archetypal "dreamer" trying to fit into the exploitative scene of the rising American middle class. Like most songwriters and composers, Foster was almost always underpaid by his publishers; his songs were often pirated. He became an alcoholic and died broke and alone in New York. Having provided the necessary musical ethos for a homesick nineteenth-century industrial society, he was among the first whom that society considered expendable.

It is good to know that a century earlier, composers like Billings and Justin Morgan had many admirers and that their works were often published in "tune books" which were used in singing schools and village choirs. Since the nineteenth century, however, these compositions have been continually critized for their supposedly faulty voice leading, an incorrect use of leading tones and diminished sevenths, archaic constructions, and the overuse of parallel fifths. Compared to the sturdy eighteenth-century American Moravivan musical tradition which was influenced by Handel and Haydn, the music of Billings and his colleagues does sound slightly "off." But choral societies which have tried to "improve and correct" the harmony and voice leading of this early music are obviously missing the point—much as literary "experts" once unconvincingly tried to alter the bizarre and personal metrics of poets like Sir Thomas Wyatt and John Donne. For as Wilfrid Mellers has suggested, Billings and other New Englanders—along with composers of eighteenth-century southern folk hymns—had in fact developed an "instinctive folk-organum," one which displayed an extraordinary admixture of English medieval and Renaissance musical characteristics, half-remembered Reformation musical forms, and a rich and independent melodic modal invention that occasioned some amazing harmonic textures.

Three recordings give us distinct and fascinating perspectives on the music. *The New England Harmony* presents works of Billings, Justin Morgan, Jeremiah Ingalls, and others of the period as performed by the Old Sturbridge Singers—an amateur group which consists of mechanics, storekeepers, doctors, and housewives. And their clear, straightforward, but sometimes rhythmically heavy interpretations are probably quite similar to those heard during eighteenth-century village choir presentations.

The Continental Harmony features nineteen anthems and fuging tunes by Billings as sung by the professionally precise and spirited Gregg Smith Singers. Aside from a lovely rendition of the patriotic song "Chester," the chorus gives us versions of rarely performed songs like "The Bird," "Kittery," "Cobham," and, most surprising of all, a short piece entitled "Jargon" which is perhaps the first totally dissonant work ever written by an American and which sounds as if it were composed by Charles Ives himself.

The most extraordinary of these three albums is *Early American Vocal Music*—to my mind the most beautiful and important recorded contribution to the performance of early American anthems, plain tunes, set pieces, fuging tunes, and folk hymns. The performers are the Western Wind, a group of young singers who specialize in medieval and Renaissance music. And here they perform these pieces with an expressive shading and dramatic approach usually reserved for the works of medieval motet composers and the compositions of Thomas Tallis and Orlando Gibbons—thereby opening the veils which heretofore often seemed to hide a music of astonishing directness, iridescence, and spiritual depth. Justin Morgan's brief plaintune "Amanda," with its ravishing cross-relations, and his epic-sounding "Judgment Anthem"; Billings's "I Am the Rose of Sharon" and "I Am Come into My Garden"; and various short and haunting southern folk hymns like "Power," "Canaan," and "Animation" (the last of which features a terrific hoedown duo between a countrified bass viol and violin) are all given subtle and totally sympathetic performances.

Hearing these southern hymns, moreover, we are reminded of the almost forgotten interrelationships between and mutual interpenetrations of the white and black "spiritual" and "revivalist" traditions, which seem to have their roots in the Baptist backwoods of New England as well as in Africa. And the ecstatic white folk-hymn is still preserved and practiced today in parts of the Deep South. Known as Fasola or Shape-Note Singing, this four-part communal singing can be heard on a primitively recorded but joyfully performed album presenting the *All-Day Sacred Harp Singing at Stewart's Chapel in Houston, Mississippi*— attesting again to the irreducible and ineradicable power of what we now often cynically call the American musical heritage.

(1973)

CHARLES IVES ON THE 100TH ANNIVERSARY OF HIS BIRTH

An Appreciation

IT IS BY NOW A COMMONPLACE that the one man who established and transmitted the laws of American music—single-handedly and seemingly parthenogenetically—was Charles Ives (1874–1954), the hundredth anniversary of whose birth we celebrate today. In an appropriately pragmatic American manner, Ives created a musical tradition simply by abrogating the prevailing *esprit de clocher* provincialisms and the cozy Teutonic harmonies and forms of orthodox composers like Paine, Chadwick, Foot, and Ives's own teacher Horatio Parker.

In their place, Ives produced, within an incredibly brief period of not more than twelve years (1902–1914), hundreds of compositions that not only stand alone as the only musical parallels to our nineteenth-century literary masterpieces, but which also anticipate almost every technique and development of twentieth-century musical practice: neoclassicism, twelve-tone writing, serialism, tone clusters, quartal harmonics, static pitch structure, "noise," counterpoints of sound masses, provisional and open-ended composition, collage, quotation, stylistic juxtapositions, foreground-background contrasts, aleatoric methods, choice of "special" ensembles, nonsynchronizing groups, spatial music, and the use of polyrhythms, polyharmonies, and polytonalities.

The Ives legend is well-known: A "normal" all-American boy from Danbury, Connecticut, raised on military and ragtime tunes, church and camp-meeting hymns, barn-dance and minstrel-show melodies . . . played drums at seven (later piano and organ), as well as high school baseball and football . . . attended Yale University, after which he became a clerk at the Mutual Life Insurance Co. until he and his friend Julian Myrick opened their own insurance agency, from which Ives retired in 1929, a multimillionaire.

Ives was wary of politicians, and his idea of patriotism—a mixed bag of participatory democracy, constitutionally enforced limited private income, the League of Nations—was, as he once said, "nearer kin to nature than to jingoism." And in extraordinary songs like "Majority (or The Masses)," "They Are There," "An Election," and "Lincoln, the Great Commoner" he conveyed his ecumenical belief that "if local color, national color, any color, is a true pigment of the universal color, it is a divine quality, it is a part of substance in art—not of manner."

It should be remembered, however, that Ives was the last (and perhaps even the first) American composer to believe seriously in the possible identification of the Community of Love with the Nation-State. That this great vision of the American potential—a vision that was being developed ideologically by people like Louis Sullivan, Frank Lloyd Wright, Vachel Lindsay, and others between the Spanish-American and the First World Wars—was in the process of being co-opted by commodity-minded hucksters must have added to his depression, occasioned by his failing health and the dimming of his creativity after 1914. Still, his social, aesthetic, and spiritual vision never really left him. He even invited composers of the future to collaborate with him on an open-ended composition—never realized—entitled the *Universe Symphony*, in which he planned to "paint the creation, the mysterious beginnings of all things known through God to man, to trace with tonal imprints the vastness, the evolution of all life to the spiritual eternities, from the great unknown to the great inknown."

While Ives claimed symbiotic benefits from his complementary lives as businessman and composer ("I have experienced a great fullness of life in business. The fabric of existence weaves itself whole. My work in music helped my business and my work in business helped my music"), there is little question that this "split" allowed him to render unto his musical life an uncompromising freedom to fulfill the laws which he continually discovered and created, even though his work was for the most part unrecognized or disparaged during most of his lifetime.

Well grounded at Yale in European musical practices, Ives was fortunate to have had as his first and most open-minded and sympathetic teacher his own father, George Ives—the Danbury town bandleader and an audacious music teacher who experimented with quarter tones and who made his family sing tunes like "Swanee River" in one key while he played the accompaniment in another in order to make them "stretch their ears." When asked how he could bear to hear the local stonemason bellowing off key at camp meetings, George Ives replied: "Old John is a supreme musician. Look into his face and hear the music of the ages. Don't pay too much attention to the sounds. If you do, you may miss the music."

Strangely, this remark was later to be echoed in his son's "Essays Before a Sonata" (Ives's literary reveries about Emerson, Hawthorne, the Alcotts, and Thoreau, which served as an explanation of and a complement to his *Concord* Piano Sonata): "Why can't music go out in the same way it comes in to a man, without having to crawl over a fence of sounds, thoraxes, catguts, wire, wood, and brass? . . . That music must be heard is not essential—what it *sounds* like may not be what it *is*." This kind of Platonic statement has been taken by a number of critics and composers to suggest that because of public and professional neglect, Ives, who only had the chance to hear a few of his works performed during his lifetime, was forced into a private world of dissociated musical discourse in which his metaphysics undermined his desire or ability to develop a coherent sense of musical continuity.

Nothing could be less true. As the composer Robert P. Morgan has simply pointed out: "Whereas the main thrust of compositional activity in the first half of the century was devoted to finding a way of reconciling new compositional 'content' with traditional form, what Ives attempted was to develop a new kind of form for traditional musical content." But it is important to add to this that, for Ives, form was indissolubly wedded to transcendental and conceptual thinking. As he once wrote, "Coherence, to a certain extent, must bear some relation to the listener's subconscious perspective. But is this its only function? Has it not another of bringing outer or new things into wider coherence? . . . Nature loves analogy and abhors repetition and explanation. Unity is too generally conceived of, or too readily accepted as, analogous to form, and form as analogous to custom, and custom to habit."

These ideas, of course, come straight out of Emerson. And it is worth noting that there has been no other composer who has so thoroughly and effortlessly embodied the substance (not only the system) of philosophical thought as Ives did with the philosophy of Emerson. Consider the following gleanings from Emerson—chosen almost at random: "The feat of the imagination is in showing the convertibility of every thing into every other thing". . . . "The new virtue which constitutes a thing beautiful is a certain cosmical quality, or a power to suggest relation to the whole world, and so lift the object out of a pitiful individuality". . . . "Nothing interests us which is stark or bounded, but only what streams with life, what is in act or endeavor to reach somewhat beyond". . . . "The nature of things is flowing, a metamorphosis. The free spirit sympathizes not only with the actual form, but with the power of possible forms. Hence the shudder of joy with which in each clear moment we recognize the metamorphosis, because it is always a conquest, a surprise from the heart of things."

These quotations not only explain why Ives—an enemy of systemization—never thought of using his technical discoveries (pitch and rhythmic series, twelve-tone rows) as the foci of new musical systems (instead of as just a number of several means of organization), but in fact also suggest and justify the intent and procedures of almost all of Ives's compositions.

The composer's often-repeated reminiscence about his having been influenced as a child by hearing four groups of band musicians playing different music simultaneously as they stood in various parts of the Danbury town square has been used to account for Ives's interest in textural multidimensionality. The composer remembers the story told by the bandmaster about "a man who, living nearer the *variations*, insisted that they were the *real music* and that it was more beautiful to hear the tune come sifting through them than the other way round" (*emphasis added*).

Beyond the fact that Ives organized his famous quotations of hymns, marches, and ragtime tunes so as to establish certain structural relationships in his work, it is equally true that these omnipresent songs, dances, and hymns—continually decomposed and recombined—come to play a role as significant vehicles by which the world of mere successiveness is transformed and metamorphosed. As Ives said about Emerson, "He seems to use the great definite interest of humanity to express the greater, indefinite, spiritual values—to fulfill what he can in his realms of revelation." Thus the Fourth Violin Sonata concludes with the violin quietly playing the line: "Shall we gather at the river," leaving the completion of the couplet to the listener: "That flows by the throne of God."

Perhaps the real secret of Ives's music resides in the area of polytonality, polyrhythms, polyharmonies, and polytextures. His use of these suggests not only our polyvalent universe, but also interdimensional worlds which the composer allows us to perceive at different levels of awareness. In fact, Ives's method of simultaneous presentation discloses nothing less than a world of profound synchronicity.

The sounds of river, mist, and leaves created by the "interweaving in an uneven way" of the notes and phrases of "The Housatonic at Stockbridge"; the confluence of military and ragtime tunes played together in different rhythms, tempi, and keys in "General Putnam's Camp"; the congeries of transpositions, loops, multiple meters, and disintegrating hymns in the second movement of the Fourth Symphony and the emerging and receding transcendental music of the solo violins and harp in the last movement of this same symphony; the hum of night insects, a ragtime piano heard far away, and the clatter of a runaway horse in "Central Park in the Dark"—all of these passages are kept from buckling under the weight of information overload by means of a textural transparency, an uncanny use of overtone modulation and a shifting of compositional materials as if through musical canal locks. These passages also reveal, as the Sufi master Hazrat Inayat Khan once said, that "one person lives only in this external world, another person lives in two worlds, and third person lives in many worlds at the same time. When a person says: 'Where are those worlds? Are they above the sky, or down below the earth?' the answer is that all these worlds are in the same place as that person is himself."

Using James Gibbons Huneker's wonderful phrase, we might say that Ives built his work on the "bases of eternity." In the simplest sense of this phrase, think of the oscillating strands of orchestral texture in "Washington's Birthday" or "The Pond," the "eternal presence" of the low organ C in "Psalm 90," or the lightest sound of bells that concludes many of Ives's works, the Third Symphony in particular—all suggesting a world of infinite and audible silence.

In a mysterious sentence in his *Essays*, Ives writes: "Emerson tells, as few bards could, of what will happen in the past, for his future is eternity and the past is a part of that." This statement conveys a remarkable understanding on Ives's part of his own method; his music ineluctably anticipates the future because it originates from a perspective that sees time as laid out simultaneously, not successively, in space. And in this sense we can understand that the nostalgic, homespun third movements both of the *Concord* Sonata and the Fourth Symphony—two of Ives's most visionary works—reveal the breathtaking logic and conception of a composer whose music goes both forward and backward to eternity. In every moment lies the possibility of eschatological revelation. The music of Charles Ives awakes these moments, presenting us with "the holy carelessness of the eternal now."

(1974)

ON EDGARD VARÈSE

". . . a menagerie or two . . . a catastrophe in a boiler factory."
—Olin Downes on a 1926 performance of Varèse's *Amériques*

SINNERS CONSCIOUS OF THE CONSEQUENCE of their deeds and musicians aware of the power of the sounds with which they work might be said to share the same general assumption, suggested in the formulation of an English Calvinist poet: "We are born under one law and are to the other bound."

The musical world into which Edgard Varèse (1883–1965) was born was that of the basically academic tradition of d'Indy, Chausson, Lalo, and Charles Widor. Yet from an early age, Varèse felt that the exploration of the possibilities of musical materials must necessarily point the way to that which was *beyond*.

Describing his "quest" in 1917, the composer wrote: "I dream of instruments obedient to my thought and which, with their contribution to a whole new world of unsuspected sounds, will lend themselves to the exigencies of my inner rhythm." But in keeping with his idea of an existing correlation between art and science ("Art," Varèse once said, "means keeping up with the speed of light"), he later added: "The composer should, in building his sonorous constructions, have a thorough knowledge of the laws governing the vibratory system, of the possibilities that science has abundantly placed, and continues to place, at the service of his imagination. The last word is: Imagination."

Imagination was to be the link between art and science, the magical and the ordinary, a new heaven and a new earth—as his quote from Paracelsus' *Hermetic Astronomy* on the title page of the score to *Arcana* makes clear: "One star exists higher than all the rest. This is the apocalyptic star; the second star is that of the ascendant. The third is that of the elements, and of these there are four, so that six stars are established. Besides these there is still another star, imagination, which begets a new star and a new heaven."

The apposite image with which we most easily imagine what is "beyond" (unseen, unheard, far out) is of course that of *outer space*. Interestingly, Varèse spent a number of years imagining two unrealized musical conceptions: first, *L'Astronome*, a work for which he began to make sketches in 1928 that was to present an astronomer who, on receiving extraterrestrial signals, dared to respond to them and was finally taken up by otherworldly beings into outer space; and second, a gigantic multilingual work entitled *Espace* which was to feature "voices in the sky, as though magic, invisible hands turning on and off the knobs of fantastic radios, filling all space, crisscrossing, overlapping, penetrating each other, splitting up, superimposing, repulsing each other, colliding, crashing." And the composer imagined *Espace* being performed and broadcast simultaneously in different parts of the world, the choirs singing in their own languages with a "humming, yelling, chanting, mumbling, hammered declamation."

Lacking the means to realize such ideas, Varèse often felt an enormous creative frustration. "I became a sort of diabolical Parsifal on a quest, not for the Holy Grail, but for the bomb that would explode the musical world and allow all sounds to come rushing into it through the resulting breach." And eventually, in three compositions—*Intégrales* (1925), *Arcana* (1927), and *Ionisation* (1931)—Varèse proceeded, with the forces available, to set off a series of musical thermonuclear explosions.

Paracelsus' motto was: "Be not another if thou canst be thyself." In 1895, when Varèse was twelve years old, he wrote an opera based on a work by Jules Verne. Brought up in Burgundy, France and Turin, Italy, he was forced by his father to study engineering, but secretly taught himself the basics of musical composition. Leaving his family, he eventually arrived in Paris to become a composer and conductor. But even as he was writing late-Romantic tone poems (all of which are now lost or destroyed), Varèse became increasingly interested in investigating the possibilities of musical sound, questioning the accepted distinctions between sound and noise, sound and silence.

"When I was around twenty," Varèse recalled, "I became interested in a book by Wronsky, a disciple of Kant. . . . I was struck by a phrase he coined to describe music. It was this: 'The corporealization of the intelligence in sounds.' I liked that phrase, and later it set me to wondering what, if anything, existed between sounds . . . was there a sound between the C key and C#? . . . The question led me to Helmholtz's *Physiology of Sounds*: I then began to think of the opposite of sound, of silence, and of how it can be used. . . . Now, to me, the climax of a crescendo can be a space of absolute silence."

Later on, reading *A New Esthetic of Music* by the composer Ferruccio Busoni (with whom Varèse later studied in Berlin), he came across Busoni's dictum: "Music was born free and to win freedom is its destiny." It was Busoni who had questioned both the ideas of the unassailability and purity of musical notation and of the equal-tempered scale: "What we now call our Tonal System,"

Busoni had written, "is nothing more than a set of 'signs'; an ingenious device to grasp somewhat of that eternal harmony . . . artificial light instead of the sun . . . . For our whole system of tone, key, and tonality, taken in its entirety, is only a part of a fraction of one differentiated ray from that Sun."

Busoni himself never really applied these theories in his compositional practice (though his opera *Doktor Faust* contains some extremely "advanced" moments). It was Varèse who insisted on attempting to "liberate" sound to "throw open the whole world of sound to music," to see musical space as "open" rather than "bounded."

The seminal notion of "spatial music"—which the composer was to be concerned with throughout his life—was in fact revealed to him at a concert in Paris as he sat listening to the Scherzo movement of Beethoven's Seventh Symphony. As he recalled it: "Probably because the hall happened to be overresonant, I became conscious of an entirely new effect produced by this familiar music. I seemed to feel the music detaching itself and projecting itself in space. I became conscious of a third dimension in the music. I call this phenomenon 'sound projection', the feeling given us by certain blocks of sound. Probably I should call them beams of sound, since the feeling is akin to that aroused by beams of light sent forth by a powerful searchlight. For the ear—just as for the eye—it gives a sense of prolongation, a journey into space."

Taking off from Debussy's use of the chord as an independent musical event or action, free of its harmonic context, Varèse broke with the tonal system's harmonic expectations and demands, as well as with the developmental idea propelling the musical tradition represented by Bach-Beethoven-Schoenberg-Elliott Carter ("populating time with pitches," as Carter described this idea).

Instead of developing "motives" or providing for an interplay between melody and harmony, Varèse froze the pitch structure, suspending it in time and locating it in space, and, as Robert Morgan has pointed out, put an emphasis on the "material's own inherent quality. . . . In Varèse one feels almost as if the material has been 'projected' in time, hurled out by virtue of its own intrinsic character, rather than because of any inherent tendency toward forward (temporal) motion." Varèse himself talked of a "counterpoint of masses" which were "mixed" to form various "planes" that interacted with each other in different kinds of combinations. (*Arcana* and *Intégrales*—the latter originally conceived for "spatial projection"—present the best illustration of these conceptions.)

Varèse compared this "counterpoint of masses" and "polyphony of timbres," with their gradual permutations and evolutions of planes and volumes, to crystal formations. And he continually talked about his music using terms such as "collision," "penetration," "repulsion," and "transmutation" of sound masses. This is, remarkably, the vocabulary not only of atomic-particle physics and of the developmental processes of the universe itself, but also, on a more mundane level, of the forces of urban social interaction as well.

Not surprisingly, on arriving in the United States in 1915, Varèse seized the idea of the New World and realized its metaphorical possibilities in a "new world of sound." His first important work, *Amériques* (1922), required 142 instruments including two sirens and twenty-one percussion instruments. In one of his greatest compositions, *Ionisation* (1931), he had thirteen musicians playing thirty-seven percussion instruments (the choice of the instrumental unit, Varèse taught us, is as important as the "formal" idea of the work itself) including a gong, two sirens, crash cymbals, bongos, guiros, slapsticks, Chinese blocks, maracas, sleigh bells, anvils—and, finally, the three pitch-producing instruments (chimes, celesta, and piano) that appear at the conclusion of the work. As Wilfred Mellers has written: "As the hissings, bangings, and scrapings gradually slow down Time's pulse into one eternal-seeming reverberation, pitch becomes equated with an ultimate stillness."

After a twenty-year period of critical neglect and compositional "stillness," Varèse finally composed *Poème électronique*—his first completely electronic work, written for the Brussels World Fair and presented at the Phillips Pavilion over 150 loudspeakers—and *Déserts* for orchestra and prerecorded tape (with sounds collected from ironworks, sawmills, and factories). Of the latter piece, the composer wrote that *desert* was to be understood as suggesting not merely "all physical deserts (of sand, sea, snow, of empty space, of empty city streets), but also the deserts in the mind of man; not only those stripped aspects of Nature that suggest bareness, aloofness, timelessness, but also that remote inner space no telescope can reach, where man is alone, a world of mystery and essential loneliness."

As the composer Otto Luening once said, Varèse was our first astronaut. But he was an astronaut not of our outer but of our inner spaces. Possessing an embracing musical mind—seeing correspondences everywhere—Varèse wanted to make everything audible and palpable because, like Paracelsus, he trusted Imagination and had faith in Nature. He lived in the future because he saw it at every moment in the present. "Farewell, Varèse," Pierre Boulez said in 1965, the year of the composer's death. "Your time is finished and now it begins."

(1975)

ON DON CARLO GESUALDO

FOR OVER 300 YEARS, the late-Renaissance composer Don Carlo Gesualdo, prince of Venosa (c. 1560–1613), was considered to be one of the embarrassing lunatics of musical history—a creator of unsingable music who supposedly wrote the way he did because of an obviously distempered state of mind. A descendent of the King Roger II of Normandy, Gesualdo's titles made him prince, duke, count, lord, and marquis many times over, and consequently much has been recorded about his life. Like his painter-contemporary Caravaggio—with whom Gesualdo shares many similar "mannerist" aesthetic tendencies—the composer was a notorious, conscience-stricken murderer. He caught his first wife Maria d'Avalos (the first of whose three husbands, it was whispered, had died of sexual hyperesthesia) in flagrante delicto with her lover, the duke of Andria, and, accompanied by three of his retainers armed with swords, halberds, and harquebuses, Gesualdo had the couple butchered in bed. Hiding out in one of his castles to avoid the professional stiletto men attached to his wife's revenge-seeking noble Neopolitan family—the noble Gesualdo, and not his low-born lackeys, should have done the job himself, after all—Gesualdo, apparently doubting the paternity of his second child, supposedly suffocated it in its cradle.

A few years before his death, Gesualdo endowed a Capuchin friary in his native town of Gesualdo and commissioned a huge altar painting—still surviving—in the church, painted to his specifications, showing Christ the Judge on high surrounded by the Blessed Virgin, the Archangel Michael, and various saints such as Saint Francis and Saint Dominic—all interceding with Christ on behalf of none other than Carlo Gesualdo, who is himself shown kneeling in black velvet and ruff at the lower-left-hand corner, protected by his aunt and maternal uncle, the recently canonized Cardinal Carlo Borromeo. At the bottom center of the painting is Gesualdo's murdered child, portrayed as a heavenly cherub, and below them all, Donna Maria and the duke of Andria, burning everlastingly in the flames of a hell from which Gesualdo himself hoped to be saved.

This story, straight out of Dante or John Webster, must be seen as an extreme working out of the Spanish ideas of honor that were operative in southern Italy (Naples was then a Spanish colony, and Spain was ruled by the sadistic Philip II), as well as of the courtly butchery that passed for problem solving among the sixteenth-century Italian aristocracy. Most of the murderers of the period washed their hands of their deeds, but Gesualdo, like Lady Macbeth, seems to have embodied his guilt irrevocably in his autonomic nervous system.

A prototype of some of Krafft-Ebing's case histories in *Psychopathia Sexualis*, Gesualdo was an insomniac, asthmatic manic depressive who submitted joyfully to frequent flagellation. He was also an "old man mad about music" (to use Hokusai's words) and probably never before—and hardly since—has hypertension been so directly and powerfully revealed in this medium.

The psychoanalyst Wilhelm Reich wrote that the "organism can perceive only what it itself expresses." And Reich furthermore revealed how certain stereotyped and rigidified facial expressions and bodily postures could be shown to be compromises between two opposing forces—a wish to express anger or grief, for example, and the wish to repress it. Almost all of Gesualdo's madrigal texts significantly feature oxymora, the poetic equivalents of this kind of tension: living death, dying live, loving hate, hateful love. In fact, all of the great sixteenth-century madrigalists—Marenzio, Monteverdi—used these "conceits," but in none of them does one feel the unmitigated immediacy of the ecstasy of pain as totally as one does in Gesualdo's madrigals. For Gesualdo reveals in the clichéd mannerist technique of *effetti meravigliosi* the vestments of an irredeemable confusion between eroticism and death.

Words like *morte, ancide, respiro* set Gesualdo off in breathtaking harmonic constructions that convey experientially a sense of what armored life really feels like. "Armored life," Reich says, "encounters unarmored life with anxiety and hatred." Thus Gesualdo's anguished and astonishing setting of *Morro Lasso*: "Dying, I am miserable in my pain, and that which can give me life is that which is killing me."

The greatness of Gesualdo's music derives not from the listener's detached, vicarious fascination with the metabolic melodrama of a composer who goes about killing himself softly with his own songs, but rather from the sensations one gets experiencing the energies released by the exploding musical torsion, whose life expressions, as Reich would say, "communicate with the world as if through gaps or holes in the armor." This is what Gesualdo's music is all about— harmonic spasms opening toward light and sexual ecstasy, psychic and musical functions manifesting themselves as rapid change and a continual shifting of energy.

What makes Gesualdo's music so difficult to perform is also its most obvious source of tension: the use of double suspensions, unprepared sevenths, and a technique of harmonic construction in which seventeen modulations can sometimes occur in not so many more beats—a modulation from A minor to F-sharp major, for example, the originality and rightness of which would not be equaled until Wagner.

But in addition to this chromatic complexity, Gesualdo's six books of madrigals and four books of sacred music demand a vocal technique of precise and varied articulative and dynamic shadings, perfect timbral balances and registral coordination, and a subtle choice of diverse, if any, vibratos—a technique that has more in common with the performance qualities of early Webern than with the usual approach and vocabulary of mainstream madrigal and choral singing.

What is usually never mentioned, moreover, is that Gesualdo's perfect and functional use of diminution-augmentation (analogous to the manic-depressive nature of the composer's musical characterology) is wedded to a radically new conception of the possibilities of musical continuity. Gesualdo's rapid changes of mood, textures, and musical ideas within a given madrigal and his sophisticated use of juxtaposed blocks—defined by shifting parametric emphases—foreshadow aspects of Beethoven's last quartets, as well as the formal procedures in Stravinsky's *Symphonies of Wind Instruments*, for example—which, in turn, share amazing similarities to Eisenstein's montage theories.

It was Stravinsky himself who put forward Gesualdo's claim as one of our major composers, and Robert Craft who first began recording Gesualdo's music with any consistency. (David Randolph had, in fact, released some madrigals a few years before Craft.) But as late as 1970, Stravinsky was writing that there were still two goals remaining for the attainment of a correct presentation of Gesualdo's music: "The recovery of performance style (a by-no-means-impossible quest) and the recording of the complete music."

If you want to hear Gesualdo as he should be heard, listen to the Deller Consort's performances of *"Belta poi che t'assenti"* and *"Morro Lasso."* Here, as not always with Deller's performances, the Consort's textures and sustained vocal tension produce the two most beautiful interpretations available of these amazing works. The other excellent presentations of Gesualdo's music appear on the middle two (of four) recordings conducted by Robert Craft. The third of these albums, which features madrigals, Responses, a Gagliarda for organ, and Stravinsky's modest, beautiful orchestration of three Gesualdo madrigals, *Monumentum pro Gesualdo,* is a collection of rapturous music, rigorously and intensely interpreted by Craft—as is his second and even more exciting Columbia album of canzonettas, madrigals, galliards, and psalms. They are a necessary introduction to this extraordinary music.

(1975)

BUDDY HOLLY

ACCORDING TO AMERICAN MYTHOLOGY, psychopaths and rock 'n' roll stars have almost invisible origins, springing parthenogenetically out of the headlines or onto the record charts as if they had no past. "I taught him once," one of Buddy Holly's high school teachers recalls, "but to be honest, it was only after the news was in the paper about his death that I remembered that he had been in my class. He was a quiet kid—wasn't any great student, but didn't cause any trouble either, you understand. So I really don't remember anything about him."

Killed at the age of twenty-two on February 3, 1959 ("The day the music died"), in the still-memorialized plane crash that also took the lives of the Big Bopper and Ritchie Valens, Buddy Holly was born in Lubbock, Texas, on September 7, 1936. He made his first appearance onstage when he was five years old, at a local talent show, singing "Down the River of Memories"—a song his mother had taught him—and winning a five-dollar prize for the performance. After forming the Western and Bop Band with his high school friends Bob Montgomery and Larry Welborn, he signed with Decca, cut several uncommercial discs, and then, under the supervision of producer Norman Petty in Clovis, New Mexico, made his famous series of recordings, both with his group the Crickets and as a soloist; between 1957 and 1958, he enjoyed seven Top 40 hits in the United States, and scored several more in England. Late in 1958, he broke with Petty and the Crickets, moved to a Greenwich Village apartment, and married Maria Elena Santiago, a New Yorker whom he proposed to on their first date.

Buddy Holly was one of the few fifties rock 'n' roll stars never to be filmed (although he did appear in several home movies and television programs). So we remember his photographs—all variations of the archetypal high school graduation yearbook picture showing the "shy Texan" in his horn-rimmed glasses. Onstage, he came across like a frenetic raver, yet his songs and vocal presentation often belied and went against the grain of this stylized pose. As writer Dave Laing has observed about Holly's rendition of "Rock Around with Ollie Vee": "There is a notable vocal touch on the line 'I'm gonna shake it just a bit *in the middle of the night*,' where the voice suddenly drops an octave for the italicized words. But while Presley manages to get a menacing sexual growl by a similar effect, Buddy Holly comes across here as playful rather than sensual; it is a wink, not a snarl." And it is this playfully ironic, childlike quality that defines and gives the key to Buddy Holly's style.

When adults communicate with infants, they use the language of baby talk, exaggerating changes in pitch, speaking almost in singsong, uttering their words more slowly, reduplicating syllables and rhymes, and employing simple sentences. It is clear that Buddy Holly absorbed, transformed, and revitalized this mode of expression in his use of titles and phrases like "Maybe Baby," "Oh Boy," "oops a daisy," "riddle dee pat," and "hey a hey hey"; in his embellished, rollicking six-syllable delivery of the word *well* at the beginning of "Rave On"; in lines like "Pretty, pretty, pretty, pretty Peggy Sue" (reminding you of a child talking to a little animal) or

"You know my love not fade away" (telegraphing its message like a Chinese ideogram); and, most obviously, in his famous "hiccup" signature or in the sudden glides from deep bass to falsetto (and back again).

It is Buddy Holly's childlike vocal timbre and phrasing, suggesting the insouciance of a choirboy who doesn't realize his voice is changing, which serves to express his almost prayerful expectancy of a love that will surely come his way . . . because it already exists in his heart. "Take your time," he sings in one of his loveliest songs, "and take mine, too." The mood of the song makes it seem as if the young singer has all the time in the world, but he is at the same time actually urging his girl to take (seize) the ripened moment of love.

And in "I'm Gonna Love You Too," Buddy Holly—like a little boy confusing the present and the hoped-for future, reality and anticipation—sings: "You're gonna say you've missed me / You're gonna say you'll kiss me." The irrepressible optimism of this song, like the adolescent confidence of "That'll Be the Day" and "Think It Over" or the incantatory trance of "Listen to Me" and "Words of Love," conveys Holly's magical notion that the insistent repetition of one's wishes ("The dreams and wishes you wish / In the night when lights are low"—"Well All Right") is in fact the *fulfillment* of the wish itself; as in ritual, the rapture of song becomes the proof of this magic and, in the end, the magic itself.

In an essay entitled "Pop as Ritual in Modern Culture," the English critic Wilfrid Mellers writes about the Australian aborigines who "make a music consisting of isolated words and phrases—invocations of sun, moon, cloud, and other natural phenomena—yelled against the everlasting drone of the dijiridu and accompanied by the rhythmic beating of sticks. In the silent emptiness the aborigine dramatizes the basic fact of his life: the beating of the pulse, the thudding of the heart." And in today's era of sophisticated production techniques, it is important to remember that Holly's most moving songs—whether accompanied by the Crickets, background vocalists, or strings—attest to the fact that he was one of the first white rock 'n' roll musicians to keep alive and draw inspiration from the simplest ritual gestures, phrases, and forms of musical expression.

Several of Holly's friends recall that some of his most memorable playing occurred in 1956–57 when he and fellow Cricket Jerry Allison performed regularly at the Lubbock youth center—Holly's vocals and guitar supported only by Allison's drumming. And even later, Holly's rhythm section often consisted of just a tom-tom or jelly. From the slapping-hands-on-knees accompaniment on "Everyday" to the modal plainness and almost shamanistic cymbal drumming on "Well All Right," from the light incantations of "Crying, Waiting, Hoping" to Waylon Jennings's and Slim Corbin's hand-clapping on the original version of "You're the One," Holly's deepest, wisest, and seemingly least complicated songs express the unadorned confrontation of beauty and love with time. The women of fifties rock 'n' roll—about whom songs were written and to whom they were addressed—almost always fell into two categories: the fast and earthy (Lucille, Fannie Mae, Hank Ballard's Annie) and the slow and dreamy (Donna, Denise, and Sheila). In most cases, they were like the emblematic and conventional ladies of the courtly and Petrarchan schools—as interchangeable as hurricanes or spring showers, Party Doll ornaments of the song.

With Peggy Sue, however, Buddy Holly created the first rock 'n' roll folk heroine (Chuck Berry's Johnny B. Goode is her male counterpart). And yet it is difficult to say how Holly did it. Unlike the "Sad-Eyed Lady of the Lowlands," whom Bob Dylan fills in as he invents and discovers her, Peggy Sue is hardly there at all. Most fifties singers let it be known that they liked the way their women walked and talked; sometimes they even let on as to the color of their sweethearts' eyes and hair. But Buddy Holly didn't even give you this much information. Instead, he colluded with his listeners, suggesting that they imagine and create Peggy Sue *for* him.

Singing in his characteristically shy, coy, ingenuous tone of voice, Holly seems to let us in on a secret—just as later, in "Peggy Sue Got Married," he continues his complicit arrangement with his listeners, half pleading with them, and with himself, not to reveal something which he himself must hesitatingly disclose. In this brilliantly constructed equivocation, Holly asks us to suspend belief (just as, contrarily, Wendy in *Peter Pan* beseeches the children in the audience to give credence to fairies in order to keep them alive) until that inexorable last stanza when we realize that no longer can Holly sing: "You're the one," but only that "She's the one." He has become one of his own listeners as Peggy Sue vanishes, like Humbert Humbert's Lolita, into the mythology of American romance.

In his invaluable biography of Holly, John Goldrosen informs us that Holly originally composed a song called "Cindy Lou," and that Jerry Allison suggested he change the title to the name of Allison's girlfriend (whom Allison married and later divorced). But the Peggy Sue of our hearts continued to live on, making an appearance not only at the living room party in "Splish Splash" but also in Bobby Darin's "Queen of the Hop" and Ritchie Valens's "Ooh My Head"—finally to be scorned and discarded for a younger rival in the insolent "Barbara Ann": "Played our favorite tune / Danced with Betty Lou / Tried Peggy Sue but I knew she wouldn't do— / Barbara Ann."

"Love is not love / Which alters when it alteration finds / Or bends with the remover to remove," wrote William Shakespeare.

And some of us would like to think that Peggy Sue is still with us, as we keep alive the vibration of her life—and that of her creator— rediscovering her presence in the coded personal-column message from the English rock group Buddy Holly influenced so strongly: P.S. I LOVE YOU.

"You recall a girl that's been in nearly every song," Buddy Holly sang. And it's tempting to imagine that the *idea* of Peggy Sue permeated all of Holly's compositions. Similarly, it is tempting to view all of Holly's recordings as one long song, all the more tempting in that the early Western and Bop demo tapes made by Holly and Bob Montgomery in 1953–54, as well as the scores of radio and garage tapes which were rediscovered and issued after Holly's death (some untouched, most with overdubbed backings), are among his greatest performances.

His first recordings for Decca—including songs like "Modern Don Juan," "Midnight Shift," "Girl on My Mind," and the first version of "That'll Be the Day"—were either commercial failures or unreleased, and have long been criticized for their poor instrumental balance and overemphasized echo effects. Today, they strike oversatiated ears as some of Holly's freshest and most unpretentious work. Likewise, the often-criticized overdubbed recordings of the slow version of "Slippin' and Slidin' " (backed by the Fireballs), the string-drenched "Love Is Strange," and the version of "Peggy Sue Got Married" overdubbed with New York City studio musicians (in contrast to the forced-ebullient Clovis studio arrangement) are masterpieces, achieving a seemingly effortless clarity. The early Holly/Montgomery recordings of songs like "I Wanna Play House with You" and "Down the Line," as well as this duo's later consummate songwriting collaborations ("Wishing" and "Love's Made a Fool of You"—both recordings featuring the extraordinary lead guitar work of Tommy Allsup), are still too little known. And no one should overlook "Because I Love You," one of Holly's most haunted and haunting ballads—a song which, along with "Love's Made a Fool of You," represents the darker side of Buddy Holly's emotional world.

All of Holly's compositions and performances reflect his amazing capacity to synthesize musical influences as diverse as Hank Williams, Hank Snow, the Louvin Brothers, western swing bands, Elvis Presley, Bo Diddley, Carl Perkins, Tony Williams, Ray Charles, black gospel, and Baptist church tunes. And through Holly, all these musical strands were later taken up and developed in the music of the sixties.

During the Crickets' first cross-country package tour in 1957, Buddy Holly and Chuck Berry used to spend their time traveling together at the back of the bus, kneeling on the floor and shooting craps with their night's earnings. And in hindsight, it is clear today that Holly and Berry were major influences on the rock music of the sixties. But Holly's specific contribution is too often underestimated. He was certainly the main inspiration for the Beatles (think of songs like "I'll Follow the Sun," "Every Little Thing," "I'll Cry Instead," "Here Comes the Sun," and "One After 909"—the last of which is almost an exact imitation of the early Holly/Montgomery recordings), as well as for the entire English Mersey school, the Kinks (think of "I'll Remember" or "Starstruck"), and the Hollies (he gave them their name). In the States, of course, he directly influenced singers and groups like Bobby Vee, Tommy Roe, the Bobby Fuller Four, the Everly Brothers, Skeeter Davis, Creedence Clearwater Revival, Tom Paxton, and Bob Dylan.

In the words of Malcolm Jones, Holly "scored with a dazzling series of firsts in an era when everyone followed the flock. He was one of the first white rock stars to rely almost exclusively on his own material. The Crickets were probably the first white group to feature the lead/rhythm/bass/drums lineup. He was the first rock singer to double-track his voice and guitar. He was the first to use strings on a rock 'n' roll record. In addition, he popularized the Fender Stratocaster and was probably the only rock star to wear glasses onstage!"

These were no mean accomplishments for a twenty-two-year-old who, as an "unmemorable" high school student six years before his death, had written in an autobiography for his sophomore English course: "My life has been what you might call an uneventful one, and it seems there is not much of interest to tell. . . . I have many hobbies. Some of these are hunting, fishing, leatherwork, reading, painting, and playing western music. I have thought about making a career out of western music if I am good enough but I will just have to wait to see how that turns out. . . . Well, that's my life to the present date, and even though it may seem awful and full of calamities, I'd sure be in a bad shape without it."

As Bob Dylan once confessed: "I just carry that other time around with me. . . . The music of the late fifties and early sixties when music was at that root level—that for me is meaningful music. The singers and musicians I grew up with transcend nostalgia—Buddy Holly and Johnny Ace are just as valid to me today as then."

(1976)

MARION WILLIAMS

IT WAS IN 1973 IN NORTH PHILADELPHIA—on the corner of
seventh and Jefferson—that I first saw Marion Williams. The B. M.
Oakley Memorial Temple, where the singer worships and where
she was to sing a service that late-fall afternoon, was originally a
synagogue but has since been converted to the Greater Zion
Church of God in Christ. It seemed somehow fitting that Marion
Williams—true Christian that she is—would be singing her
biblical songs in this temple/church, for as she herself once said:
"Jesus came out of that Old Testament lineage. When I pray, I love
to say aloud: 'The God of Abraham, the God of Isaac and the God
of Jacob, Oooh *yes*! When I say *that*, it looks like something's really
happening.'"

Backed by a forty-voice chorus, piano, organ, and percussion,
Marion Williams Suzy-Q'ed, sashayed, and strutted through the
aisles as several worshipers fell out at the sound—once described
as "seraphic funk"—of her inspired gospel chants and arias. In an
overwhelming ten-minute litany entitled "Jesus, Jesus," Marion—to
the accompaniment of minatory drums, affirming chorus, and
ritual clapping—re-created and relived the trial of Jesus. Shouting
and sighing, defying and admonishing, her voice dropping from
incandescent falsetto to sanctified whine, she momentarily became
Pilate's wife, singing: "I've suffered many things in a dream because

of Him," then laughing, as if possessed, and proudly declaiming: "*That's* a woman for you! Don't you tell me God don't speak to women. Ha! Yes, sir!" Only a deaf recusant would have been unmoved and unconvinced.

When I visited Marion Williams at her Philadelphia home, I asked her about these lines from "Jesus, Jesus." "They're not in the Bible," Marion told me, "I just thought of them and put them in the song. I've always tried to figure out why women are the greatest carriers of the message. It even happened in Jesus' time— think of the woman at the well exciting the people and telling the whole town about Jesus. That was a *real* revival. Where do you read about the disciples ever doing anything like that? And remember Deborah—she was one of the greatest judges. It goes way back."

Marion Williams speaks her words in a whisper, interspersed with light laughter. So it seems incredible that this barely audible person is the same saved, sanctified, and Holy Ghost–filled woman whose growling, hollering, hands-on-the-hips vocal style directly influenced both Little Richard and the Isley Brothers (their "Shout" is a deliberate imitation of Marion's style) . . . and whose rhythmic control, perfect timing and remarkable use of portamento, falsetto, and ornamentation rival the techniques of the most renowned of classical singers. As Tony Heilbut once wrote: "The more saved Marion becomes, the more unpredictable her improvisations."

Before she is anything else, however, Marion Williams is simply the greatest of contemporary gospel singers, combining the directness of Clara Ward, the wit of Sister Rosetta Tharpe, the fervor of Dorothy Love Coates, and the vocal grandeur of Bessie Griffin and Mahalia Jackson. A natural, untrained vocalist, Marion remembers singing her first a cappella song ("Yes, Jesus Loves Me") in a Miami church when she was three years old, and bowling everyone over. Clara and Gertrude Ward heard her sing "What Could I Do?" when she was eighteen, and a year later she accepted their invitation to go on the road with the Ward Singers, with whom she made her first important Savoy recordings ("Surely God Is Able" and "Packin' Up"). After leaving the Ward Singers, Marion starred in *Black Nativity*, toured Europe and Africa, and performed at many colleges. In the early seventies she recorded several pop spiritual-type albums for Atlantic (all out of print), including songs like Dylan's "I Shall Be Released" and "The Wicked Messenger"— whose last, pure-gospel line is: "If ye cannot bring good news, then don't bring any."

But Marion's most adventurous, imaginative, and fulfilled album, *Prayer Changes Things*, was released just over a year ago [1976]. Accompanied only by piano, organ, and percussion, her enormous range of techniques and moods is revealed in a cantatalike sequence of songs, including the sanctified, upbeat "Prayer Changes Things," the breathtaking a cappella "Shall These Cheeks Go Dry," and the almost sultry, perfectly sustained "Nobody but You Lord."

During my visit with Marion, I noticed that the Bible in her living room was open, and the following passage from Psalm 57 caught my eye: "My heart is steadfast, O God, / My heart is steadfast! / I will sing and make melody! / Awake, my soul! / Awake, O harp and lyre! / I will awake the dawn."

In other countries, Marion Williams would already have been acknowledged as a priceless national treasure. Over here, we still have to start waking up the record industry.

(1977)

STÉPHANE GRAPPELLI
The Prince of Violins

MY GRANDMOTHER USED to tell me that once when I was three years old and on an outing with her to a toy store, I grabbed and tried to make off with a pretty stuffed violin-playing monkey—much like the storybook chimpanzee that throws itself on ladies' hats decorated with artificial fruit. In fact, it wasn't the monkey I wanted, but rather that irresistible violin which I tried, unsuccessfully, to wrest from the prehensile grasp and chin of that obdurate and well-made creature.

Three years old is the beginning of the end. At home I pined away, comforting myself with a little 78 rpm phonograph on which I incessantly played a recording of Mischa Mischakoff performing treacly standards like Dvořák's *Humoresque* and Fritz Kreisler medleys. Six months later, however, my anguish vanished upon receiving from my grandmother an eleven-inch-long Mexican wooden toy violin (a relic which my mother, obviously sensing a legendary career in its formative stages, still keeps in one of her closets).

At seven, two things happened to change my life: First, I discovered Jascha Heifetz, whose electrifying recordings suggested to me, then and even now, the possibility of perfection. And second, my mother bought me a quarter-size violin, and I began taking lessons and practicing, scratchily and irritably, those miserable

Ševčik exercises that are the bane of parents and next-door neighbors. And I progressed from first to fifth positions, but prodigy I was not. Moreover, aside from the Beethoven, Brahms, Schoenberg, Berg, and Stravinsky violin concertos, I began to lose interest in what I considered to be the mostly sentimental Romantic violin repertoire. And when at fourteen I flubbed my way through a Vivaldi concerto in front of an audience of parents and peers, I turned to "Heartbreak Hotel" and "Roll Over Beethoven" for solace. I started having fantasies about and casting furtive glances at sensual-sounding oboes and English horns, and realized that the love affair between me and the violin was over.

Or so I thought until January of 1976 when, almost by accident, I went to Carnegie Hall to hear the great jazz violinist Stéphane Grappelli performing with the Diz Disley Trio. I had earlier admired Django Reinhardt's and Grappelli's Quintet of the Hot Club of France recordings of "Mystery Pacific," "Nuages," "Ain't Misbehavin'," and "Hot Lips," among others. But I hadn't quite expected the faultless intonation, crisp upper-register sonorities, wine-dark lower-string timbres, rhapsodic phrasing, and vespertine lyricism of that shining, graceful, Pierrot-like figure—reminding me lightly of my grandmother in former times—playing the most inspired version of "Body and Soul" I had ever heard.

That night at Carnegie Hall brought on one of those Proustian moments of involuntary memory, taking me body and soul back to my three-year-old obsession, as I repressed the thought of dashing onstage to pry loose and run off with that beautiful violin.

In December of 1976 I was on the phone to Paris.

"Hello, is this Stéphane Grappelli?" . . .

"You're calling from New York? You want to see me in Paris? *Incroyable! Bien sûr*, you're invited, my dear, and bring Rockefeller Cent*aire* when you come!"

"Jazz violinists have always had to be unusually resilient to survive," Nat Hentoff has put the matter bluntly, "because until recent years their instrument has not been regarded as a legitimate jazz axe." Considering the dominant position held by the piano and reed instruments, however, it is important to remember the efflorescence in the twenties and thirties of such inventive pioneer jazz violinists as Joe Venuti, Eddie South, and Stuff Smith (once described as the "palpitating Paganini"), who in turn inspired Svend Asmussen and Ray Nance, and, more recently, Michael White, Leroy Jenkins, and Jean-Luc Ponty.

Stéphane Grappelli not only partakes of this hardly super-annuated tradition—a tradition he himself has shaped and developed—but, today [1977], at sixty-nine, the violinist is at the height of his imaginative and technical powers. He lives in a compact, modest Upper West Side–looking apartment on the Rue de Dunquerque—an apartment filled with books, records, and souvenirs from his travels. It is just one of Stéphane's home bases (he has a room in Amsterdam and apartments in London and Cannes, where his daughter lives), and, in fact, he is continually traveling at a clip that would exhaust a person half his years. During the last three months of 1976, for example, Stéphane played in eight American and seven Canadian cities, then flew off for performances in Edinburgh, London, Amsterdam, Lyon, Stuttgart, and Hamburg.

"We are all Gypsies, my dear," Stéphane says to me as we sit down in his study. "As a matter of fact, I don't like living in any one place. I don't like doing the same thing every day. The only thing in this life is to find people to have a little talk to . . . *that's* agreeable. I really don't envy [*pronounced "en*-vee;" *lovely is "love-lee," chopped liver is "shopped lee*-vair"] people staying in the same place. I'm not blasé at all. I prefer to be an ignorant and be amazed when I see something that's new to me. Sometimes it helps to be an imbecile: you don't need a name, or a tax collector coming after you.

"I like New York in June (though I once got the most celebrated flu of my life there), San Francisco in the summer. But best of all I love New Orleans in the fall. I was there a few weeks ago, and it's the best thing I ever saw in my life. We played at Rosy's. Rosy is the woman who owns the club, she likes music very much and she even sang 'Summertime' with us. Summertime in a cool night."

"The French writer, jazz critic, and singer Boris Vian, who died in 1959, loved New Orleans, too," I mention to Stéphane.

"Oh, I knew him and loved his books," Grappelli says enthusiastically.

"Do you know about the Clavicocktail Machine that he describes in his novel *L'Écume des Jours* [The Froth of Days]? It reminds me of your playing."

"I read that book so long ago. It's a machine?"

"A machine that makes drinks to music," I say. "For each note there's a corresponding drink—either a wine, spirit, liqueur, or fruit juice. The loud pedal puts in egg flip, and the soft pedal adds ice. For soda you play a cadenza in F-sharp. And if you feel like a dash of fresh cream, you just play a chord in G major. The quantities depend on how long a note is held, but the alcoholic content remains unchanged. So you can make a 'Weather Bird' drink or a 'Loveless Love' potion. Imagine what cocktails you could concoct with your music!"

"A marvelous contraption," says Stéphane. "You know, Boris Vian used to play the trumpet, and I was pinching myself not to laugh. But what a brain! He was a very spiritual man, and he used to compose some very light but amusing songs. In fact, I have a rare edition of *I Spit on Your Grave*, the detective novel he wrote which was banned in France. He used to come to Club St. Germain about twenty years ago almost every night when I was playing there. I'll never forget him. Near the end, he was completely white. I think he was suffering with his art [heart] a long time before. It was not very *solide*.

"Me, I'm A-okay. I was just checked up. I used to smoke a lot, but no more. I started when I was ten. It was during World War I, so, *alors*, when I see an American I ask him, but they didn't often give a cigarette to me because I was too small. So I smoked the leaf of the chestnut tree—*maronnier*. But I stopped cigarettes in 1970. It was easy, and now my cere*bral* is clearer.

"Do I smoke anything else? Well, I've tried like everybody, but I'm not a *dope*. One thing that helps me through when I'm playing something that I've done over and over for fifty-four years is a couple of whiskeys before I go on the stage. When I'm at Carnegie Hall, for example, I get a little nervous, it's normal. But when you must *attack*—bang!—you need a little support behind. I always arrive one hour before I'm supposed to perform, put my fingers into good order—maybe it sounds pretentious—I take a little drink, some quick conversation like that, and then I'm onstage. Maurice Chevalier once told me: "You must start very well, finish very well, and in the middle it's nobody's business. But me, I try to do the business in the middle, too."

"Whiskeys or no," I say to Stéphane, "I'm amazed that you can play those same pieces and make them sound new after all these years."

"The big groups of today," he replies, "like the Rolling Stones, always do the same thing: 'I love you, I love you, I love you' . . . you see what I mean? Anytime you go to see those people they're always saying, 'I love you, baby.' I try to catch them changing, but it's *impossible*. I can't bear those screams for nothing at all without *nécessité*. If I did that on my violin, it would be in pieces! I recently heard Morgana King singing "You Are the Sunshine of My Life.' Now, I could listen to *her* say 'I love you' for one month! But she's intelligent, she doesn't say 'I love you' for one month. She says, 'You are the sunshine of my life,' which at least is a change. But I don't want to criticize too much because these people do their best to please a certain clientele.

"*Alors*, me . . . I, too, am saying 'I love you' or 'I don't love you' with my violin. It's basically the same program every night, but sometimes we start with the entrée and end up with the appetizer. And we've got the dessert as well. No dessert in the middle, though—that would be a bad menu. And when the public is nice, we add a little salt, pepper, and a better bottle of wine. *Voilà*!

"I prefer performing for young people than for the people who ask for mustard when I'm playing 'Nuages.' That's why I like performing at the Bottom Line in New York or at the Great American Music Hall in San Francisco. A lot of atmosphere and no soup. I like my programs to have something *soft*, something *energetic*, something *slow*, something *blue*, something *red*, something *burning*. And it's quite difficult to do that with just two guitars, string bass, and violin. We are a bit victimized by the new aspects of electric music. We're playing like classical people except that we're doing jazz music. Segovia or Ike Isaacs—one of the guitarists I play with—is to me the same sound. I don't dare to say I'm playing like Heifetz. I play my own style—I bought it myself from my body—but I'm trying to get that sound. Those classical guys go very fast, but I go fast, too, in my music. Why not? It keeps you alive."

Stéphane has some errands to do and asks if I'd mind joining him on a little walk around the neighborhood. When we get outside— a chilly December day—he mentions that we're just a couple of minutes away from the first apartment he ever lived in as a child.

"My childhood was like a Dickens novel," Stéphane says as we start walking. "I lose my mother, who was French, in 1911 when I was three. And my father had no choice but to put me in a very poor *catholique* orphanage. My father, who was Italian, was a very strange and interesting person. He was the first *hee*pie I ever met, a Latinist and a teacher of philosophy. He did translations from Virgil and Italian into French, and he spent most of his time in the Bibliothèque Nationale. Occasionally he worked as an instructor in a place like Berlitz, but he was incapable of making a penny. We were very good friends. But I'm the opposite of him. I'm very practical, he was *théorique*, always reading and writing. He thought he could get well by reading a book instead of going to a doctor, but he died in 1939. You know, my father got remarried, but I didn't get on with my stepmother. It's probably the reason I never got married.

"My first impression of live music was when I was six. My father wanted to take me out of that orphanage, and since he knew Isadora Duncan, who had a school then, he asked her if she wanted another student. 'Bring me the child,' she said. Of course, in those days, I was not looking like what I look like today. So she said, 'Oh, yes, I like him!' But I wasn't very successful as a dancer. I played an angel, but when you're not an angel it's *difficile*. I did, however, hear some grand music there. Musicians used to play in her garden, and I remember hearing Debussy's *Afternoon of a Faun* and the music made me *feel* the faun.

"After Isadora Duncan I had to go to another orphanage because the war was breaking out. We slept on the floor and I suffered from undernutrition. That's why I like desserts now. I never ate much of anything there, and I wasn't very sunny. So I escaped that damned place and wandered in the streets. Finally I move back with my father. And because of him I become a musician. Every Sunday he used to take me to hear orchestras, and that's when I first become acquainted with a lot of Debussy and Ravel. I wanted to play something. And my father wanted to distract me and keep me a bit quiet. So he took me into a store on Rue Rochechouart and bought me a three-quarter violin. All the way home I hugged it so hard I almost broke it. In fact, I still have that violin in my desk at home— there are no cracks in it and it is one of the only things of mine that wasn't destroyed during World War II. I'll show it to you when we go back. It's my only fetish.

"There was no money for lessons, so my father takes out a book from the *bibliothèque*, and we learn solfeggio together. I never had a teacher, so I learn good position and posture from sheer luck. The technique came along slowly. When I needed some more notes I had to wait. I can't play the notes with the correct classical fingering. On the other hand, a classical musician can't play jazz easily either. It's a different way. Maybe if I practiced I could succeed in playing the Beethoven concerto from beginning to end, but I'd never play like Isaac Stern or Menuhin because my hand is deformed, my brain is deformed. I love bluegrass fiddling, but maybe I could catch it if I lived down South for six months. Because learning to play music is like a language—you've got to learn it on the spot. But you can't catch anything on the street except a cold.

"At fourteen I got job in a pit band in a cinema. That's where I really learned to play and to read music—three hours during the day, three in the evening. I played in tune, and that's why they kept me."

We reach Stéphane's dentist's office, and he goes upstairs to give the dentist—"a nice guy"—two of his albums (*Stéphane Grappelli Plays Cole Porter* and *Stéphane Grappelli Plays George Gershwin*). When he comes smiling back down the stairs, I suddenly realize how much his bearing and music remind me of Charlie Chaplin and Buster Keaton.

"Did you ever play music for Chaplin films?" I asked Stéphane.

"Oh, yes, my dear, I was dying of laughter from his films. I used to laugh so deeply that sometimes I was sick. But I can't laugh like that today. Rarely do I have what we call *fou rire*. But, you know, the only kind of movie I don't like is those family-affair films in which they dispute and go back with everybody kissing at the end. I can't bear that.

"It's interesting that just about this time I heard my first jazz. I don't want to sound stupid or pretentious, but I think I'm more near the black beat than the white. I was first attracted to black musical interpretation and atmosphere by chance. I remember hearing a tune called 'Stumbling' on a record performed by a group called Mitchell's Jazz Kings. It drive me insane. Soon after that I listen through the door of a nightclub to a pianist, saxophone, and drums playing 'Hot Lips,' and that drive me mad, too. Practically just two notes and the chords change all the time. So when Charlie Chaplin comes on the screen in that cinema, I start playing 'Stumbling' with the other musicians.

"Then one day I went out and saw musicians playing in a courtyard and decided I wanted to earn some pocket money for some pastry, so why don't I try it? I remember concierges chasing me out with their brooms, but one or two accepted me, and I got a little money. I did this two years—though I never tell my father—and I earn more than I make from playing in silent-movie cinemas.

"In the courtyards I play little classical tunes—"Berceuses" by Fauré, melodies from Thaïs, and the "Serenade" by Toselli, which was a great success. It was the 'You Are the Sunshine of My Life' at the time, and if you wanted to make money you had to play that. So I begin to make some money, and my father and I move into a bigger apartment. About this time I hear Louis Armstrong and Bix Beiderbecke and teach myself the piano. I like its *harmonique* aspect and discover that I can make money playing it at private parties."

Stéphane and I have now arrived at the office of the local optometrist, who chats with Stéphane as he loosens the violinist's glasses ("I'm very farsighted"), and out we go again.

"When did you meet Django Reinhardt?" I ask.

"Oooh, more questions about Zhango! Information about him is *everywhere*. In the subways even! One day I may sit down and write things no one knows about him. He was a very secret person. In the early thirties, I had been playing piano at the Ambassadeurs in Paris—where I hear Paul Whiteman, Bing Crosby, Oscar Levant, and George Gershwin perform—and then with Gregor and his Gregorians in Nice. Gregor got me playing the violin again. And then one day, back in Paris, I meet Zhango at a club in Montparnasse. He was looking for a violinist to 'play hot.' But I lose touch with him. Then at Hotel Claridge in Paris in 1933 we both met up again in the same hotel orchestra. One day when the tango orchestra was on we find each other backstage. I had broken a string and was tuning up, and all of a sudden we start fooling around playing 'Dinah' together—pretending we are Eddie Lang and Joe Venuti."

Stéphane is tired of telling Django stories, so I fill in the rest. Django, his brother, his cousin, Stéphane, and bassist Louis Vola formed the legendary Quintet of the Hot Club of France which, as Ralph Gleason once wrote, was the first and only European group of that time "accorded major-league status in jazz by musicians and fans alike."

Reinhardt was a Gypsy whose third and fourth fingers on his fretting hand were left withered and paralyzed by a fire in his caravan, forcing the guitarist to develop a unique "cross-fingering" technique with which he created a dazzling musical style. A man who told time by the sun, Django, more often than not, was off playing billiards, fishing, or painting when he was supposed to be onstage.

In fascinating interviews with Whitney Balliett in *The New Yorker* and with Dan Forte in *Guitar Player*, Stéphane remembered Django as "a great artist but a difficult man. His chords were always there, but he was not there himself." Stéphane was constantly trying to get Django to gigs on time. "But when he was annoyed with me," Stéphane recalls, "he would give me some funny chords."

They were in London together just about the time the Germans invaded France. "I used to get up very late," Stéphane told Dan Forte, "six o'clock in the afternoon. Django, as a Gypsy, would always get up early. Anytime, he'd get up. Three o'clock in the morning, he'd go be listening to a bird somewhere. He'd hear a bird and say, 'Oh, it's the spring.' The spring was my worst enemy, because when the new leaves came on the trees, no Django. . . . During the war we were in London, but the first siren Django heard, he said, 'We must go, we must go!' He was in the street when he called me, and I said, 'Fuck off, I'm not going to get up. We'll see you later on.' But when I got up, it was too late. And that was good for me, because at least I was not with the Germans."

During the war, Stéphane played in London with pianist George Shearing. "I played with George for the troops. And the bombs dropped quite often. I remember one time we finished up playing in a club in Golders Green. The sirens started, so we flew out of there to get to the deepest underground station nearby, which was Hampstead Heath. We started walking fast down the street, and George said: 'There's no need to run, we're underground.' He didn't know where we were because he was blind.

"One Friday night when we were performing, there was a terrible bombing. I didn't want to disturb George, who was playing his solo, so I ask the manager of the club if we should stop. 'Keep blowing forever!' he shouted. And I didn't dare go because he had our check! Another time I remember a singer we were accompanying who was singing 'As Time Goes By' as the bombs came down. You should have heard the tremor—'Ti-iy-i-me go-oo-oo-es bi-yi.' It was awful! We laugh now, but those damn V-2s could drop anywhere. Always that bloody blitz started when *we* started. It was a signal."

After the war Stéphane rejoined Reinhardt in Paris, but they played less and less frequently together. In 1953, Reinhardt died of a cerebral hemorrhage while playing billiards. Stéphane kept a low profile for a while, performing at nightclubs, then for five years at the Paris Hilton, and later at Ronnie Scott's Jazz Club in London. During the past ten years he has performed all over the world and recorded prolifically, releasing at least five albums a year with musicians as diverse as Duke Ellington, Jean-Luc Ponty, Gary Burton, Bill Coleman, Paul Simon, Stuff Smith, Baden Powell,

Barney Kessel, George Shearing, and Yehudi Menuhin. With Menuhin he has collaborated on two scintillating albums of music of the thirties (*Jalousie* and *Fascinating Rhythm*), eliciting the following comments from his classical friend: "Stéphane Grappelli is a colleague whom I admire and would love to emulate. Although his repertoire is entirely different from mine and he plays the violin in a different style, he brings to it an imagination, a perfection of technique, and a spontaneous expression of feeling which would be the envy of every violinist."

"Where will you be playing next?" I ask Stéphane as we continue our walk.

"A trip to Tunisia and then in March I'll be performing at the Hong Kong festival; back to the States in April. I do get about. By being hectic I keep young. But here we are at Anvers Square—it's the highlight of our little stroll. I wanted to show you this square because I used to play here as a child. It's changed a lot since then: there's an underground parking lot now, and the statues have been torn down. I used to hang around here and do little things to earn some money, like opening doors of taxis, helping people with luggage, working in a laundry nearby, and delivering hats. One day I delivered a hat to a prostitute at her home. Her boyfriend and a friend of his were there playing banjos, and that woman had a violin around, so the three of us had a wonderful concert that afternoon."

Back in Stéphane's study, I notice on the wall a framed photograph of a beautiful woman. "She was a close friend of mine," Stéphane says, "a hostess in one of the clubs I played at in London during the war. One night a bomb dropped and killed her. I lost another friend—an ice-skating champion—at that time, but in a different way. I was the Prince of Violins, but one day she met the King of Sardines, and I couldn't compete. He was an American colonel and he took her to America after the war, but a year later I received an announcement from her saying that she was marrying *another* guy. By that time I forget.

"In 1975 I was confined in New Zealand and Australia, the most faraway places in the world. And for some reason I had a desire to read something, anything—it could have been the telephone directory. I was feeling homesick and worried about my daughter and grandsons. And by chance I found a copy of *Madame Bovary*, which I read as a child. But in New Zealand I came across two lines in the book which told me exactly what I was feeling: 'How to describe that elusive sickness whose aspects change like clouds in the sky and which whirl around like the wind.' When you feel something like that, it's an impalpable disease. It's a dreadful feeling. But it wasn't too bad and I soon forget. One gets fed up with the same thing.

"Unlike Zhango, I like a classical life. I like everything classical. I don't like that abstract business. I like Louis Quatorze, the music of Couperin and Rameau. But I always come back to jazz music. Not so much to other jazz violinists, but rather to pianist Art Tatum. For me, my god is Art Tatum [*pronounced "Tay-*toom"]. Tatum's melodic line is influenced by Ravel and Debussy, you know, and by orchestral work. Art Tatum *is* an orchestra. I've played with Count Basie, Joe Turner, John Lewis, Duke Ellington, Oscar Peterson, Errol Garner, Fats Waller—but never Art Tatum. My greatest ambition is to be the Art Tatum of the violin. That's why I want to keep good health and try to go on."

It was time for me to leave. Stéphane, too, had an appointment across town, so we walked to the Métro station together, and he treated me to a ticket for the first-class section.

"It's our type of *chic*," he said smiling, as we got into the train and sat down.

I noticed the red French Legion of Honor stripe in the lapel of his jacket.

"I wear it, my dear, so that I don't have to carry identification papers on me."

For some reason I also noticed what large ears Stéphane has.

"Did you know, Stéphane, that Stravinsky once said that musicians have bigger ears than most other people?"

"A donkey as well," he replied, giving me a warm bear hug as the train pulled into the station and he got up to say goodbye— beaming the way my grandmother used to, the way Stéphane always does when he plays his beautiful violin.

"When I'm playing I'm blissful, I'm happy, I improvise."

(1977)

PATTI SMITH
Rock and Rimbaud

THE WRITER GRACE PALEY once talked in an interview about the fact that many women missed the sense of boyhood when they were children, "the freedom and excitement of boyhood," and that girls would try "to invent some kind of risky, boyhood life for [their] girlhood – which creates imagination, which means imagination."

Patti Smith – poet and rock 'n' roll star – accepted her boyhood life right from the beginning. "Female. feel male," she wrote in her little book *Seventh Heaven.* "Ever since I felt the need to choose/I'd choose male." And her concomitant childhood imagination was apparently both overstimulated and overstimulating. As her hyperkinetic Arista Records biography describes her: "It's nigh irrelevant knowing that this child visionary, Patti Smith, is by birth one of December's children – Chicago, '46; that she grew up a gawky, shy, spaced-out schoolgirl, eldest of four, in South Jersey;… that she'd hallucinate kelly green tortoises which materialized out of viscous azure air and encounter extra-terrestrial wayfarers, so beset by hallucinations she'd blank out and lose all track of time…"

A kind of cross between Alice in Wonderland and Huck Finn – a working-class kid who took off from the New Jersey backwater to become a poète maudit in New York City – Patti Smith seems to have nurtured her contradictions not so much with "joy and terror" – as Baudelaire said he nurtured his hysteria – but with a tomboyish sense of comedy and curiosity. "When I was young," she told Dave Marsh in *Rolling Stone*, "what we read was the Bible and UFO magazines. Just like I say I'm equal parts of Balenciaga and Brando, well, my dad was equal parts of God and Hagar the Spaceman in Mega City. My mother taught me fantasy; my mother's like a real hip Scheherazade. Between the Two of 'em, I developed a sensibility."

Her sensibility is one that borrows and embraces Gnostic-tinged, heterodoxical ideas and feelings that have appeared in the cosmogony of William Blake, the ritualism and paranoia of Baudelaire, the illuminations of Rimbaud, the menacing sexual fantasies of Lautréamont, Bataille, and Genet. And her esthetic program is one that owes and incalculable debt to Antonin Artaud, who, in the words of Roger Shattuck, "concocted a magic amalgam of theatrical style, occult and esoteric knowledge... antiliterary pronouncements, drug cultism, and revolutionary rhetoric without politics."

Patti Smith has taken this magic amalgam and manifested it in what she calls "3 chord rock merged with the power of the word," claiming that rock 'n' roll is "the highest and most universal form of expression since the lost tongue (time: pre-Babel)." Certainly, since the 1960's, "rock 'n' roll has been a perfect arena for sympathetic magic and convulsive theatrics, for ecstatic poetry and collective transcendence. As with Artaud, however, it is hard to separate Smith's poetry and recordings from her public persona, for she has been producing – as Susan Sontag has said of Artaud – not so much a literary and musical body of work as a "self." And it is a self that consciously draws on the mythological presence of rock stars such as Jim Morrison and Lou Reed (both of whom are published poets), Mick Jagger, Bob Dylan, and Jimi Hendrix.

As an intense, thin, almost etiolated figure – performing on stage in black (pegged pants, ribbon satin tie, silk shirt) and white (cotton T-shirt, shoes) – she imitates and mirrors the image of the androgynous male rock 'n' roll hero, which allows her to avoid the stereotyped victim-or-vamp role-playing of most female performers. And by adopting a paradoxical theatrical stance – one that confuses male and female roles and that combines the acoustic magic of Rimbaud and the Ronettes – Patti Smith has been able to develop, explore, and create a certain shamanistic presence that has eluded many aspiring rock 'n' roll seers and heroes. In the words of critic Robert Christgau, she has become "the first credible rock shaman, the one intelligent hold-out/throwback in a music whose mystics all pretend to have IQs around 90."

And in the role of shaman she bridges this world, the underworld, and the heavens, and brings back news from the shadows; she contacts ghosts, makes love with the dead, and transforms herself into animals (a black-haired, blue-eyed skunk dog in one poem). As she said in an interview with Amy Gross in *Mademoiselle*: "I get into so many genders I couldn't even tell you. I've written from the mouth of a dog, a horse, dead people, anything. I don't limit myself. Some of the best sex I ever had was with Rimbaud or Jimi Hendrix. I call them my brainiac-amours. Nothing sick about it, ya know. I get a lot of good poetry out of it. Me and Rimbaud have made it a million times."

To many people, most or all of the above will sound demented if not pretentious. And to them, her new book *Babel* – about 60 lyrics, poems and prose poems (most of them previously unpublished) that are set in lower case typeface with expressive but intentionally crude punctuation and spelling – will prove to be the work of an overwrought poetaster suffering from dysphoria and delirium tremens. To me, it is an alternately dazzling, uneven, arousing, annoying, imitative, original work.

Of course, Patti Smith sounds like everyone who has influenced her – especially Lautréamont, Rimbaud, Bataille, Burroughs, and Paul Bowles – and even like those who probably haven't – Mina Loy and Else von Freytag-Loringhoven come to mind. Of course her obsession with "love/and sex drugs and death," with "the freedom to be intense," with her pantheon of heroines including Joan of Arc and Marianne Faithfull, and with the ideas that vision places one in a state of grace and that "the cross is just the true shape of a tortured woman" are hyperalgesic, pubescent, and adolescent concerns. As Baron von Hügel once wrote, true illumination results in a special sweetness of temper; and in Babel there is more violence than grace, more bravado, swagger, machine-like lovemaking, "cooked" lesbian encounters, embodiments of rapists, masturbatory fantasies of sexual vengeance, reveries of saints and studs, Ethiopians and lepers, "disintegration and bending notes."

But out of the "realm of dreams and of fever" and in the "forbidden cinema" of her naturally hallucinating mind, Patti Smith has also given us some wonderful passages: Rimbaud's limb walking through a forest as children cruelly mock and assail the poet's crippled body in song ("rimbaud dead"); a garden envisioned in a mirror held up to a head of a young boy whose blood streams through and colors of a filed of poppies ("sohl"); God dreaming, the poet's father searching, humans worshipping so deeply that they connect themselves to the divine consciousness, only to be separated from their perfect union with the Creator ("grant"); a series of ecstatic poems of praise to "neo-boy," a kind of Blakean child of untrammeled joy and energy; a meditation that connects the rape of the heroine in Bresson's film *Au Hazard*

Balthazar – via the image of black jacket-black oil slick – to an entranced description of the work and death of Jackson Pollock ("robert bresson"); and a dream of an escape by the poet-heroine ("a misfit full of faith") from a colony of women ("i imagine the women in their starched linens, heads shaven, assigned and numbered, punctured and drained") who crave order (death) at the hands of "doctor love" who, in fact, "craves flaws, distinction. the challenge of the wrath and whims of a real woman" – upon whose escape the heroine is transformed into a mythic queen of sexual bliss ("doctor love").

The 16th-century Venetian courtesan poet Gaspara Stampa used outworn Petrarchan forms and imagery to write powerful sonnets on the themes of "fever and love." Patti Smith employs such overused surrealistic ideas as "the omnipotence of dream" and "the disinterested play of thought" to give us a number of poems, and two wonderful records, that have more energy and passion than many well-regarded works by American surrealists like Parker Tyler and Philip Lamantia. Patti Smith must certainly be praised for her insistence that one "never let go of the fiery sadness called desire," for her striving to attain the kind of vision Rimbaud nicknamed *voyance* – and this at a time when many writers settle simply for being voyeurs.

(1978)

JOHN LENNON
How He Became Who He Was

Say the word and be like me.
—John Lennon and Paul McCartney, "The Word"

"IS THERE ANYBODY GOING to listen to my story?" John Lennon asked in his song "Girl" on the 1965 *Rubber Soul* album. And it was one of the most ironic questions in the history of popular music, for it seemed as if everybody wanted to listen to his story—or at least to the ongoing story of the four Beatles.

"None of us would've made it alone," Lennon once explained, "because Paul wasn't quite strong enough, I didn't have enough girl-appeal, George was too quiet, and Ringo was the drummer. But we thought everyone would be able to dig at least one of us, and that's how it turned out." In fact, each of the Beatles came to be seen and thought of symbolically—like the four evangelists or the four elements. And in an elementary sense, each Beatle—in the way each became defined by his face, gestures, voice, and songs— took on an archetypal role: Paul, sweet and sensitive; John, sly and skeptical; George, mysterious and mystical; Ringo, childish but commonsensical (these roles were fixed forever in the film *A Hard Day's Night* and sanctified in the animated feature *Yellow Submarine*). But, at the risk of slighting the composers of beautiful songs like "Here, There and Everywhere" (Paul) and "Here Comes the Sun" (George), it seems clear in hindsight that there was one Beatle who embodied all of the above-named characteristics and qualities, and that was John Lennon.

The more he developed as a person and an artist, the more facets of himself he revealed. Alluding to the well-known image of the giraffe going by a window, he once said: "People are always just seeing little bits of it, but I try and see the whole . . . not just in my own life, but the whole universe, the whole game." He was both Nowhere Man and Eggman, he contained multitudes ("I am he as you are he as you are me and we are all together"), and of these one and all, he wove the song of himself. It was a song that included anthems ("Give Peace a Chance") and dream collages ("Revolution 9"), portraits ("Mean Mr. Mustard") and statements ("I Want You"), meditations ("Strawberry Fields Forever") and calls to action ("Power to the People"); it was a song of contrasting states of feeling and emotion—weariness ("I'm So Tired") and wakefulness ("Instant Karma!"), need ("Help!") and independence ("Good Morning, Good Morning"), depression ("You've Got to Hide Your Love Away") and elation ("Whatever Gets You Thru the Night"), reflectiveness ("In My Life") and anger ("How Do You Sleep?"), pain ("Yer Blues") and pleasure ("I Feel Fine"), toughness ("Run for Your Life") and gentleness ("Julia"); it was a song featuring different modes of expression—irony ("Happiness Is a Warm Gun"), primal screaming ("Mother"), sermons ("The Word"), political protest ("John Sinclair"), and nonsense ("I Am the Walrus"); and it was a song manifesting different states of being—the tragic ("Isolation"), the comic ("Polythene Pam"), and the cosmic, ("Across the Universe").

As Walt Whitman knew, the art and life of a person who contains multitudes is usually filled with contradictions. John Lennon was a born leader. It was he who brought Paul into the Quarrymen (Paul brought George, and George, Ringo), and it was he who, early on, had a sense of being out of the ordinary ("I was hip in kindergarten. I was different from the others. . . . When I was about twelve I used to think: I must be a genius, but nobody's noticed"). But he was a leader who also unstintingly shared his creative powers in collaboration with Paul McCartney and Yoko Ono.

He was an unreconstructible rock 'n' roller whose life was forever changed by "Heartbreak Hotel" ("When I heard it I dropped everything") and "Long Tall Sally" ("When I heard it, it was so great I couldn't speak") and who once thought that "avant-garde" was French for "bullshit." Yet he was always experimenting, even as a Beatle, with tapes played backward, tape loops, sound montages, and nonnarrative eight-millimeter films; and he produced an avant-garde masterwork in "Revolution 9." He furthermore came to rhapsodize about Yoko's music ("She makes music like you've never heard on earth. . . . It's as important as anything we ever did . . . as anything the Stones or Townshend ever did"), and often used to compare some of her most outré songs to "Tutti-Frutti"!

He grew up not only tough and angry but also gentle and vulnerable ("I was torn between being Marlon Brando and being the sensitive poet—the Oscar Wilde part of me with the velvet, feminine side"). He was a compassionate, pacifistic human being who was so in touch with his feelings that he could lash out verbally at those he felt had acted hypocritically or who had abused him or, especially, Yoko ("People want me to . . . be lovable. But I was never that. Even at school I was just 'Lennon.' Nobody ever thought of me as cuddly").

He was sometimes insecure and sometimes boastful ("Part of me suspects that I'm a loser and the other part of me thinks I'm God almighty"). He was a trusting and believing person who frequently—and, as it turned out, presciently—spoke of his sense of paranoia and mistrust ("The way things are going / They're going to crucify me"). And if he occasionally seemed stubborn, he at the same time developed a high degree of flexibility that allowed him to move on, to take risks—personally and artistically—and to live continually in the present ("Some people like Ping-Pong, other people like digging over graves. Some people will do anything rather than be here now. . . . *I don't believe in yesterday*"). And, finally, he was a leader who renounced his crown and empire in order to be true to himself ("It's pretty hard when you are Caesar and everyone is saying how wonderful you are and they are giving you all the goodies and the girls, it's pretty hard to break out of that to say, 'Well, I don't want to be king, I want to be real' ").

"I left the Beatles physically when I fell in love with Yoko," Lennon said a short time before his death, "but mentally it took the last ten years of struggling. I learned everything from her." In fact, Yoko became his teacher, his guru, his soul guide (like Dante's Beatrice), and as he told us in "One Day (at a Time)," he was the door and she was the key. Simply, Yoko enabled John to become what he was.

After they met at Yoko's 1966 Indica Gallery show in London, John used to receive "instructions" from Yoko in the mail (BREATHE, HIT A WALL WITH YOUR HEAD); he was perplexed but intrigued. They became lovers in 1968 after he and she stayed up one night and, at dawn, created the lovely East/West musical symbiosis they called *Two Virgins*, for whose album cover they posed naked together. She had led him where he would not go. "I always wanted to be an eccentric millionaire, and now I am," John said a short time later. "It was Yoko who changed me. She forced me to become avant-garde and take my clothes off when all I wanted to be was Tom Jones. And now look at me." But he also said: "People have got to become aware . . . that being nude is not obscene. Being ourselves is what's important. If everyone practiced being themselves instead of pretending to be what they aren't, there would be peace." And on the Beatles' White Album, John, inspired by Yoko, sang his much-neglected, exhilarating song of liberation, telling the world of his newfound energy, fearlessness, and openness:

> *The deeper you go the higher you fly.*
> *The higher you fly the deeper you go.*
> *So come on, come on . . .*
> — John Lennon and Paul McCartney, "Everybody's Got
> Something to Hide Except Me and My Monkey"

John Lennon had surrendered to his love for Yoko Ono ("*Yes* is surrender, you got to let it, you got to let it go," he would sing later in one of his most haunting songs, "Mind Games"). And from the moment he and Yoko became a couple, John Lennon, Beatle, began to learn how to become "John Lennon" again. On his first solo album, for instance (*John Lennon/Plastic Ono Band*), he jettisoned the extravagant imagery of songs such as "I Am the Walrus" and "Come Together." As he once explained it: "I started from the "Mother" album onward trying to shave off all imagery, pretensions of poetry, illusions of grandeur, [what] I call à la Dylan Dylan-esque. . . . Just say what it is, simple English, make it rhyme and put a backbeat on it and express yourself as simply and straightforwardly as possible."

On "Girl," Lennon had sung: "Was she told when she was young that pain would lead to pleasure?" But it was on this explosive new record—what I like to call his Howlin' Wolf album, inspired, in part, by John's and Yoko's primal-scream therapy with Arthur Janov—that he stripped down words and music and entered and explored, emotionally naked, an unmediated and undiluted world of pain. It became the subject of almost every song: "Don't let them fool you with dope and cocaine / Can't do you no harm to feel your own pain" ("I Found Out"); "God is a concept / By which we measure / Our pain" ("God"). And in a very real way, his pain was his waking up—from the world of personal illusion and the Social Lie ("As soon as you're born they make you feel small / By giving you no time instead of it all"—"Working Class Hero"). The record was certainly one of the most extraordinary creations in the history of rock 'n' roll.

On his next solo album, *Imagine*, Lennon presented a more lyrical and accessible musical "package," but his songs were still unsettling and subversive, for his pain was still forcing him to open his eyes to everything—politically ("No short-haired, yellow-bellied son of Tricky Dicky / Is gonna Mother Hubbard soft-soap me / With just a pocketful of hope"—"Gimme Some Truth") and psychologically ("You can wear a mask and paint your face / You can call yourself the human race / You can wear a collar and a tie / One thing you can't hide / Is when you're crippled inside"— "Crippled Inside").

His pain could lead to anger, as in his attack on Paul McCartney for falling creatively asleep in the vitriolic "How Do You Sleep?"; as an explanation he said: "I felt resentment, so I used that situation, the same as I used withdrawing from heroin to write 'Cold Turkey.'" And he took on the subject of his own irrepressible jealousy—a subject he had dealt with in previous Beatles songs like "No Reply," "Run for Your Life," and "You Can't Do That"—and attempted to understand its ravaging power by entering into its realm and describing the manner and process by which jealousy manifests itself in our bodies. In so doing, he allowed jealousy to be experienced as something rich and strange:

I was dreaming of the past
And my heart was beating fast
I began to lose control
I began to lose control

I was feeling insecure
You might not love me anymore
I was shivering inside
I was shivering inside

I was trying to catch your eyes
Thought that you was trying to hide
I was swallowing my pain
I was swallowing my pain
   —John Lennon, "Jealous Guy"

But pain also led him to see noble truths, as in his song "Imagine," one of the most beautiful visions—"antireligious, antinationalistic, anticonventional, anticapitalistic," as John termed it—of our possibilities as human beings: "You may say I'm a dreamer / But I'm not the only one / I hope someday you'll join us / And the world will be as one."

The muse of the *Imagine* album was, of course, Yoko, whose cover design showed John's face in the clouds, and to whom he wrote one of his most heartfelt ("Oh My Love") and one of his most joyous ("Oh Yoko!") songs. But it was she who sent him on his way in 1973 for what he called his eighteen-month Lost Weekend, and also on a trip by himself to Hong Kong in the late seventies, when he wandered around the city on his own, waking up at five in the morning to see the dawn, and during which, in the middle of a bath one day, he rediscovered *himself*. "I just got very,

very relaxed," he recalled. "And it was like a recognition. God! It's me! This relaxed person is *me*. I remember this guy from way back when! So I called Yoko. I said, 'Guess who, it's *me*! It's *me* here.' I was John Lennon before the Beatles, and after the Beatles, and so be it."

"Out of such abysses," Nietzsche once wrote—as if to describe the moment—"also out of the abyss of great suspicion, one returns newborn, having shed one's skin, more ticklish and sarcastic, with a more delicate taste for joy, with a more tender tongue for all good things, with gayer senses, with a second dangerous innocence in joy, more childlike and yet a hundred times more subtle than one has ever seen before." And in John and Yoko's last collaboration, *Double Fantasy*, they clearly revealed this joy and subtlety.

Aside from the beauty of individual songs like "Beautiful Boy" and "Every Man Has a Woman Who Loves Him," one might notice the mysterious little sound-collage segue on side two—it lasts less than a minute—between John's "Watching the Wheels" (a thematic variation on his wonderful Beatles song "I'm Only Sleeping") and Yoko's charming, thirties-like "I'm Your Angel." One hears what seems to be a hawker's voice, then an arresting few seconds of Greek balalaika music, followed by the sounds of a horse-driven carriage and footsteps, then a door slamming and a few phrases played by a piano and violin in a restaurant.

When I asked John about this collage shortly before he died, he told me: "One of the voices is me, going, 'God bless you, man, thank you, you've got a lucky face,' which is what the English guys who beg or want a tip say, so that's what you hear me mumbling. And then we re-created the sounds of what Yoko and I call the Strawberries and Violin Room—the Palm Court at the Plaza Hotel. We like to sit there occasionally and listen to the old violin and have a cup of tea and some strawberries. It's romantic. And so the picture is: There's this kind of street prophet, Hyde Park Corner–type guy who just watches the wheels going around, pronouncing on whatever he's pronouncing on. And people are throwing money in the hat. (We faked that in the studio, we had people walking up and down dropping coins in a hat.) And they're throwing money in his hat, and he's saying, 'Thank you, Thank you,' and then you get in the horse carriage and you go around New York and go into the hotel and the violins are playing and then this woman comes on and sings about being an angel."

And in "I'm Your Angel," Yoko sings: "I'm in your pocket / You're in my locket / And we're so lucky in every way." They must have had a guardian angel watching over their relationship, for, starting over after thirteen years as a couple, they seemed happier than ever before.

"All for love and the world well lost" has always been the motto of romantic lovers. But in the early years of their relationship John and Yoko might have said: "All for love and the world we'll win" ("Just a boy and a little girl / Trying to change the whole wide world" is what John *did* say in his song "Isolation"), as they performed their bag events and bed-ins for peace—"in the tradition of Gandhi, only with a sense of humor," as John put it. The *London Daily Mirror* described him as 1969's Clown of the Year, and he and Yoko were laughed at, patronized, and scorned by many people. Taking off one's clothes, greeting journalists in bed, and planting acorns wasn't exactly the appropriate image for two great romantic lovers. But it was exactly their naive and comic behavior that made them so real and believable a modern romantic couple—only two fools could be so much in love! And in their own tongue-in-cheek way, and like few others in history, John and Yoko lived lives that acted out in the everyday world archetypal dramas of the imagination. I have always thought of them whenever I read the letters of Abelard and Héloïse, the ill-starred twelfth-century lovers—he a famous philosopher, theologian, poet, and musician; she his pupil, paramour, wife, then abbess of a convent. As she wrote to Abelard: "You had besides, I admit, two special gifts whereby to win at once the heart of any woman—your gifts for composing verse and song, in which we know other philosophers have rarely been successful. . . . The beauty of the airs ensured that even the unlettered did not forget you; more than anything this made women sigh for love of you. And as most of these songs told of our love, they soon made me widely known and roused the envy of many women against me. For your manhood was adorned by every grace of mind and body, and among the women who envied me then, could there be one now who does not feel compelled by my misfortune to sympathize with my loss of such joys? Who is there who was once my enemy, whether man or woman, who is not moved now by the compassion which is my due?"

It is a letter that Yoko Ono might have written after John's death.

But John and Yoko also acted out the mythology of the gods and goddesses. Lennon once described Yoko as his "goddess of love and the fulfillment of my whole life." And in her song "Mother of the Universe," on *Season of Glass*, Yoko sings a hymn to the Mother Goddess, saying: "You gave us life and protection / And see us through our confusion / Teach us love and freedom / As it is to be."

It is interesting to find out that Yoko was deeply interested in Egyptian art and antiques—a large collection of which, including a full-size mummy in a case, she bought for their home. As she said: "I make sure to get all the Egyptian things, not for their value but for their magic power." And it is the ancient Egyptian goddess Isis that Yoko seems most to revere—the goddess who considered cows sacred to her (think of Yoko's interest in buying cows!) and who was at once wife and sister to Osiris, the supreme god and king of eternity (his name means "many-eyed") who was slain, dismembered, revived by Isis, and resurrected.

John's Isis was both mother and wife. "I occasionally call her Mother," he once said, "because I used to call her Mother Superior—remember 'Happiness Is a Warm Gun.' She is Mother Superior, she is Mother Earth, she is the mother of my child, she's my mother, she's my daughter. . . . The relationship goes through many levels, as in most relationships; it does not have any deep-seated strangeness about it." But the mythical Isis-Osiris resonance is there—as is the similarity to Héloïse's famous salutation to Abelard: "To her master, or rather her father, husband, or rather brother; his handmaid, or rather his daughter, wife, or rather sister; to Abelard, Héloïse."

And one further thinks of a seventeenth-century engraving of the "Soul of the World" that shows some of the symbols associated with Isis: long flowing hair; half-moon on her womb and one foot on water, the other on land. She is standing naked, chained to God, while man (pictured as an ape) is chained to her—and one recalls the photograph taken by Annie Leibovitz shortly before Lennon was killed, showing a naked John in fetal position clinging onto Yoko's body. "You've captured our relationship exactly," was what he said when he saw the test Polaroids.

John Lennon was a worshiper of the goddess. He was also a househusband for five years, while Yoko took care of all business and legal concerns. One thinks of Herodotus writing about Egypt in the fifth century B.C.: "Women attend market and are employed in trade, while men stay at home and do the weaving." The Lenonos—to use the name of John and Yoko's music-publishing company—seem to have run an ancient Egyptian household! Or a topsy-turvy nursery-rhyme one, for, as Lennon sang on "Cleanup Time": "The queen is in the counting house / Counting out the money / The king is in the kitchen / Making bread and honey."

Watching the wheels or baking bread, John Lennon had become who he was. Then, one night while at a disco in Bermuda in 1980, where he was vacationing with his son Sean, John heard a song called "Rock Lobster" by the B-52's for the first time. It sounded like Yoko's music, so he said to himself: "It's time to get out the old ax and wake the wife up!" In Bermuda he also had taken Sean to the Botanical Gardens and come across a flower called a Double Fantasy. "It's a type of freesia," John said, "but what it means to us is that if two people picture the same image at the same time, that is the secret." In "The Ballad of John and Yoko," he sang: "Last night the wife said, / Oh boy, when you're dead / You don't take nothing with you but your soul"—but he didn't leave it at that, for, pausing after the word *soul*, he added another word: "Think!" His message always was that each one of us should wake up.

"Produce your own dream," he said at the end of his life. "You have to do it yourself . . . . I can't wake you up. *You* can wake you up." But he pointed the way. "Why in the world are we here? / Surely not to live in pain and fear," he sang in "Instant Karma!" adding: "Well we all shine on like the moon and the stars and the sun. . . . Come on and on and on on"—and ending, in inimitable John Lennon fashion, "Yeah yeah, all right, ah ha."

(1982)

GLENN GOULD

"THE NUT'S A GENIUS," the conductor George Szell once remarked after attending a performance in Cleveland by the Canadian pianist Glenn Gould. Since 1947, when he first publicly performed Beethoven's Fourth Piano Concerto at fourteen, Glenn Gould continually amazed and astonished audiences, critics, and professional colleagues alike. He was called a musician of "divine guidance" and the greatest pianist since Busoni. He was also castigated for, 1, his unconventional performing mannerisms—loping onstage like a misplaced eland with unpressed tails, sometimes wearing gloves, playing almost at floor level on a sawed-down, short-legged wooden folding chair and conducting, humming, singing, combating, cajoling, and making love to his piano as it were Lewis Carroll's Snark ("I engage with the snark / Every night after dark / In a dreamy, delirious fight"); 2, his uncompromisingly imaginative choice of repertoire (William Byrd, Bach, Hindemith, and Schoenberg instead of Chopin and Rachmaninoff . . . and more Rachmaninoff); 3, his obsessive search and preference for a tight-actioned piano, meant to facilitate a musical approach that emphasized clarity of definition and textures and a rarely equaled analytical subtlety and acuity —as well as for certain startling but revelatory interpretations of such "standards" as the Brahms First Piano Concerto. (When Gould first performed this piece with Leonard Bernstein and the New York Philharmonic, for instance, Bernstein—with the pianist's approval—got up before the audience to disassociate himself gently with Gould's approach, which featured slow tempi and a profound structural design that, for the first time I could remember, truly revealed the work's pent-up emotional rapture.)

And finally, Gould was criticized for his eccentric and hermetic lifestyle (the pianist refused to fly, liked taking car trips by himself to the far north of Canada, and spent most of the last half-dozen years of his life sequestered in a claustral hotel studio on the outskirts of Toronto); for his bizarre getup (gloves, mittens, T-shirt, shirt, vest, sweater, coat, and scarf, all in warm weather); and, to cap it all off, for his having retired, at the wizened age of thirty-two from any and all public concert recitals.

Gould's retirement, in fact, allowed him to try to realize and make good his claims that the functions of concerts had been—or would soon be—taken over by electronic media and that it was the recording medium itself that allowed for an unparalleled analytic clarity, immediacy, tactile proximity, and catholicity of repertoire. The "analytic dissection by microphone" enabled Gould to present the music from a "strongly biased conceptual viewpoint," just as it permitted the music to emerge with an untrammeled force and luminescence. As Gould's recorded performances demonstrated, structural clarification always released new energy.

After his retirement from the stage in 1964, Gould continued to produce one extraordinary album after another. And he interspersed his unsurpassed Bach realizations with "first" recordings of Richard Strauss's *Enoch Arden* (accompanying the actor Claude Rains, who recited Tennyson's sentimental drawing-room poem), the Liszt piant transcription of Beethoven's Fifth Symphony, Bizet's *Variations Chromatiqes*, sublime piano realizations of virginal pieces by Byrd and Gibbons, and an astonishingly beautiful piano transcription of Wagner's *Siegfried Idyll*.

Along with his transcriptions, Gould also composed. His works include a string quartet Opus 1, written between 1953 and 1955—an unabashed romantic composition showing the pianist's predilection for the fin-de-siècle works of Bruckner and Richard Strauss; *So You Want to Write a Fugue* for vocal and string quartets—a jocular tour de force that was originally recorded in the early sixties by the Juilliard String Quartet for the plastic insert disc in *HiFi/Stereo Review* and later released on *The Glenn Gould Silver Jubilee Album*; and two dazzling cadenzas to Beethoven's C-Major Piano Concerto.

In addition to his recording career, Gould made a number of pathbreaking programs of "contrapuntal radio" for the Canadian Broadcasting Corporation (using voices in trio sonata form and employing the sounds of a train and the sea as a basso continuo); narrated and performed on—and was the subject of—innumerable radio and television programs; and assembled and arranged music for several shorts and feature films.

Throughout his career, Gould also wrote brilliant and provocative lectures, magazine articles, reviews, and self-interviews on such subjects as the forger as hero of electronic culture, Artur Rubinstein, Petula Clark versus the Beatles, Barbra Streisand and Elizabeth Schwarzkopf, Beethoven as the exemplar of a composer whose "professional development skills" conflicted with an "amateur's motivic bluntness," and the analytical importance of the "flipside overlap" (the four-minute demarcation points at the ends of 78 rpm records). These essays and articles were an extension of Gould's brilliant and witty liner-note extravaganzas— similar in style and approach to the eighteenth-century *Spectator* and *Tatler* newssheets—in which the pianist informed his listeners of the state of health of his piano; commented on and theorized about a wide range of musical matters; and offered advice to his critics as to how to write about certain of his performances.

In the notes accompanying his recording of Bizet and Grieg piano pieces, for example, Gould explained that Grieg was a cousin of his maternal great-grandfather, thus affording him a not-to-be-begrudged interpretive authority. And the pianist went on to suggest to record reviewers that, since no previous recordings of the Bizet works existed, "for those of you who greet the release with enthusiasm, I should like to propose a phrase such as '— vividly and forcefully, as only a first reading can, it partakes of that freshness, innocence, and freedom from tradition that, as the late Arthus Schnabel so deftly remarked, is but a "collection of bad habits." ' On the other hand, for those in doubt as to the validity of the interpretation involved, I venture to recommend a conceit such as '—regrettably, a performance that has not as yet jelled; an interpretation that is still in search of an architectural overview.' "

And on his Liszt-Beethoven album, Gould printed four parody "reviews" of his interpretation of the Fifth Symphony by four of the pianist's most entertaining critical personae: Sir Humphrey Price-Davies of *The Phonograph* Magazine, Professor Dr. Karlheinz Heinkel of *Münch'ner Müskilologische Gesellschaft*, S. F. Lemming, M.D., of North Dakota Psychiatrists Association, and, finally, Zoltan Mostanyi of *Rhapsodya: Journal of the All-Union Musical Workers of Budapest*. (Gould was, incidentally, awarded a Grammy in 1974 for his liner notes to his recording of Hindemith's three piano sonatas.)

When it was suggested several years ago that Gould collect his liner notes, articles, and essays into a book, the pianist replied that if he reread what he had previously written, he would feel compelled to emend, correct, annotate, amplify, and redo everything—so much so that he would wind up with completely new texts! (Many of Gould's original writings have now been collected in *The Glenn Gould Reader*, edited by Tim Page.) The Canadian music critic William Littler further reports that the pianist "took positive pride in the fact that he had to submit the first draft of a two-minute, forth-three-second speed in his radio commentary on Richard Strauss to no fewer that one hundred and thirty-one edits—about one per second." In a certain parlance, one might well say that Glenn Gould was a classic "control freak." As John Lee Roberts, former head of the Music Department of CBC Radio, once stated, Gould "liked to feel he was in total control of himself in every instant of his life." And as Anthony Storr has described the obsessional artistic personality: "Perhaps the most striking feature of the obsessional temperament is the compulsive need to control both the self and the environment. Disorder and spontaneity must be avoided so far as possible, since both appear threatening and unpredictable."

In a sense, Gould set up and organized his personal and professional life like a series of games with intractable rules. But unlike most obsessive types, whose rigidity and lack of humor foreclosed the possibility of spontaneity, the pianist's seemingly restricting games of life allowed him to manifest *exactly* a spontaneous and unpredicable sense of being and creating. In claustral hotel room and recording engineer's control (!) booth, Gould created his *temenos*, his sacred grove—a hidden place where he could *play* and explore his musical and technological obsessions, far from minatory onlookers and an admonishing outside world.

A philosopher once said that if art were to redeem man, "it could do so only by saving him from the seriousness of life and restoring him to an unexpected boyishness." And on the jacket of

Gould's debut Columbia recording—a 1955 performance of Bach's *Goldberg Variations*—were thirty contact-sheet-size photographs (one per variation), each showing various aspects and expressions of a boyish-looking young man. And taken together, the photos expressed visually the grace, wit, speed, clarity, passion, daring, and almost androgynous beauty of the astonishing performance of a work that, originally intended to while away the nighttime hours of the insomniac eighteenth-century Russian Count Kayserling, awoke us all to the presence of a musical genius.

"The Sound of Genius" was the phrase with which Columbia Records immodestly designated and advertised its classical-music artists in the late fifties and sixties; but never was it more accurately applied than to Glenn Gould, whose progress from record to record (and, for those lucky enough to see him, from concert to concert) created the kind of excitement that teenagers long ago used to feel when anticipating the publication of a new Tom Swift or Nancy Drew adventure book. For every album that Glenn Gould proceeded to release gave evidence not only of the possibilities of a more vital and rewarding pianistic repertoire (as well as the concomitant ongoing revelation of Gould's musical personality) but also of an interpretive audaciousness free from the preconditioning and preconceptions of all received cultural canons and performance "norms." Beethoven's last three sonatas; music by Mozart and Haydn; piano works by Berg, Schoenberg, and Ernst Krenek; Brahms's *Intermezzi*; and the ongoing Bach recordings almost every new recording was accompanied by scintillating, Gould-authored liner notes and ever-changing record-jacket photographs of our hero (looking alternately entranced, relaxed, sensual, dreamy), and each album promised and fulfilled our longing for adventure and discovery.

Gould fulfilled our expectations because he was a musical explorer who revealed as he created his own artistic path, noticing things on it that few before him had ever seen because he observed and heard with the eyes and ears of a child. "Children," the Italian poet Leopardi once said, "see everything in nothing; adults, nothing in everything." And with this childlike sense, Gould perceived, for instance, that the inner lines of a William Byrd pavane, a Bach fugue, a Beethoven bagatelle, a Brahms intermezzo, a Scriabin sonata, a Schoenberg suite contained their own beauty and energy—as well as contributing to the integrity and power of the whole composition—qualities awaiting the discovery and release that could be conferred only by Gould's special touch of magic, a kind of magic that enabled the pianist to connect himself, as well as his listeners, to the roots of artistic creation. And here lies the ultimate Gouldian paradox: by distancing and isolating himself from his audience, he got ever closer to and more in touch with it . . . and by allowing himself undistractedly to enter and surrender himself to his music, he revealed and gave both it and himself totally to us.

A personal note: At the age of thirteen—filled with typical adolescent turmoil and angst—I heard Glenn Gould's recording of the *Goldberg Variations* and attained what I took to be a moment of musical, emotional, and spiritual enlightenment. For it was as if the pianist's performance had truly embodied and brought to fruition Nietzsche's conception of art—"that sorceress expert in healing"— about which and whom the philosopher had written: "Only she can turn [our] fits of nausea into imaginations with which it is possible to live. These are on the one hand the spirit of the *sublime*, which subjugates terror by means of art; on the other hand the *comic* spirit, which releases us, through art, from the tedium of absurdity."

365

Throughout my teenage years, I attended every concert performance by Glenn Gould—both as a solo recitalist and as a guest artist with several orchestras—in the New York City area. I remember, for example, traveling up to Westchester to see the pianist perform Beethoven's *Emperor* Concerto with a makeshift suburban orchestra, whose conductor (may he remain nameless) was so inept that Gould, score in hand and playing in a semi-crouching position, decided to half perform and half lead the stranded musicians, who gratefully took their cues from their keyboard artist guest, while their *chef d'orchestre*, standing on the podium, obliviously went about waving his arms to the sounds of a different drummer (or pianist)!

I also remember being one of the three or four privileged observers at a Carnegie Hall rehearsal session of the Schoenberg Piano Concerto (with Dimitri Mitropoulos leading the New York Philharmonic), at which a shoelesss Gould emerged from the wings almost *gliding* onto the stage in his stocking feet, wearing a scarf, carrying a bottle of Poland Spring Water, and warming his hands in a basin of hot water in preparation for what turned out to be the most assured and vital performance of this concerto I have ever heard.

In 1960, I was actually invited to meet my hero in the office of a New York City television station where the pianist had come to discuss the possibility of his doing a series of live performance broadcasts (a project that ultimately fell through). Before the meeting started, I was introduced to Gould, who, in spite of the summer season, was wearing his customary outer and inner polar garments. The pianist warily held out his hand to me (a practice that the self-protective Gould was known to avoid). I shook it and heard him give a quiet yell, as I quickly withdrew and uttered my deepest apologies. Gould shrugged, smiled, and quickly forgave me—especially so when I told him of my enthusiasm for his recently released album featuring music by Berg, Schoenberg, and Krenek.

In the mid- to late sixties, living in California, I occasionally wrote the pianist unabashed fan letters that thanked him for his inspiring and revelatory recordings—in particular his six-record *Well-Tempered Clavier* project—and received an occasional note back from him. Then, in 1974, I had the opportunity of talking to Gould on the telephone for six hours over a three-day period, the results of which were published as a two-part interview in *Rolling Stone* magazine. It was in fact, during these phone conversations that Gould and I became friends—the phone made it easier for the pianist to make contact and keep in touch with people he liked. And after the interviews were published, whenever I found myself answering the phone at some odd hour and hearing someone asking for me in various strange-sounding accents (German, French, Russian), I knew it was Herr Gould, Monsieur Gould, or Gospodin Gould on the line.

In 1979, the pianist called me one evening and said: "You know, in three years I'll be fifty, and I've been thinking that that would be a good year for me to give up making piano recordings." "You can't do that!" I found myself involuntarily pleading with him. "Well," he tried to console me, "I'll have finished recording the complete Bach for keyboard, most of the Beethoven sonatas . . ." "What about the Sonata No. 28 in A, Op. 101?" I asked. "I heard you perform that once in concert, and *no one* has ever done it so beautifully." "Well, I thank you, sir," Gould laughed. "But if I don't get around to recording it, you can come up to Toronto and I'll play it for you here."

That same year I began two years of full-time work on a book, and had to travel everywhere *but* to Toronto, so I missed that promised private recital—and, unfortunately, Gould never did get around to recording Op. 101. But in 1981, the pianist informed me that, for the first time in his career, he had agreed to allow the French director Bruno Monsaingeon to film an entire series of his recording sessions, during which he planned to make a new version of the *Goldberg Variations* for CBS Records. When the album was released in the middle of 1982, I mentioned to a friend that the front jacket photo of Gould was extremely disturbing, for never had the pianist adorned a cover looking so haunted, pained, and sad. (The back jacket photo ominously showed only Gould's piano and his empty, pillowless chair.)

These photographs had been taken in 1982. But a year earlier, as the recording of Monsaingeon's remarkable film makes clear, Gould—balding and bespectacled and no longer the thin and boyish pianist of 1955—had nevertheless given us the deepest and most joyful Bach interpretation of his career. Supported by and accountable to a simultaneously overarching and underlying musical pulse—inaudile but felt—Gould's new *Goldberg* encapsulated and manifested a lifetime's worth of wisdom and understanding about the music of Johann Sebastian Bach, and particularly about what is probably the greatest set of keyboard variations ever written.

On October 4, 1982—several months after the album's release—Glenn Gould died. He was fifty years old. Although the pianist had made three additional recordings before his death, of music by Brahms, Beethoven, and Richard Strauss (albums that—with the exception of the magnificent performances of the Strauss *Five Piano Pieces*, Op. 3—are uncharacteristically gloomy and funereal in tone, approach, and execution), and although Gould had just begun a new career as a conductor (he led a chamber orchestra in a recording of Wagner's *Siegfried Idyll*), I prefer to remember that his last will and testament was also his first—the *Goldberg Variations*, whose opening Aria also concludes this work that, as Gould described it (and, I like to think, his own playing as well) in his almost thirty-year-old liner notes, "observes neither end nor real resolution, music which, like Baudelaire's lovers, 'rests lightly on the wings of the unchecked wind.' It has, then, unity through intuitive perception, unity born of craft and scrutiny, mellowed by mastery achieved, and revealed to us here, as so rarely in art, in the vision of subconscious design exulting upon a pinnacle of potency."

(1984)

KURT WEILL

THERE IS ALWAYS AN UNFORGETTABLE DAY when one comes across *The Threepenny Opera* for the first time. In his autobiography *The Magic Lantern*, the director Ingmar Bergman recalls what was for him that epiphanic moment: the summer of 1936 in Weimar, Germany, when, as a sixteen-year-old Swedish exchange student, he found himself at an open-air rally for the Führer one summer afternoon, then, later that evening—in a candle-lit tower room of a banker's mansion—smoking Turkish cigarettes and sipping brandy dizzily in the company of the two sons and daughter of one of his aunt's best friends.

"A small portable gramophone stood on a small gilded table, [Bergman writes,]wound up and ready. David, the younger of the brothers, stuffed a couple of socks into the sound box. A record with a blue Telefunken label on it lay on the turntable. The needle was dropped into the track and the harsh but subdued notes of the overture of *The Threepenny Opera* rose out of the black box, revealing a whole world of which I had never had an inkling, despair without tears, desperation that wept! . . . Why all this secrecy with nighttime concerts, closed doors, soft gramophone needles, and socks in the soundbox? 'It's banned music,' Horst said. 'Brecht and Weill are banned. We found the records in London and smuggled them over.' . . . I didn't understand the words, anyhow not many of them, but I have always, like a shrewd animal, understood tone of voice, and I understood this tone of voice. It sank into my deepest consciousness, to remain there as a part of me."

Once heard, *The Threepenny Opera*—first performed in Berlin on August 31, 1928—is never forgotten. What *is* often forgotten, however is that Kurt Weill is the composer not just of this *one* masterpiece, and not just of this play-with-music's *one* "catchy" tune ("Mack the Knife"), turned into an American "classic" by the likes of Bobby Darin, Louis Armstrong, Jimmy Durante, Liberace, and Frank Sinatra—as well as into the "Mac Tonight" jingle for the McDonald Corporation. (To what other glory could a composer aspire?) Rather, as we approach this ninetieth anniversary year of Kurt Weill's birth (on March 2, 1900, in Dessau, Germany) and the fortieth anniversary of his death (on April 3, 1950, in New York City), we can clearly see this creator of about fifty concert-hall compositions, seven collaborations with Bertolt Brecht, and nine works for the Broadway stage as one of the most risk-taking and influential composers of the first half of our century.

The son of a Jewish cantor who was able to trace his family's ancestry (mostly rabbinical) back to fouteenth-century Dessau, Kurt Weill was brought up as an assimilated Reform Jew who considered himself a humanist in chaotic Weimar Republic Germany. Composing and playing the piano in his early teens, he moved, at eighteen, to Berlin—"a carnival of jazz bands and rattling machine guns," as someone then described the city—where he studied musical composition with Engelbert Humperdinck and the composer and theorist Ferruccio Busoni.

Short in stature, prematurely bald, sensitive-looking with a charming, ironical smile and dark brown eyes behind thick-lensed glasses—and continually smoking a pipe—the introverted Weill gave the impression of a preoccupied Talmudic scholar. His earliest concert-hall compositions are accordingly serious, intense, rigorously structured works, displaying an atonal lyricism and *Gebrauchsmusik* ("functional-music")-type rhythms. (The Violin Concerto, Cello Sonata, Second String Quartet, and First Symphony are among the best of these pieces.) But they ultimately lack a true musical profile. Take any few bars, for instance, of almost any work of the 1920s by Schoenberg, Berg, Stravinsky, or Hindemith, and one can immediately identify the composer; take any few bars from one of the above-mentioned compositions by Weill—however forceful and beautiful in parts— and it is difficult to guess who is behind it all.

During his early years in Berlin, Weill supported himself by teaching music theory, writing weekly music criticism for a radio-station journal, and playing organ in a synagogue and piano in a beer hall. In hotel bars, dance halls, and cabarets, Weill heard and was drawn irresistibly to American jazz, big band music, and dances like the Boston, the foxtrot, the shimmy, the Charleston, the tango. For him, it all comprised an "international folk music of the broadest consequences," he wrote, adding: "Why should art-music isolate itself from such an influence? . . . Jazz is as precisely the external expression of our time as was the waltz of the nineteenth century."

By 1926—a year before he met Brecht—Weill was speaking of a "very different kind of music that I feel is slowly growing within me." No longer interested in composing elite music for concert halls or in "working toward solution of aesthetic problems as if behind closed doors," Weill (metaphorically) opened his blinds, his windows, his door, and went out searching, not for "new forms or new theories" but rather "for a new public." To that end, he emphasized his need to develop in his music a "clarity of language, precision of expression, and simplicity of feeling" that soon allowed him to create works for the radio (*The Berlin Requiem*), for children's schools (*Der Jasager*), and a masterpiece for the music-theater (*The Threepenny Opera*).

With continually waffing major/minor chords, marching-band rhythms intertwining with jazz syncopations, and an instrumental palette featuring the sensual, dark-hued timbres of a ragtag German version of a seven-piece jazz ensemble (alto and tenor sax, harmonium, banjo, bandoneon, trumpet, trombone, percussion), Weill's *Threepenny* score colored in Brecht's mordant ironies to convey and distill, in a voice all his own, the bittersweet gaiety, dance-hall decadence, sardonic wit, and romantic wistfulness characteristic of late-twenties Berlin— one of the great, electric, dying cities of the world.

In the mid-1920s, Kurt Weill had met a girl who seemed to him a true expression of the time—a bit of an embodiment of Pirate Jenny herself. Born Karoline Wilhelmine Blamauer, the Catholic daughter of a coachman and a laundress from Vienna, this girl had a beauty, sensuality, and vivacity that caught his eye . . . and even made him lose his glasses. As Lotte Lenya (the name the girl had adopted for her ballet-dancing and acting career) later recalled: "One Sunday afternoon I took Weill on a boat on the lake. He was very nearsighted; he wore thick, thick glasses and I did something and hit his glasses and they fell in the lake. That was the time he proposed marriage. I said later on, 'Kurt, would you have married me with the glasses on?' He replied, 'Yes, I think so, yes.'"

Like his then-and-future audience, Weill was obsessed with Lenya's voice. "When I long for you," he once wrote to her, "I think most of all about the sound of your voice, which I love like a very force of nature, like an element. You are entirely contained within this sound; everything else is only part of you; and when I envelop myself in your voice, then you are with me in every way."

They lived together for two years before getting married in 1926. They had a stormy relationship (she demanded attention, while he would compose from eight in the morning until midnight, and then responded to her accusations of neglect by saying, "But darling, you *know* you come right after my music!"); and they led a bohemian-style "open" marriage that ended in divorce in 1933 . . . though they later got remarried in 1937 and remained companions and devoted collaborators until the end of his life. "She is a terrible housewife but a wonderful actress," Weill once said about Lenya. "She can't read a note of music but when she sings it sounds like Caruso. . . . She married me because she wanted a taste of the horrors—a wish which, she maintains, has been granted many times over."

But the real horror was everywhere around them. Brown shirts incited full-scale riots at the premieres of Weill's works; writers connected with the Nazi *Kampfbund für Deutsche Kultur* attacked everything he composed; and it is said that Weill himself stumbled inadvertently onto a rally presided over by the Maestro of the Master Race, and heard himself—along with Albert Einstein and Thomas Mann—accused of corrupting and besmirching the purity of the *Volk*. Being Jewish, an associate of the Bolshevik Brecht, an intellectual, and a composer whose works were popular with the masses, Weill was officially placed close to the top of the Nazi hit list. So on March 21, 1933, he and Lenya drove from Berlin to Paris, where he lived and composed until September 1935, when he and Lenya again headed west—this time on an ocean liner for New York.

Booking themselves into the St. Moritz Hotel, they immediately went to see a film. In Lenya's words: "We were ardent readers of people like Hemingway and Scott Fitzgerald, and we saw all the movies. So when we arrived, we dropped our bags and went to Broadway into a movie. We saw *The Dark Angel* with Ronald Colman and Vilma Banky. That was the first thing and from then on there was really nothing strange or unfamiliar."

From that moment on, Kurt Weill (now pronounced "Curt Wile") never looked back. Never again would he speak German—not even to Lenya—the language of the country that had betrayed him; and he refused to keep in touch with nostalgic émigré friends. Simply but courageously, he adopted and embodied the adage: "The man who finds his homeland sweet is still a tender beginner; he to whom every soil is as his native one is already strong; but he is perfect to whom the entire world is as a foreign land" (Hugo of St. Victor).

Weill now considered himself an American composer: he contributed propaganda songs for the American war effort; and beginning with the musical play *Johnny Johnson* (1936), he collaborated with writers such as Ira Gershwin, Langston Hughes, Ogden Nash, and Maxwell Anderson in a series of works for Broadway (including *Lady in the Dark*, *Street Scene*, *Love Life*, and *Lost in the Stars*). Once again, as in Berlin, he hoped to find a "new public," and, at the same time, to create a new type of American opera. As he remarked in 1937: "Broadway represents the living theater in this country, and American opera, as I imagine it, should be part of the living theater"—a notion he found even more compelling after attending a performance of *Porgy and Bess*.

Weill himself—who is honored in Dessau by a piffling plaque that remembers him only as the collaborator of Bertolt Brecht (whose statue dominates the city's main square)—would certainly have felt vindicated (and pleased) to have found himself described in 1978 by *The New Yorker's* Andrew Porter as "a master American musician, master musical dramatist, and large soul who found song for the people of his adopted country, learned its idioms, joined them to his own, and composed music of international importance." (Undoubtedly, he would have also enjoyed the "Brechtian" irony of knowing that his echt-American *Street Scene*, with its New York City tenement setting, was rapturously received by German audiences when presented in March 1988 in three English-language concert performances to sellout crowds in Duisburg, Recklinghausen, and Cologne.)

As Professor Kim H. Kowalke, president of the Kurt Weill Foundation, recently stated: "In 1990 there will be more performances of Weill's works than at any other time since *The Threepenny Opera* had its premiere in Germany—and I don't think that's an exaggeration. And yes, I *do* think that in *that* sense, you could say Weill is more alive now than before.

"When he *was* alive, Weill was seeking an audience; and when he did find one, he was criticized for doing so. His early concert-hall works were dismissed by some music critics as too dissonant and atonal; his later Second Symphony was considered too cheap, too tuneful. Schoënberg and his followers attacked him viciously; Brecht and *his* followers wanted to bury him as well. And Weill's American musical competitors weren't too happy with him either; they thought of him as a foreigner and an interloper. Someone supposedly once asked Richard Rodgers, 'What are you going to do now that Weill is writing these big finales?' And Rodgers was supposed to have flippantly responded, 'What's a finale?'

"Today, however, Weill is allowed to be his complete self. We can enjoy 'September Song' *and* the Cello Sonata, and not have to say, 'My God, those pieces are written by two different persons, one of whom had to suppress the other.' No, the works of Kurt Weill are by one remarkable talent."

"I want to use whatever gifts I have for practical purposes," Kurt Weill once said, "not waste them on things which have no life, or which have to be kept alive by artificial means. . . . I have never acknowledged the difference between 'serious' music and 'light' music. There is only good music and bad music."

(1989)

HILDEGARD OF BINGEN

SEVERAL YEARS AGO, the once-Dominican, now-Episcopalian theologian and priest Matthew Fox recalls giving a workshop in Oregon. The subject was the twelfth-century German Benedictine nun Hildegard of Bingen (1098–1179)—mystic, preacher, oracle, healer, and the first (and possibly the greatest) female composer in the Western classical-music tradition. "If Hildegard had been a man," Fox asserts, "she would be well known as one of the greatest artists and intellectuals the world has ever seen."

In his workshop, Fox spoke of Hildegard's "woman wisdom" in a patriarchal culture and male-run church; discussed her marrying of science, art, and religion; described her spiritual awakening at the age of forty-two; and showed slides depicting her astonishing visions of living light, greening love, flowing water, and burning spheres that appear in her book *Scivias* ("Know the Ways of the Lord"). At the conclusion of the workshop, Fox remembers, "a woman came up to me and commented, 'I'm a Catholic, I have two daughters, and you know, I think Mary is fine and everything, but Mary didn't do that much. This Hildegard was a visionary and a healer and a musician . . . and I can't wait to run home to tell my daughters about Hildegard of Bingen.' Hildegard *is* a wonderful role model," Fox declares. "She's a giant, someone to usher us into the new millennium."

Until recently, however, there was little if any attention paid in the English-speaking world to "the Sibyl of the Rhine," as Hildegard was known in her time. In the late 1970s Judy Chicago paid homage to Hildegard in her monumental sculpture "The Dinner Party," a symbolic history of women's achievements told through embroidered runners and china painted plates on a triangular table. And suddenly in the past ten years, more than a score of critical studies and translations of Hildegard's work, originally written in Latin, have been published here and in England. Several recordings of her hypnotic, candent music are currently, and surprisingly, on the classical best-seller charts. A small healing center in Allensbach, Germany, is employing Hildegard's homeopathic cures and remedies. And the International Society of Hildegard von Bingen Studies, founded in 1984 at Ball State University in Muncie, Indiana, now has more than 300 members in twenty-five countries. Why this unprecedented revival of interest in this "poor little figure of a woman" (as Hildegard of Bingen once called herself), who once wrote:

> Listen: There was once a king sitting on his throne. Around him stood great and wonderfully beautiful columns ornamented with ivory, bearing the banners of the king with great honor. Then it pleased the king to raise a small feather from the ground and he commanded it to fly. The feather flew, not because of anything in itself but because the air bore it along. Thus am I . . . "

That the "Hildegardian" feather is blowing in the wind today as noticeably as it is can undoubtedly be attrituted to a recording that was released at the end of 1994 by the aptly-named Angel Records. Entitled *Vision: The Music of Hildegard von Bingen*, it immediately became the number-one album for sixteen weeks on *Billboard's* chart for classical crossover music, and has sold 450,000 CDs and tapes worldwide.

On *Vision*, sixteen of Hildegard's rapturous melodies are alternately sung by Sister Germaine Fritz, a Benedictine prioress at Saint Walburga Monastery in Elizabeth, New Jersey, and by the early-music vocalist Emily Van Evera, and these have been given a New Age, worldbeat, techno-pop overlay by arranger and producer Richard Souther. The result—a cross between Enya and Canteloube's *Songs of the Auvergne*—is admittedly a far cry from Hildegard's pristine, luminous monodic compositions. One critic said of Vision that it was "like putting ketchup on caviar." Another considered it "a great CD to chainsaw by." The majority of the critics, however, were enthusiastic. And Sister Germaine loved it. "Through *Vision*," she said, "I came to appreciate the beauty both of the music and of Hildegard as a person. She is a person for all ages and a model of how one responds to the call."

It is a sunny April day in New Jersey, and Sister Germaine Fritz, O.S.B., is leading a visitor around Saint Walburga Monastery, housed behind an enormous brick mansion originally designed by Sanford White, where she is the prioress of seventy-five nuns. Sister Germaine, who wears glasses and has short gray hair, is dressed in a blue skirt and a blue-and-white-striped blouse on which is pinned a Benedictine medal—much her normal attire, since she has chosen not to wear a veil, which is optional at Saint Walburga. The old church across the street, she says, collapsed several years ago; and she now proudly points out the monastery's recently built, ultramodern Eucharist Chapel and cavernous Gathering Space with some of the Rules of Saint Benedict painted on stained- glass windows (PRAY AND WORK, SPEAK TRUTH FROM THE HEART). And when she opens her mouth to sing—as she does for a moment in the Gathering Space to demonstrate its remarkable acoustics—it is clear that she belongs in the first circle of the angels.

"Kind of neat, isn't it?" she exclaims enthusiastically about the new additions to the monastery. Sister Germaine is nothing if not enthusiastic—a word, after all, that derives from the Greek for "having the god within." Every other week throughout the year she presides as cantor at the Eucharist and Liturgy of the Hours. In addition, her duties include ministry and community work— teaching, child care, a hospice, guidance services. She is high-spirited, gracious, charming.

Brought up in Maplewood, New Jersey, Sister Germaine taught Catholic elementary and high schools, and received an M.A. in music from the New York University School of Education. She was elected prioress of the monastery by her sister nuns in 1985. "One day," she says, "someone told me that Angel Records, which was coming off its big success with *Chant: The Benedictine Monks of Santo Domingo de Silos*, was looking for 'a real nun who sings chant' on an album of music of Hildegard of Bingen.

"My first reaction was: Chant is sacred music, it's part of my prayer life, it's part of my community's prayer life, is this recording going to cheapen the music? Then I met up with the people from Angel Records, and they impressed me with their excitement about Hildegard's songs. So I talked to the sisters and said: It's Hildegard. Hildegard was a Benedictine. I'm a Benedictine. And I knew she was an extraordinary woman. Though she's not formally canonized—she is accepted as a saint in Germany—there's a Mass that commemorates her. So my sisters told me to go ahead.

"Angel wanted a demo tape of my voice, so I went down to the Gathering Space, sat down right next to the holy water font with a two-bit tape machine, and recorded six of Hildegard's songs a cappella. It's a great space, my voice was rolling around the room, and it sounded good. So I put the tape in the mail the Wednesday of Holy Week last year and got a call the Tuesday after Easter. And we went on from there."

Driving her visitor back to New York City in the monastery car—a '92 black Dodge Spirit—Sister Germaine searches through her collection of cassette tapes, which include recordings by Neil Diamond and Phil Coulter, Vangelis' *Chariots of Fire* ("my first introduction to electronic music," she says), a choral collection of Ave Marias . . . and finally finds what she's been looking for. A copy of *Vision* goes into the car tape deck. "Sure, it's not an authentic version of Hildegard, but I cannot fault Richard Souther's intention. He's a spiritual guy and he's enraptured by Hildegard's dialogue with God. Just listen to this antiphon 'Unde Quocumque' . . ."

Against a slow-motion cascade of gentle, synthesized polyphonic lines and the calming sounds of harp and chimes, Sister Germaine's clear voice rises and falls in a florid, wide-ranging melody. And as the car heads down the New Jersey Turnpike, the driver's heavenly voice begins to accompany the voice on the tape:

> And so wherever the travelers went
> They were received
> With the joy of heavenly paradise . . .

• • •

Late in her life, Hildegard of Bingen recalled that when she was three years old she had been overwhelmed by the vision of what she called "the living Light." At five she astonished her nurse by predicting the color of a pregnant cow's unborn calf. Throughout her early years she continually foretold the future and claimed she could see pictures from out of the past. At eight, this frail tenth child of noble parents was given as a tithe to God and placed in a hermitage within the walls of the monastery of Saint Disibod where she shared a cell with the anchoress Jutta of Sponheim. Hildegard became her handmaid, and Jutta taught her the rudiments of Latin and how to chant the monastic Office. When Jutta died, Hildegard was elected her successor as abbess.

In 1141 Hildegard received a prophetic call. She stated: "And it came to pass . . . when I was forty-two years and seven months old, Heaven was opened and a fiery light of exceeding brilliance came and permeated my whole brain, and inflamed my whole heart and my whole breast, not like a burning but like a warming flame." Commanded three times by a voice from Heaven to "cry out and write, therefore, the things you see and hear," Hildegard held back because of "doubt" and a sense of unworthiness, until "laid low by the scourge of God, I fell upon a bed of sickness." The only cure was to obey the voice. Encouraged and assisted by the monk Volmar, her secretary-scribe, she began dictating in her idiosyncratic Latin the texts of three volumes of her visions concerning theology, moral psychology, and cosmology—a forty-four-year undertaking that confirms the critic Walter Benjamin's notion that "insight only occurs as a lightning-bolt; the text is the thunder-peal rolling long behind."

In the first of these works, *Scivias*, Hildegard presents, describes, and explains twenty-six of her visions with accompanying miniature paintings completed under her supervision. Through her words and astonishing images, many of which are reproduced in Matthew Fox's *Illuminations of Hildegard of Bingen* and which uncannily remind one of mandalas or even the Dreamtime paintings of the Australian Aborigines, we see the universe imagined as a subtly erotic cosmic egg, a golden kite filled with "fireballs," Adam falling into a black shadow that is both lake and serpent, the Mother Church with souls going in and out of her womb, the bones of the dead leaping together at the end of time, and the beauty of the heavens filled with light and celestial song.

It has been asserted by Charles Singer and Oliver Sacks that Hildegard suffered from migraine and that some of her images, in particular her visions of shimmering and extinguished stars and fortification figures radiating from luminous points, are a result of the flickering spectra and visual auras associated with this disorder. In the words of Oliver Sacks: "Hildegard's visions were instrumental in directing her toward a life of holiness and mysticism. They provide a unique example of the manner in which a physiological event, banal, hateful, or meaningless to the vast majority of people, can become, in a privileged consciousness, the substrate of a supreme ecstatic inspiration."

In her visions Hildegard often spoke of her concept of *veriditas* (greenness), which for her meant not just the color but what might be understood as the élan vital that radiates throughout the cosmos and from human bodies, plants, and crystals. It is the life-creating power of God that the Hindus called *prana* and that Dylan Thomas strikingly referred to as "the force that through the green fuse drives the flower." As Hildegard wrote:

Good People,
Most royal greening verdancy,
rooted in the sun,
you shine with radiant light.

In this circle of earthly existence
you shine
so finely,
it surpasses understanding.

God hugs you.
You are encircled
by the arms
of the mystery of God.

And in her visions Hildegard exults not only in "greening power" but also in the Feminine Divine, praising and drawing inspiration from female, almost goddesslike figures such as Sophia (Wisdom), Caritas (Love), Ecclesia (the Church), the Virtues (Humility, Chastity), and of course Mary, whom Hildegard refers to as "you glowing, most green, verdant sprout."

Part of Hildegard's modern appeal derives from her ardor for and connection with the divine Mother-of-all-that-lives and her seeming absorption of both mainstream Catholic and pagan ideas. This has led, on the one hand, to Hildegard being called a "fruitcake" (by the *Catholic Reporter*) and, on the other, to her being adopted by many people—ecologists, feminists, goddess worshipers—as a kind of New Age avatar.

Matthew Fox, who was dismissed from the Dominican order by the Vatican in 1993 and who is currently the director of the Institute in Culture and Creation Spirituality at Holy Names

College in Oakland, California, and who has written extensively about Hildegard as a purveyor of the "cosmic Christ," is repeatedly pointed to as a "guru" of the New Age worldview. But Fox, who prefers to think of himself as a "post-denominational" rather than a New Age theologian, unabashedly views Hildegard as a great mystic and prophet.

"I think that people who are raised on an exclusively modern way of seeing the world are intrinsically antimystical," Fox declares, "so when they come across someone like Hildegard they think she's a fruitcake. As with the Native Americans, anything that's 'pre-modern' is fruitcake . . . even though, of course, the pre-moderns have a wisdom we're desperate for. The first time I translated some things by Hildegard and gave them to my students, one guy spoke up and said, 'I've just spent sixteen years in a Lakota Indian reservation. And this Hildegard sounds exactly like the medicine man who was my spiritual teacher!'

"Remember," adds Fox, "Hildegard was raised in a Celtic monastery—Disibode was an Irish saint who lived in the seventh century as a hermit on the site of Hildegard's first monastery. And the Celts never bought into Augustine's ideas of original sin that much; they were always much more conscious of cosmology and the cosmic Christ. It's much more earth-based, really much more like Native American religion than the southern European tradition represented by someone like Augustine who was dualistic in his thinking. There's an erotic dimension in Hildegard that we don't get much of during the past few centuries of theology. She talks about the creator 'kissing' creation—blessing creation with a kiss."

Barbara Newman, a professor of English and religion at Northwestern University and the author of *Sister of Wisdom: St. Hildegard's Theology of the Feminine*, refuses to join the party of those who embrace the abbess and prophet as a kind of New Age mystic, asserting rather that Hildegard combined holistic cosmology with a dualistic system of ethics. "Matthew Fox," she says, "speaks of creation-centered spirituality, and he opposes it to a theology of redemption. But to Hildegard, as to other medieval thinkers, these were not opposed. Within the tradition of monasticism, Hildegard was, of course, a consecrated virgin and she thought that consecrated virgins were living the life of paradise here on earth.

"She's indeed a highly original writer, but that doesn't mean she's a writer without a context. You can talk about Hildegard's 'goddess' language as long as you realize the limits of that. I mean, she wouldn't use the word 'goddess' in her vocabulary, and she doesn't see Wisdom and Charity as independent of God. She's not a polytheist. She believed strongly in original sin, in the existence of hell, in the damnation of the unbaptized, and all those very 'unpopular' Christian doctrines. And yet at the same time she conveys this spirituality of the Feminine Divine, which is something that people today are extremely interested in."

Today, there is also enormous interest in Hildegard's fascinating writings on nutrition, pharmacology, and medicine—including some remarkable gynecological remedies—which originally appeared in two volumes, *Liber simplicis medicinae* and *Causae et curae*. In this country, a number of psychotherapists, endocrinologists, and nutritionists are applying some of Hildegard's approaches in their practices. In the Czech Republic, a holistic practitioner is using Hildegardian "soul therapy" in her work with paraplegic patients. And in Allensbach, Germany, Dr. Wighard Strehlow, a pharmaceutical-research chemist and co-author of *Hildegard of Bingen's Medicine*, has been practicing for the last ten years what he calls "Hildegard medicine" at his Hildegard Kurhaus.

To Hildegard, Lucifer is the origin of sickness, a separation from God that results in a state devoid of wetness, moistness, and greenness. God's power is the key to wellness. (It is significant that the Latin word for healing, *salus*, is the root of *salvation*.) And in her writings on healing, Hildegard particularly recommends foods like spelt (a kind of wheat), chestnut, and fennel; and proscribes strawberries, pork, and coffee as nutritional poisons. Her cures— some 2,000 of them—include powdered English geranium for the common cold, a violet salve for headaches, parsley-honey wine for heart pain, gold paste for arthritis, a blue sapphire for eye inflammation, and the liver of a young male goat for male sterility.

At the Hildegard Kurhaus in Allensbach, patients can stay from two to three weeks partaking of detoxification procedures such as bloodletting, cupping, kidney massages in front of a fire; a diet including hot spelt porridge, chestnut cream soup, and fennel au gratin; a kind of psychotherapy based on thirty-five Hildegardian virtues (among them, faith, charity, discretion, blessedness, devotion, heavenly joy); and daily meditations in the Kurhaus chapel using Hildegard's poems and songs. "For me," states Dr. Strehlow, "Hildegard combines theology, medicine, visions, and music into one whole, inseparable world. And on this universal continuity, health is dependent."

Perhaps the most healing of all of Hildegard's arts is her music, a body of work consisting of seventy-seven modal and monophonic songs that she collected under the title *Symphony of the Harmony of Celestial Revelations*. If the *Vision* CD provided only a peek into the Hildegardian musical palace, the radiant splendor of the interior is best approached by two remarkable recordings. The first—also a recent best-selling album—is *Canticles of Ecstasy*, featuring sixteen responses and antiphons performed by the distinguished early-music ensemble Sequentia, which is based in

Cologne. According to the group's co-founder Barbara Thornton, "Hildegard's music bursts beyond the normal limits of medieval music because her vision was much larger and more extended. Some of her compositions are thickly ornamental and melismatic and very daring in the way they move from mode to mode in a single work; there's almost that modern sense of walking into another key in the middle of a piece. With regard to their range, some of her compositions start high and get higher, some start low and get lower, though it was common in the music of the Middle Ages to balance these out. Hildegard is absolutely not shy of trying things that are outrageous, and really succeeding at them too. She is a magnificent composer, satisfying beyond belief to work with, and her music is perfect for the female voice."

The other indispensable Hildegard recording, first released as an LP in 1983 and now available on CD, is *A Feather on the Breath of God*. The disc presents eight sequences and hymns sung by the marvelous Gothic Voices, directed by Christopher Page and featuring the soprano voices of Emma Kirkby and Emily Van Evera (who appears along with Sister Germaine on *Vision*). It was this recording that introduced most people to Hildegard of Bingen's musical genius. According to Melvin Jahn, manager of Tower Classics in Berkeley, California, "We've sold more copies of the Gothic Voices album than any other store worldwide. What happened was that about twelve years ago, Heuwell Tircuit, the then–classical-music critic of the *San Francisco Chronicle*, reviewed the album glowingly and at length. We cut out the review, posted it, and all of a sudden we couldn't keep the album in stock. We started with ten, our next order was for fifteen, then twenty-five. The distributor couldn't believe it. Soon we were ordering fifty a month. Come Christmas, during the LP days, we would stack 200 of the Pavarotti Christmas albums; and the stack of the Hildegard was as high as Pavarotti and outsold it. Today we order 300 copies a month . . . and we've been doing this for twelve years!

"On my way home every day, I generally go to a local bar called Henry's, which is where a lot of people from the Cal athletic department hang out. Over the years I've given a couple of the bartenders copies of *Chant* and the Hildegard CD. And one Thursday night, one of the guys put the Hildegard on the CD player, and about fifteen people came up and said, 'What is that?' And the next day they all showed up at our store.

"So what is it about Hildegard's music? It's relaxing, mesmerizing, it makes you focus your thoughts and drive utter clatter from your brain. It's like the English having a cup of tea."

One wonders whether the composer shouldn't be called Hildegard of Berkeley.

"They might as well call her that now," says Jahn. "I think we should make her our patron saint. A remarkable woman. I love the old girl!"

(1994)

NORMAN GREENBAUM

"OKAY, GOOD EVENING AMERICA, and welcome aboard Apollo 13," says Tom Hanks, who plays astronaut Jim Lovell in the film about the ill-fated moon mission. Holding a handheld camera for the crew's first video transmission from space, he turns to astronaut Fred Haise (played by Bill Paxton) and says, "We're broadcasting tonight at an altitude of about 200,000 miles away from the face of the earth. We have a pretty good show in store for you tonight. . . . One of the first things we'd like to do is provide you with the appropriate background music. So hit it there, Freddo . . . " And as we see a portable tape recorder floating giddily about the space capsule, we suddenly hear what was once described as "the dirtiest heavy-industrial fuzz-tone outside a machine shop," then a hypnotic hand-clapping/snare drum rhythm, and finally those memorable words written and sung by Norman Greenbaum:

> When I die and they lay me to rest,
> Gonna go to the place that's the best,
> When they lay me down to die,
> Going up to the spirit in the sky,
> That's where I'm gonna go when I die,
> When I die and they lay me to rest,
> Gonna go to the place that's the best.

"Spirit in the Sky" was Norman Greenbaum's first and last hit. Written in 1969 and produced by Erik Jacobsen (who has been responsible for albums by the Lovin' Spoonful, Tim Hardin, and Chris Isaak), the song was featured on Greenbaum's 1970 solo debut album of the same name; as a single, "Spirit in the Sky" became the fastest selling 45 rpm in Warner Bros. history, and it eventually sold more than two million copies. The song has been covered by a number of artists, most successfully by the English glam group Doctor and the Medics; it has been used by American Express and Mitsubishi for ad campaigns and by Indian Nation to promote its gambling casinos; and it can be heard in films such as *Wayne's World II, Miami Blues, Maid to Order, The War*, and now *Apollo 13*.

" 'Spirit in the Sky' made my life and destroyed my life at the same moment," Norman Greenbaum told me when I recently tracked him down to Santa Rosa, California where he has lived for the past fifteen years as a short-order cook and, more recently, in his own words, as "a consultant for anything you want." The royalties on "Spirit in the Sky" have provided Greenbaum with a modest but steady income for twenty-five years.

I had always wanted to find out what had happened to this legendary musician who had disappeared from the music scene shortly after he released his third and last album, *Petaluma*, in 1972. At the end of 1995, Varèse Sarabande Records brought out *Spirit in the Sky: The Best of Norman Greenbaum*, a wonderful collection of fifteen songs—some previously unavailable and unreleased. I had heard that Greenbaum was a bit of a recluse and did not give interviews. But roused last June by the presence of "Spirit in the Sky" in *Apollo 13* and the promise of the forthcoming compilation CD, I thought that perhaps Norman Greenbaum might consider talking about his work and life.

I called his producer Erik Jacobsen in San Francisco and asked him if he might give Greenbaum my telephone number. Jacobsen sounded doubtful, told me that Greenbaum was incapacitated with two broken legs, but said that he would do what he could. Six months went by. No Norman. Then one day in late November, on a trip abroad, I called home for my telephone messages and heard someone saying that he was Norman Greenbaum and that I should get back to him. I did, and heard the melodious, slightly breathless, almost little-boy voice on his machine saying, "This is Norman. As most of you know, I have a broken leg. I can get to the phone but I can't get to it fast. Leave a message and I'll get back to you sooner or later. Thanks." That "sooner or later" didn't sound promising, but I stayed on the line, began leaving a kind of rambling message . . . when suddenly Norman's real voice broke in. He said his legs were improving slightly and suggested that we meet in three weeks for lunch at a restaurant in Santa Rosa.

He arrived at the restaurant in a wheelchair. I found out that Norman is recovering from having broken his legs *twice* during the past year. Apparently, the first day after having been in a wheelchair for several months after his first mishap, he decided, at his doctor's suggestion, to go downstairs and out of the house for a walk, when his cat darted between his legs, and unbalanced him, and he fell down the steps and broke everything once again. Norman stepped gingerly out of the wheelchair, greeted me, and slowly sat down in a seat by a table. "I've got so much metal in my legs," he said with a courageous grin, "that I can pick up the reruns of Wolfman Jack broadcasts from Del Rio, Texas!" He was wearing a gray sports jacket, jeans, a purple T-shirt, and a Native American Dreamcatcher necklace. At fifty-three, Norman still has the characteristic look of his earlier years—handlebar mustache and impish smile—but now augmented with rabbinic-looking gray hair.

"'Spirit in the Sky' really did make and destroy my life simultaneously," he said to me. "It was like a Cecil B. De Mille thing. It became too big. It was a total fluke. Usually, you have a hit, and then another one, and *then* you die. With me it happened right away."

"How did you happen to write the song?" I asked him.

"Believe it or not," he told me, "the song came about because of the country singer Porter Wagoner. He used to have a half-hour TV show in Los Angeles in the late 1960s—I was living there at that time—and one night I tuned in and there was Porter Wagoner with his pompadour haircut, wearing his tailored cowboy suit from Nudies with sequins and spangles and stuff. And the song he sang against this huge stained-glass backdrop was about a man who had spent twenty years panning for gold in the mountains, and one day he decides he needs religion. He hasn't been to church in twenty years. So he heads into town with his mule, rides up to the church, walks up the steps, and sees this sign that reads: 'The Preacher Is on Vacation.'

"And I thought, God, that's a *killer*. That guy wanted salvation and the preacher was on vacation! And that's why I wrote 'Spirit in the Sky.' I'd never done anything like that before. Up to that point I was writing things like 'The Eggplant That Ate Chicago'— humorous things, jug-band skits. And I'm Jewish, though I'm not affiliated with any religion now. But without thinking about it, I wrote the lyrics to the song in fifteen minutes, and then I spent the next six months trying to figure what music went with it. Actually, the music would never make you think of a religious-type of song—it's blues, it's boogie . . . though in a way it is kind of like gospel: the girls singing in the background were from a gospel church in Oakland, and later they recorded a version of the song themselves. Erik Jacobsen produced it, I had input in the arrangement, and we recorded it in San Francisco with the simple equipment we had back then in 1969; there was nothing digital or state-of-the-art, just square microphones, a small Fender Twin amp, a couple of overdubs, and that was about it."

"What about that astonishing fuzz-tone?" I asked.

"A friend of mine named Robbie Robbinson built it right into my guitar—it's just a tiny little chip. It has this incredible reverberation, it just went *zhzhzhzhzh* and sent shivers up your spine, and the louder you play it the bigger the shiver is. Robbie never put a chip in another guitar, that was the one and only, and I don't have that guitar anymore, I'm afraid to say.

"So yeah, the preacher was on vacation, and without thinking about it, I made up for what didn't exist in Porter Wagoner's song: In 'Spirit in the Sky,' the preacher *isn't* on vacation."

"In 'Spirit in the Sky,'" said, "you sing: 'I've got a friend in Jesus / So you know that when I die / He's going to set me up with the Spirit in the Sky.' Some people have wondered if you are or have been a Jew for Jesus or even a follower of a Native American religion?"

"My mother," replied Norman, "who's an Orthodox Jew, did get gray hair when she first heard the song: 'What have you done?' But I was a writer, I just used my imagination. And I am not a Jew for Jesus. It's funny though that you mentioned the Native American connection. I didn't know it at the time, but when I was buying Christmas cards shortly after the song came out, I discovered a card with a Hopi painting of a bird, and inside the card it said 'Spirit in the Sky.' That's how things are in my life."

"Someone," I commented, "once said jokingly that the line 'Gonna go to the place that's the best' sounded like a heavenly Holiday Inn."

"No," replied Norman, "that's a *different* song of mine called 'Can I Book a Room in Heaven Before It's Time to Go?' The idea of the song was: Is it as busy up there as it is down here? . . . So is 'Spirit in the Sky' tongue in cheek? It's hard to say. If I say it's tongue in cheek, then people are going to be offended. If I say it's real, though I'm not a Jew for Jesus, I'm just a writer who came upon a thought that happened to turn out to do well . . . well, that would be the truth. I just wrote it and did my best.

"When 'Spirit' became a hit, I got a lot of mail, and some of it was hate mail. From Christians saying, 'What's a goddamn Jew doing singing a song about our Lord Jesus? Where do you get off?' Others said that it was the greatest song they ever heard. I remember a letter from Japan saying, 'I love your song 'Spill It In The Sky.' And recently a guy wrote to me: 'I'm fifty years old, I loved that song when I was a kid. My parents loved it, too. They died, and I played it at their funeral.'

"When I played with a band at clubs after 'Spirit in the Sky' was released, I didn't need a second song. I could go out on stage and do sixty minutes of 'Spirit'—playing it, singing it, jamming it, then playing it again. And it wasn't enough. . . . I don't know, I'm still amazed about how big it got."

Erik Jacobsen once stated, "Norman is one of the furthest-out guys in the history of the world. Anyone who would follow up 'Spirit in the Sky' with 'Canned Ham' will give you a small indication right there." That song, a two-step, good-timey rocker that asks the question "When are you going to buy me a canned ham? / I've been waiting so long" was, as Norman says, "not well received. They just thought I was crazy. What happened was that on Friday I was watching TV, and here comes Porter Wagoner; on Saturday I'm at Safeway and there's a person on the checkout line in front of me with this big canned ham.

"What did 'Canned Ham' really mean? Was it sexual? Was I not getting any? I don't know. Was it a metaphor? But for what? Who knows. I don't even eat canned ham. It's not easy growing up Jewish, it's very frustrating.

"In a Jewish synagogue you need a daily minyan [*a quorum of ten male adults*]. Sometimes it's hard to get a minyan, the old guys die off and sometimes there were only eight. But when I was going to Jewish school, I noticed that there was always a bottle of Seagrams 7 downstairs because after the men did their davening, they'd go down and have a couple of shots before going home. That never escaped me. To get kids to the services they'd give them a pin and a candy bar. Religion is just like Macy's, it's the same thing, you just sell it in a different way.

"That's what my song 'The Day They Sold Beer in Church,' which is appearing for the first time on my new CD, is about. People said, 'You have to write another song like "Spirit in the Sky." But they don't know whom they're talking to, they're talking to Mr. Demented here who takes everything and twists it into the way he wants it to be and goes, 'Okay, here it is.' And they go, 'Huh?' "

At twenty-one, Norman broke with the traditions of his Orthodox Jewish family in Malden, Massachusetts, and took off for the promised land of Los Angeles, where, as Norman says, "there were blond girls and swimming pools and palm trees and warm weather . . . and Mom was gone!" His first group was Dr. West's Medicine Show & Junk Band, supposedly the world's first psychedelic jug band, which featured light shows and a percussion section consisting of, among other things, a whiskey jug, a washtub, a Taiwan finger piano, a Tibetan temple block, and a 1949 Buick bumper bracket. For this legendary group Norman wrote songs like "The Eggplant That Ate Chicago" and "Weird."

When the band broke up in the late sixties, Norman performed solo and was discovered by Erik Jacobsen while playing Hoot Night at the Troubadour. According to the singer, "Eric came up after the show and said, 'You're good. I'm Erik Jacobsen.' And I said, 'You're the Erik Jacobsen who did all those Lovin' Spoonful hits and Tim Hardin's "If I Were a Carpenter"?' And he said, 'Yeah, that's me.' And I said, 'Where do I sign?' "

Norman moved to Mill Valley, where Jacobsen lived, and recorded three albums with him for Warner/Reprise: *Spirit in the Sky*, *Back Home Again*, and *Petaluma*, the last of which featured Ry Cooder on mandolin and which gives a musical picture of Norman and his new family's bucolic life on his farm in Petaluma—bought with royalties from "Spirit in the Sky"—known as the chicken capital of the world: "They got chickens in the houses / They got chickens in the trees," Norman sang on the album's title song. "I had everything then," Norman states. "Chickens, ducks, geese, a llama, 200 rabbits, pigs, angora goats, and sheep from Tasmania called cormos. We got a ram and some ewes. And what do you think I named the ram? Perry Cormo!" Mostly he spent his time breeding goats, and twice a week he would personally drive from Petaluma to San Jose and back delivering his Velvet Acres Goat Milk. "I used to visit Norman and his wife and kids," Erik Jacobsen recalls; "I ate the goat cheese that they made, and frankly, I haven't eaten it since then."

The Petaluma idyll fell apart. Norman's wife, according to Jacobsen, began to follow an Indian guru. The couple were divorced, the wife got the farm, and before it was eventually sold, Norman had to set up residence in a reconditioned chicken coop on the property. "It was just temporary housing," he now says philosophically. "Today, chicken coops in Petaluma have hot tubs in them!"

Shortly after *Petaluma* was released, he decided to publicize the album in an unusual manner. "I went down to San Francisco to the Party Store in Union Square," he says, "and bought about ten pounds of chicken feathers, all white and clean, and took a pair of white pants and a white shirt and spent weeks gluing each feather onto the clothes. So when it was finished it was all feathers. A girl I knew made a chicken headdress for me, I gathered together a lot of plastic eggs, and made occasional appearances by myself or with a group playing songs from the album."

Soon after these remarkable performances, Norman stopped composing and playing in public. "To tell the truth," he says, "I can't believe that my career fell apart. I don't know why, but it just did. People wanted another 'Spirit in the Sky' from me, and it couldn't be, that song was too special. So I became a sous chef, an under chef, in Petaluma and in some other places. I made a cheesecake to die for."

"So you made a sacrifice of your career to the Spirit in the Sky for having given you that song?" I commented.

"Yes," Norman replied, "my career and both my legs!"

"Do you think you'll ever start composing and playing again?" I asked.

"I'm thinking about it a lot," he told me. "I haven't figured it out yet, but I could do it, now that my legs are starting to feel better. It's hard getting around, but I feel good about myself and I like the new compilation CD of my songs—I'm glad they included things like 'California Earthquake' and 'The Day They Sold Beer in Church' that were never released on an album before. And I've started writing again. One of my latest songs is called 'Loading Zone': it's about going to dinner on Fisherman's Wharf in San Francisco, but there's no place to park, so I park in the loading zone and when I come back, the car is gone, 'towed away, I suppose / Pay a fine right through the nose.

"I think it's coming back again."

(1995)

REFLECTIONS

THE ROLLING STONES
Back to a Shadow in the Night

WHEN THE ROLLING STONES FIRST APPEARED on *Hollywood Palace* in 1964, it was none other than Dean Martin who, as the traditional bibulous compère, found himself in the unrehearsed position of messenger of ill tidings. The Visigoths were at the backstage door, and as Martin took hold of the microphone and himself—perhaps realizing at that parlous moment of delirium tremens that the era of the four-flusher and the crooner was over—he announced in a voice of forced casualness and feckless incredulity: "I've been rolled before, and I've been stoned before, but *take a look at these guys!*"

For here in Hollywood, on the turf of filmmakers like Nick Ray, Robert Aldrich, and Sam Fuller, was nothing less than the living musical embodiment of American film noir—a group which took the spectral underside vision of the American dream as revealed in films like *They Live by Night*, *Kiss Me Deadly*, and *The Naked Kiss* and latched onto it the unassimilated sexual vitality of the music of Slim Harpo, Solomon Burke, and Howlin' Wolf.

Even in that early, undifferentiated surge of rock groups that announced the English rock 'n' roll renaissance, it was easy to distinguish the Stones from the Dave Clark Five, Freddie and the Dreamers, the Kinks, or the Beatles. No other group presented (or has ever presented) that eerie quality combining the hustling menace of the spiv, the coolness of the dandy, and the unpredictable amorality and frivolity of the Greek gods. And from the moment they landed in America, these soul survivors of British imperialism, these half-scruffy, half-exotic exiles on Main Street, naturally and exuberantly took on the role of devil's advocate for what was then beginning to be thought of as the Love Generation.

It was in 1965 that I first saw the Rolling Stones perform live, on a bill with Paul Revere and the Raiders and the Byrds at a less-than-sold-out concert at the San Francisco Civic Auditorium. The Raiders played dressed in revolutionary regalia; the Byrds performed songs like "The Bells of Rhymney" with an unforgettable naïflike, street-urchin radiance. And then out came the Stones . . . glinting, disengaged, self-prepossessing—the visual incorporation of an idea: four expressionless, lean, and hungry instrumentalists, spoken for by their shining, narcissistic knight. And the words with which the poet Arthur Symons once described the famous Parisian music-hall dancer Jane Avril perfectly caught this idea as Mick Jagger and the Stones embodied it that San Francisco evening:

> Alone, apart, one dancer watches
> Her mirrored, morbid grace;
> Before the mirror, face to face,
> Alone she watches
> Her morbid, vague, ambiguous grace. . . .
> And, enigmatically smiling,
> In the mysterious night,
> She dances for her own delight,
> A shadow smiling
> Back to a shadow in the night.
> —"La Mélinite: Moulin Rouge"

The Stones began the set with "Everybody Needs Somebody to Love," and at the words, "I need *you, you, you*," Jagger danced up to the front of the stage, pointing sinuously to what everyone in the audience seemed to think was each one of them. But the wonder of that moment lay in the fact that each of us knew inside that this singer needed nobody at all. With Elvis and the Beatles, you felt you had a chance. With the Stones, you knew you didn't want one. In fact, we willed them *not* to need us, for it was only if we were kept outside would we be able to see ourselves and the world afresh—like a child accidentally overhearing the adults late at night, drunk with strangeness.

Exalted indifference. Innocent malice. Careless cruelty. It is these ambiguous mixtures of emotion which we find in songs like "Play with Fire," "Back Street Girl," and "Star Star"—a mixture revealing the disturbing yet fascinating quality of a child grown up too soon, like an eleven-year-old dragging on a cigarette. And it was this "child" who dangerously explored the ever-lurking but disapproved world of sex and drugs in songs like "Under My Thumb," "Sister Morphine," and "Monkey Man."

Yet when the Stones were at their most exploitative, they seemed their most liberating, because we became aware of the reversal of that social and psychological pathology by which the oppressed identify with their oppressors: we sensed that the Stones, from their position of indifferent power, were singing in the voice of the hurt and abused, thereby magically transcending all humiliating barriers ("But it's all right now / In fact it's a gas").

And in the guise of that distant, irresponsible child who continually rejected all appropriate modes of feeling ("I'm hiding sister and I'm dreaming"), the Stones revealed secrets about ourselves and our world. From "Get Off of My Cloud" and "19th Nervous Breakdown" to "Mother's Little Helper" and "Have You

Seen Your Mother, Baby, Standing in the Shadows," the Stones once and for all pulled open the blinds, exposing—while both celebrating and attempting to exorcise—the demonic ghosts of the Oedipal family romance and of all forms of social hypocrisy, so that we could see that the emperor and the empress were really wearing no clothes.

But when the Devil appeared at Altamont, his Satanic Majesty—with a little help from his friends—disillusioned us and helped to destroy our idea of the Stones. What had been young and distant was now too weary and too near. Art and life became commingled and confused in both the minds of the group and its audience. And it was *Exile on Main Street*—the last Stones masterpiece—that powerfully and compendiously summed up both the history of the music of the sixties and the breakdown of the culture that supported and was sustained by it.

Rock 'n' roll continues to stand—however wobbly ("It's only rock 'n' roll"). And as the media always demand some group to play the role of "Greatest Rock 'n' Roll Band," why not the Soul Survivors? Most promoters and critics agreed and the audience felt obliged—especially since a large part of this audience had never seen the Stones before.

Now, following the example of the sixteenth-century revolutionary Anabaptist commune at Münster (whose days were filled with pageants, messianic banquets, sexual parties, and public executions), rock 'n' roll has, for a number of years, tried hard to fill the vacuum caused by a lack of community by attempting to fabricate and construct the form of a dramatic ceremonial cult surrounding the likes of David Bowie, Alice Cooper, and others. Ceremonial trappings by themselves, however, can never create the sense and feeling of ritual that one can experience in just the first few bars of songs like "Honky Tonk Women" or "Gimme Shelter."

And the Stones, unfortunately, have gone the way of the ceremonial cult. Their current [1975] tour—at least the concert I saw at Madison Square Garden in New York—revealed a concern only for fancy stage spectacle, fashionable pastel lighting, muffled sound, a circuslike phallic monster ballooning into the air, buffoonery and horseplay by members of the band, Mick Jagger rolling around the floor in shepherd pajamas and occasionally coming up with a few karate-inspired dance gestures, and a generally unsurprising and unrevealing set of reinterpretations of their old songs. (Remember how the Stones used to perform "Stray Cat Blues" live a few years ago, turning their hard-edged recorded version into an almost haunting lullaby?)

In fact, this concert reminded us that the recent Stones songs have no more secrets to reveal—or conceal. "Fingerprint File" was already Yesterday's Papers when it came out. And "Luxury" is hardly Satisfaction. Moreover, what all this ceremonious cakewalk finally disclosed was simply that behind the incantation, the gestures, the charm, lay . . . nothing. The spirits did not rise. The final mystery was that there was no mystery.

This is the lesson of most ceremonial cults, and it is hardly up to the Stones to produce miracles out of a lot of props and tricks. Once an audience gets used to showy technology, it's hard to go against the grain of expectation. But as Mark wrote in the New Testament to explain why Jesus did not perform miracles in Nazareth: "He could not do it, because they did not believe in him."

Now, it must be said that most of the audience at the Garden that night really seemed to believe in the Stones. Perhaps it was just a few of us who had now become distant and indifferent ourselves. Perhaps, too, there were some persons there who were disappointed that Jagger wasn't about to stick his hand in his heart and "spill it all over the stage," as he himself sang in "It's

Only Rock 'n' Roll."

Belief requires dreams. And I'm still dreaming that the next time the Rolling Stones appear onstage, there'll be just five of them, plainly dressed in black—"Back to a shadow in the night"— with no stage effects or shining draperies behind them, just a few direct lights, and they'll be playing and singing some new songs— songs that will demand, like Salome, only our heads.

(1975)

BOB DYLAN
Back Inside the Rain

I dreamt that a great war had come upon the world, and they called me up to fight. I swore a solemn vow to God that if I returned from the war unharmed, whoever came out of my house to greet me when I returned I would offer up as a sacrifice. I returned unharmed, and it was myself who came out to greet me.

—S. Y. Agnon

I

AFTER YEARS OF COLD WAR AND COLD POETRY, Bob Dylan, in the appropriately titled *Bringing It All Back Home*, decided to earth the lightning in himself. Following the homeopathic poetic principles of Baudelaire and Rimbaud, he absorbed and refined the poisons of subterranean homesick life, inoculating himself with the disease in order to protect himself from it. In "Subterranean Homesick Blues," Dylan was "mixing up the medicine," and in songs like "Just like Tom Thumb's Blues" and "Stuck Inside of Mobile" he upped the dosage and described the scene and the results:

Now the rainman gave me two cures,
Then he said, "Jump right in."
The one was Texas medicine,
The other was just railroad gin.
And like a fool I mixed them
And it strangled up my mind,
And now people just get uglier
And I have no sense of time.
—"Stuck Inside of Mobile with the Memphis Blues Again"

Like few other persons of the mid-sixties, however, Dylan was right in time with the times. People used his poisons as a tonic and elixir. The fact that some even took enough courage from his songs to explore new ways of dealing with the world led them to picture Dylan as a bellwether for the sixties counterculture.

But Dylan, unlike Rimbaud, did not want to transform the human condition—"giving blind advice to unknown eyes," as he once wrote in *11 Outlined Epitaphs*. Having become his own sacrifice, he was both "exposed" and a subject of countless exposés. And in response to one too many slanted questions and reporters' whims—as Dylan himself complained in "Epitaphs"—he made his famous pronouncement: "My songs don't mean nothin'." (They had, of course, come to mean everything to his admirers.) And it was just at the moment of his greatest cultural (if not commercial) influence that Bob Dylan rejected the poison, sheared himself of his *Blonde on Blonde* persona, and—choosing neither to build bombs (like the Weathermen) nor to run guns (like Rimbaud in Africa)—withdrew to Woodstock, New York.

Dylan had learned that in order to bear the word, one must be totally bare: "A poem is a naked person," he had written on the liner notes for *Bringing It All Back Home*. And it is interesting, especially for someone whose songs meant "nothing," that during this period of retreat or reintegration (depending on your perspective), Dylan, in my opinion, must have been meditating on the images and themes of Shakespeare's *King Lear*, the play in which "something" comes exactly from "nothing": on the naked king and his wheel of fire, who banishes the true and prefers the false; on blind Gloucester, who ends his life between joy and grief; and on the loving Cordelia, a soul in bliss, whose word of rejection— "Nothing"—ultimately reveals the world of truth. In extraordinary songs like "This Wheel's on Fire," "Too Much of Nothing," and "Tears of Rage" (on the legendary *Basement Tapes*), Dylan revealed an unmistakable and deep understanding of this play: "Too much of nothing / Can make a man abuse a king" or "Oh what dear daughter beneath the sun / Would treat a father so / To wait upon him hand and foot / And always tell him, 'No'" ("Tears of Rage").

As Dylan himself disappeared from public view, he sacrificed his "public" poetic voice, turning not like King Lear to silence, but to a kind of audible muteness. Concerning the idea of perception in *King Lear*, it has been said that in order for one to see clearly, one has to be seen through. *Self Portrait*, released about this time, is an album whose title is ironical in the extreme, revealing, as it does, a portrait of a self fading into mostly borrowed songs whose words—as someone once said—"are only like a window that has no light of its own, but only shines forth out of the light that it admits"; and whose moods and performances shifted from enervation at worst to mellowness at best. Since Dylan's "self" had itself become absent, there was nothing in *Self Portrait* to see through.

For those who had valued Dylan for his *attentiveness*, for the exacting ways in which he described and charted the feelings, as Kafka put it, of being "seasick on dry land," his change of heart, as represented by *Self Portrait*, signaled Dylan's withdrawal from the world and from himself—much as mystics had pictured God withdrawing from his creation, leaving both himself and man in exile. This cosmic drama took a turn for the comic when A. J. Weberman began to rifle the husks of Dylan's garbage, thinking he could redeem Dylan from his exile.

II

Poets have a singular path to travel. In his haunted new song "Tangled Up in Blue"—a song of longing for the vanishing beloved, as well as for the lost spirit of the sixties—Dylan says: "And when finally the bottom fell out / I became withdrawn / The only thing I knew how to do / Was to keep on keepin' on." Dialectical thinking reveals that an awareness of contradictions can guide one on the path to truth. But, equally, poets intuit the fact that truth contains its own contradictions, and that nothing can be seen except in a context that transcends it. Rimbaud's "alchemy of the word"—or what Herbert Marcuse calls the "permanent imaginary revolution" inherent in the work or art—depends for its efficacy on the power of the negative, for "illusion is in the reality itself," as Marcuse profoundly remarks, "not in the work of art."

What this means is that the power of the "negative"—not to be confused with the "negativity" that, as Dylan tells us, couldn't pull him through in "Just Like Tom Thumb's Blues"—is the keeper and witness of the "positive." Dylan has always understood the contradictory nature of the truth, and his best songs resulted in part from the acceptance of this awareness, his worst from his denial of it. Those lesser songs mostly took the form of pictures of a world of family and country solitude that he called peace. There is, of course, a great pastoral poetic tradition that succeeds in conveying exactly this kind of repose, but Dylan's extraordinary gifts as a romantic and visionary poet often went against the grain of this gentler mode.

It would be both foolish and untrue, however, to say that songs concerned with love and family are by their very nature products of illusion. Amid the bucolic atmosphere of *Nashville Skyline* ("Peggy Day stole my poor heart away / By golly, what more can I say"), Dylan created two songs that ineradicably affirm the power of love both as a concrete and a theoretical reality: "Why wait any longer for the one you love / When he's standing in front of you"("Lay Lady Lay"); "Love is all there is, it makes the world go 'round / Love and only love, it can't be denied" ("I Threw It All Away"). And it is this second song, of course, that gives an idea of how the power of the positive can be contained within the negative.

But the song which most clearly illustrates how this "power" can give expression to an awareness of nonillusory love is Dylan's "I Want You": "Now all my fathers, they've gone down / True love they've been without it / But all their daughters put me down / 'Cause I don't think about it." In an extraordinary way, these lines suggest that the knowledge of one's being *without* love should never lead to a self-deluding and false nostalgia *for* it, since in that way lies nothing less than love's betrayal. Conversely, in the light of this awareness, when Dylan sings about a world of "guilty undertakers" and "drunken politicians," the words "I want you" simply affirm the fact that it is desire itself (not pornography or pretended love) that can be seen as the key to a connected social and spiritual universe.

When we feel removed from the present, we can either remember and recollect the past or enter the spaces of memory. Memory is deep within us—a place where things that are separate and cut off from our sense of the present always find a home. This is the world of the "night playing tricks when you're trying to be so quiet" ("Visions of Johanna"), a world of ghosts between things and of imaginary conversations with parts of the self (as in *John Wesley Harding*), a world in which what was asleep is now awake and what was once ordered and real is now disconnected and illusory:

> All the people we used to know
> They're an illusion to me now
> Some are mathematicians
> Some are carpenters' wives
> Don't know how it all got started
> I don't know what they're doin' with their lives
>
>   —"Tangled Up in Blue"

But just as we have seen that the power of the negative bears witness to the positive, so the *awareness* of the illusory—discovered in rapturous and unsettling moments in the world of memory—communicates nothing less than an ecstatic celebration of what is really real.

Needless to say, one has to enter the world of memory before any such celebration can take place. It is interesting that the psychologist Theodor Reik once concisely drew a distinction between remembrance and memory—a distinction made by everyone from Aristotle to Proust. "The function of remembrance," Reik wrote, "is the protection of impressions; memory aims at their disintegration." And if Dylan totally entered the world of memory in *Blood on the Tracks*, in *Planet Waves* he was still placing himself in *between* the realms of remembrance and memory.

While memory provides many of the images and moods of "Something There Is About You" ("All that shaking to wonder"), there is still a protective nuance in lines such as: "I was in a whirlwind / Now I'm in some better place." More than any other song on *Planet Waves*, it is Dylan's seemingly throwaway "Never Say Goodbye" that glimmers with the aura of rediscovered places: "Footprints in the snow / And the silence down below."

III

"If your memory serves you well / You'll remember you're the one," Bob Dylan has sung on "This Wheel's on Fire." And when Dylan gave his nationwide tour last year, his performance of older songs like "It's Alright, Ma" and "Gates of Eden" must have reminded him of that person who, in writing those songs, had warned and criticized others not to become what he, in part—like most of us—had become. Now the songs themselves had become reminders and warnings to the soul. "How does it feel / To be without a home / Like a complete unknown / Like a rolling stone?" The audiences at Dylan's concerts sang out the chorus as if it were a national anthem. And what had once been an aggressive and admonitory sneer was now, in 1974, simply an invitation to reexplore a world of inhabited solitude and memory which Dylan had turned his back on for many years.

"Shelter from the Storm" is a parable of the meeting of two interfused worlds that had been split off, one from the other, in Dylan's songs since *John Wesley Harding*: the formless, primordial creature of darkness, doom, and rejection embraced by the merciful sister of unquestioning love. "Well I'm livin' in a foreign country / But I'm bound to cross the line / Beauty walks a razor's edge / Someday I'll make it mine."

It is this "foreign country" whose presence we feel in almost every song on *Blood on the Tracks*. It is a world of signals crossed and of times out of joint ("Shelter"), of soul mates losing their way and each other ("Simple Twist of Fate" and "If You See Her, Say Hello"), of love that betokens separation ("You're Gonna Make Me Lonesome When You Go"), of separation that betokens pain ("You're a Big Girl Now"), of the breath no longer of life but of corruption and deceit ("Idiot Wind"), of barbed wire, hail, and a never-rising sun ("Meet Me in the Morning") and of a night journey in search of the beloved—"Looking for her everywhere in hope of finding her somewhere," as the mystics say about the Eternal Beloved ("Tangled Up in Blue").

Probably some kind of separation must have set Dylan back on the road and "back in the rain," as he says in "You're a Big Girl Now"—an image overflowing with associations from Dylan's older songs: "Lost in the rain in Juarez" ("Just like Tom Thumb's Blues") or "Nobody feels any pain / Tonight as I stand inside the rain" ("Just like a Woman"). In Dylan's world, "rain" is another word for "memory," (among other things), where persons from the past and present and where love and pain reflect and merge with each other as in "buckets of rain/buckets of tears."

Dylan's new fable "Lily, Rosemary and the Jack of Hearts" presents a mirrored cabaret as the theater of the world in which you can see: backstage women playing cards, a hanging judge, and Lily and Rosemary, both in love with a diamond-mine tycoon ("in" on a bank robbery) who is soon to be stabbed to death by a jealous Rosemary, who winds up hanging on the gallows. Hovering over and around this scene is the Jack of Hearts—perhaps a playing card like all the others, an actor beyond compare (as the song informs us), a mysterious, almost transparent presence whose power reveals as it conceals much like Bob Dylan himself. And like much of Dylan's work, this song becomes a parable whose meaning must be worked out in each listener's head: "He moved across the mirrored room / 'Set it up for everyone,' he said / Then everyone commenced to do / What they were doin' before he turned their heads."

Rimbaud said: "*I* is another," and Bob Dylan, in "You're Gonna Make Me Lonesome," sings about how his relationships have been like the one between Verlaine and Rimbaud (the "foolish virgin" meets the "hellish bridegroom" is how Rimbaud described Verlaine and himself in *A Season in Hell*), concluding: "But there's no way I can compare / All them scenes to this affair / You're gonna make me lonesome when you go." This is Rimbaud filtered through the melody and gaiety of "I don't care if it rains or freezes / As long as I've got a plastic Jesus."

But the grace and humor of this song is as much a foil as is the poison and spleen of "Idiot Wind"—which exemplifies, in Rimbaud's elegant phrase, "the refraction of grace crossed with a new violence." While "Idiot Wind" is the most obviously explosive and bitter work Dylan has released since "Positively 4th Street" and "Can You Please Crawl Out Your Window?" it is also the first such song in which he incriminates not only the person he's singing about but himself as well: "We're idiots, babe / It's a wonder we can even feed ourselves."

Any emotion lived out in full, it has been said, is a form of love. And in "Idiot Wind" Dylan does nothing less than materialize, as in Japanese legend and plays, a personalized subsistent moment of wrath which, if not made visible and exorcised, will feed on the souls it destroys: "I kissed goodbye the howling beast / On the borderline which separated you from me"—while also seeing political evil as an extension of interpersonal hatred: "Idiot wind / Blowing like a circle around my skull / From the Grand Coulee Dam to the Capitol."

Rarely has Dylan's presence seemed so full and moving as on *Blood on the Tracks*. No matter what the mood, Dylan's voice sounds as alternately rich, gentle, haunted or exacerbated as each song demands. The musicians provide what Robert Christgau has aptly called "a certain anonymous brightness." But their clean, gleaming sound is perfectly suited as a support for Dylan's wonderfully phrased harmonica, mandolin, and guitar work and for his beautifully articulated and glowing lyrics, reminiscent of a thirteenth century poem in the book of verse he reads in "Tangled Up in Blue" ("And every one of them words rang true / And glowed like burnin' coal / Pourin' off of every page / Like it was written in my soul / From me to you/Tangled up in blue").

> I find no shield she does not shatter,
> no place to hide from her look;
> because, like the flower on the stalk,
> she takes hold on the summit of my soul:
> she seems as worried by my suffering
> as a ship by a sea that lifts no wave;
> and a burden founders me no poetry is equal to.
>
> —Guido Cavalcanti

(1975)

DYLAN AT SIXTY

I N J EAN -L UC G ODARD 'S 1966 FILM *Masculin-Féminin*, the young protagonist played by Jean-Pierre Léaud picks up a French newspaper and reads a headline aloud QUI ÊTES-VOUS BOB DYLAN? It was, and is, a good question. As the American folk singer Eric von Schmidt commented in the mid-sixties: "At this time Bob had the most incredible way of changing shape, changing size, changing looks. The whole time he was in London he wore the same thing, his blue jeans and cap. And sometimes he would look big and muscular, and the next day he'd look like a little gnome, and one day he'd be kind of handsome and virile, and the following day he'd look like a thirteen-year-old child. It was really strange. . . . You'd never know what he was going to look like."

You'd also never know what his voice was going to sound like. One of the other fascinating, if obvious, things about Bob Dylan's mercurial personality was the way the timbre of his voice would change from one record or period of his life to another—as if his voice, too, couldn't stand having just one, unvarying sound. When he first arrived in New York City, he was singing like a hillbilly, sounding "like a dog with his leg caught in a barbed wire," as someone remarked at the time. And as the years went by, Dylan's voice would veer from, in his words, "that thin . . . wild mercury sound . . . metallic and bright gold" of *Blonde on Blonde* (1966) to the relaxed country sound, which some attribute to his having stopped smoking cigarettes, of *Nashville Skyline* (1969) to the openheartedness, gentleness, and anger of *Blood on the Tracks* (1975). Like the Greek sea deity Proteus, who in order to elude his pursuers continually changed shape, from dragon to lion to fire to flood—uttering prophecies along the way—Dylan has unequivocally remained true to his vision of an unlimiting, unpossessive love that, whatever its form, comes straight from the heart, from which springs a wisdom worthy of the greatest poets and teachers:

> Well, the moral of the story,
> The moral of this song,
> Is simply that one should never be
> Where one does not belong.
> So when you see your neighbor carryin' something,
> Help him with his load,
> And don't go mistaking Paradise
> For that home across the road.
> —"The Ballad of Frankie Lee and Judas Priest"

As always, Dylan has kept on keepin' on—like his hero Hank Williams's alter ego, Luke the Drifter, traveling and performing in one joint after another, night after night, literally around the world. And on his journey he never wavers from revealing and confronting the masks that all of us are wearing and that distract us from out path:

Everybody's wearing a disguise
To hide what they've got left behind their eyes.
But me, I can't cover what I am
Wherever the children go I'll follow them.

—"Abandoned Love"

Without even the "murmur of a prayer," as he sings on "Not Dark Yet," the soul turns "into steel" and the inner light is extinguished. On his sixtieth turn around the sun— still keeping the lights burning and reminding us to be a light unto ourselves ("Everythin' I'm saying' / You can say it just as good"—"One Too Many Mornings") Bob Dylan has remained true to the words of Emily Dickinson's little prayer: "Lad of Athens faithful be / To thyself / And Mystery / All the rest is Perjury."

(2001)

ROCKIN' THE CRADLE
Rock 'n' Roll As Children's Literature

ROCK 'N' ROLL HAS BEEN INSPIRED BY and has at the same time preserved and extended the magical tradition of children's literature—fables, bestiaries, ballads, wonder stories, and nursery rhymes—in ways we hardly ever notice. With few exceptions, the kind of children's literature being written today is sentimental, pallid, and overly careful, lacking the imaginative power of the mostly anonymous nursery rhymes or the work of writers like Lewis Carroll, and Edward Lear, for example, who created masterpieces equally for children and adults from their child-selves.

Surprisingly, it is rock 'n' roll which has provided us with our best children's literature: the Who's "Boris the Spider," the Beatles' "Yellow Submarine," Randy Newman's "Simon Smith and the Amazing Dancing Bear," Donovan's *A Gift from a Flower to a Garden,* the Kinks' "Phenomenal Cat," and Bob Dylan's "When the Ship Comes In" ("Oh the fishes will laugh / As they swim out of the path / And the seagulls they'll be smiling / And the rocks on the sand / Will proudly stand / The hour that the ship comes in"). And let us also remember Dylan's marvelous song "Man Gave Names to All the Animals": He saw an animal leavin' a muddy trail, / Real dirty face and a curly tail. / He wasn't too small and he wasn't too big. / Ah, think I'll call it a pig." [In 1999 the artist Scott Menchin used the text of "Man Gave Names ..." to create a charming children's picture book.]

Of course, it is easy to observe how fairy-tale characters and situations have been used as sexual conceits in songs like Sam the Sham's "Lil' Red Riding Hood" or the Rolling Stones' "Who's Been Sleeping Here?" And it's interesting to recall the various children's literary classics that have been paid homage to in songs such as Loggins and Messina's "House at Pooh Corner," the Jefferson Airplane's "White Rabbit," Elton John's "Goodbye Yellow Brick Road" or, best of all, Pink Floyd's *The Piper at the Gates of Dawn*, (*which takes its name from* The Wind in the Willows.)

But it is specifically the nursery-rhyme tradition—which itself draws upon ballads, proverbs, jests, riddles, decayed songs, sound-effect verse, mummers' plays, and forgotten rites, and which shares basic characteristics with street-game and rope-skipping rhymes—that has provided much of the best rock 'n' roll with its playfully compressed approach and tone.

Bob Dylan's "A Hard Rain's A-Gonna Fall," for example, seems to draw its inspiration and paratactic style not only from the traditional song "Lord Randall" but also from the following visionary rhyme: (I saw a peacock with a fiery tail / I saw a blazing comet drop down hail . . . / I saw the sun even in the midst of night / I saw the man that saw this wondrous sight"). Songs, moreover, like the Who's "Mary-Anne with the Shaky Hands" ("Linda can cook / Jean reads book / Cindy can sew / But I'd rather know Mary Anne with the shaky hands") and "I'm a Boy" ("One girl was called Jean Marie / Another little girl was called Felicity / Another little girl was Sally Joy / The other was me and I'm a boy") are each in the great nursery-rhyme tradition of "I had a little husband no bigger than my thumb" and "There was a madman and he had a mad wife."

The Miracles' "That's What Love Is Made Of," Aretha Franklin's "The House that Jack Built," and Simon and Garfunkel's "Scarborough Fair" are all variations on classic nursery rhymes. The

Alley Cats' "Puddin' 'n' Tain" ("Puddin' 'n' Tain / Ask me again / And I'll tell you the same"), the Dixie Cups' "Iko Iko," and Rufus Thomas's "Walkin', the Dog" have their roots in black folk and nursery tradition. Shirley Ellis's "The Name Game" is nothing but a delightfully inane infant amusement ("Shirley Shirley / Bo Birley / Banana Fana Fo Firley / Fee Fi Mo Mirley / Shirley"). And then there are the Jaynetts' "Sally, Go 'Round the Roses"—as haunting and gnomic as the most mysterious rhymes—and Jethro Tull's "Mother Goose"—a hallucinated voyage into the alternately cruel and gentle world of Nursery-Rhyme Land itself.

And in the medley that concludes *Abbey Road*, the Beatles present a slight variation of a lullaby ("Golden slumbers kiss your eyes / Smiles awake you when you rise. / Sleep, pretty wantons, do not cry / And I will sing a lullaby") written in the 16th century—and adopted soon thereafter as a children's song—by the poet and dramatist Thomas Dekker. In this same medley, it is clear that song fragments like "Polythene Pam" and the refrain, "One, two, three, four, five, six, seven / All good children go to heaven" were derived from nursery and rope-skipping rhymes. Nor should we overlook "All Together Now" from the *Yellow Submarine* soundtrack—one of the most graceful of alphabet and counting songs ("One, two, three, four, can I have a little more / Five, six, seven, eight, nine, ten I love you. / A, B, C, D, can I bring my friend to tea. / E, F, G, H, I, J, I love you").

When adults want to discard childlike parts of themselves, they go about banishing and exiling them to the far-distant region of childhood, and then belittle what they no longer want to understand: "It's only a fairy tale, it's only a nursery rhyme, it's only rock 'n' roll." But these rock 'n' roll poets and musicians can claim to be some of our most important children's writers because they continually contact the magical world of fables, folk wisdom, and disguised rites. As Ray Davies once put it in his song "The Village Green Preservation

Society": "Preserving the old ways from being abused / Protecting the new ways for me and for you / What more can we do?"

(1976)

SMOKEY ROBINSON
and My Perfect Desert-Island Record

ANY DESERT-ISLAND RECORD should be like an island one wishes to explore—an island, as in Shakespeare's *The Tempest*, "full of noises, / Sounds and sweet airs that give delight and hurt not."

No airs could be sweeter than those on Smokey Robinson and the Miracles' *Greatest Hits*. It is an album filled with the "heavenly music" that Prospero summoned up with a type of "rough magic" that allowed him to create and dissolve towers, palaces, temples, and even "the great globe itself"—leaving "not a rack behind":

> Just like the desert shows a thirsty man
> A green oasis where there's only sand,
> You lured me into something I should have dodged:
> The love I saw in you was just a mirage.
> —"The Love I Saw In You Was Just A Mirage"

The singer, too, is a magician. Tormented like Caliban and Gonzalo, Smokey Robinson sings with the voice of Ariel, transforming disillusion and trouble into wonder and amazement. And his miraculous voice—seemless in its flow, subtle in its timing, delicate in its timbre—has its source, not in Prospero's occult philosophy and mathematical mysticism, but in the magic of the music of the fifties: the Moonglows, Clyde McPhatter, Frankie Lymon and the Teenagers, Little Anthony and the Imperials. "They had a great influence on me," Smokey has said, "because those were the records I bought when I was a teenager. That high tenor kind of sound—it influenced me a lot. Jackie Wilson, too, and of course Sam Cooke, who was probably my all-time favorite singer."

"Ooh Baby Baby" gives a perfect account of Smokey Robinson's vocal technique—an exquisitely controlled and endlessly sustained swooning line of voluptuous pain that demonstrates the singer's command of high swoopings, note bendings, and a kind of melismatic ornamentation that gospel singers call "curlicues and flowers and frills." As remarkable as his voice, however, is what he does with it dramatically. In "(Come 'Round Here) I'm the One You Need," we first hear what sounds like faraway percussion (tambourine and drum) beating out an insistent 4/4 rhythm over an eerie grouping of piccolos, flutes, and violins playing heterophonically like a Javanese gamelan.

"Ooh-ooh-*oooh*," Smokey sings, as he enters with the rest of the pounding instruments and announces, with an almost out-of-body voice: "Now you say . . . " Immediately, we hear him singing in a deceptively gentle, young boy's voice: "Everytime you need some affection / The one you love goes in another direction / And you just sit there in a daze reminiscing / 'Cause you know some other lips he's been kissing." Then back Smokey comes, chanting with that first voice, combining the tones of ecstasy, complaint, and despair: "Now when you need the love he's never shown you, come round here, / And when you need some lovin' arms to hold you, come round here." Voice number two follows insistently with: "Now I may not be the one you want, / But I know I'm the one you need." After which Smokey speak-sings in a mock-haunted, vibratoless voice, against those previously heard gamelan-sounding piccolos and flutes: "Your life stands still the minute he goes, / You count the hours just hoping he shows."

The rest of the song presents the return and interchange of voices one and two within the same stanza, the same line, and even, occasionally, on the same word—as if to reveal how pleading boy and obsessed girl, demon and possessed person, are inextricably bound, both of them trying to express themselves and to escape from the singer's body, their voices rising in a climax of ecstatic pain: "Now the days, the days, the days you sit alone by yourself / He's out fooling 'round with somebody else / Leaving you alone here with nothing to do / Just waiting till he has time for you."

The fact that, as Smokey Robinson has said, he was "completely hoarse the day we overdubbed 'Come 'Round Here,' and that maybe that accounts for the effect," cannot mitigate the fact that there are few other rock 'n' roll songs—Marvin Gaye's "You" is another example—that create such a sense of shamanistic trance. It is shamans who bridge the world, the underworld, and the heavens; bring back news from the shadows; contact ghosts; and, finally, discover and explore the dividing line between male and female. Here lies the true source of Smokey Robinson's magic.

According to the first account of creation in the Bible, Adam was androgynous. And concerning *The Bacchae* of Euripides, Thomas Rosenmeyer has stated that "in the person of the god, strength mingles with softness, majestic terror with coquettish glances. To follow him or to comprehend him we must ourselves give up our precariously controlled, socially desirable sexual limitations."

In the seemingly innocuous "Shop Around"—the Miracles' first hit song—Smokey takes on the role of a boy whose mother advises him to keep his freedom for as long as he can. In the boy's voice Smokey sings her advice; but as the song progresses he begins to take on the role of the mother herself, and in Dionysian fashion she begins to possess him: "Before you take a girl and say I do now /

Make sure she's in love with-a you now, / Make sure her love is true now / I'd hate to see you sad and blue now." What the lyric sheet leaves out, moreover, is a final stanza in which the mother, now in control of the singer's being, gradually becomes hysterical: "Before you let her hold you tight, / Make sure she's all right, / Before you let her take your hand, my son, / Understand, my son, / Be a man, my son, / I know you can, my son, / I love you . . . shop around" [fade].

"I hope we get back to music *and* words," Smokey Robinson said in 1978. "Right now, people are still discoing—which is fine—but the words are lost or insignificant. I think songs *are* words." And if I have concentrated on Smokey's words—on the *Greatest Hits*, Robinson was the main writer and melodist on all songs except "Come 'Round Here," "Mickey's Monkey," and "Beauty Is Only Skin Deep"—it is because he is a remarkable poet who loves the playful ambiguities of words ("I Second That Emotion," "No Wonder Love Is a Wonder"), as well as their sounds (listen to the way Smokey sings the words "good," "bye," and "does" in "What's So Good About Goodbye,") and he is a master of colloquial talk ("Quicker than I could bat an eye, / Seems you were telling me goodbye"—"The Love I Saw in You Was Just A Mirage").

In "That's What Love Is Made Of," he takes a nursery rhyme and tells a children's story simply by using little images. Repeating and stringing them together, he charts the progression of a bittersweet love affair from meeting to breakup, and then, in an amazing turnabout, makes the imagery go backward, bringing the couple back to happiness: "Words being told with a little bit of soul, / Pride gets broken, cruel words spoken, / Hearts say goodbye, eyes have to cry, / Hearts on a tree, walks by the sea, / Snakes, snails, puppy dog tails, / Sugar, spice, everything nice, / Yeah, yeah, all right."

Things are always all right if you can understand them by dancing them. "Going to a Go Go" (with its opening deep-pitched African drums), "Mickey's Monkey," and "Come On Do the Jerk" are still among the most ecstatic dance songs of the sixties—and perfect for a rite of spring on a tropical desert island night. "Spirits to enforce, art to enchant"—every island should be filled with such noises!

(1980)

NOTES ON J.S. BACH'S
The Well-Tempered Clavier
(In Memoriam: Glenn Gould)

A LINE GOES JOURNEYING through the world, and its underlying and supporting counterpoint and harmony reveal its obstacles, travails, and longings. It cannot exist without them, nor they without it.

The end pulls the whole work, like one's life, to a close.

In the B minor fugues concluding Books I and II, the sequences of the former lead to ecstasy (are ecstasy), the latter to the final judgment.

Notes are points of light.

Listening to the entire work as if it represents and reproduces the life process of the ideal human organism, whose optimal sense of achievement and fulfilled desire is revealed in the satisfied grace of the E-flat major and E-flat minor fugues, Book II.

"And twofold always": Prelude and Fugue—a double form presenting two progressions, two facets: Bows of Mind and the Arrows of Thought.

(Prelude to fugue as "outside" to "inside.")

The fugue as *texture*, made up of motivic material and linear strands.

The fugue as *process*, compressed, dense . . . a vehicle of unceasing motion, of constant variation and transformation—continually reminding us that to remain on a given level, no matter how exalted, is a sin ("The angels praising the Lord are never the same; the Lord changes them every day").

"Fugue" from the Latin *fuga* (flight). Each subject pursues itself.

(Since we are separate, let us try to imitate each other.)

Fugues move into the future with no fear of it.

Anxious to block this streaming beauty, we are left with only a souvenir, an idol, an eidolon. (Prelude in F Major, Book II)

As the glow of the beginning of the universe fills all space, the broken harmonies of the first prelude fill all time.

As a raga expresses an "ethos" particular to time and season, so each prelude contains appropriate *Affekts* for the turnings of our hours—dawn (Prelude in E Major, Book I), dusk (Prelude in A-flat Major, Book I), midnight (Prelude in B-flat Minor, Book I)—and of our seasons—spring (Prelude in A Major, Book II), autumn (Prelude in C-sharp Minor, Book II), summer (Prelude in E Major, Book II), winter (Prelude in D Major, Book II).

Preludes often resemble each other (the D-sharp minor and E minor preludes, Book II). Occasionally, they share particular characteristics, as do members of a family (the two preludes in B-flat minor). Sometimes, however, a prelude will register a deeper connection with an unrelated composition, as when sympathetic chords reveal a shared nervous system (the nine-voiced diminished seventh chord in the Prelude in B-flat Minor, Book I; the eight-voiced "Barrabas!" from the *St. Matthew Passion*).

Dux and *comes*: as the "companion" of the fugue subject transposes the notes of the "leader" into the dominant, it becomes a "real answer"—where I no longer dominates *Thou*.

"The eighth rest in the course of the subject makes it easy for the *comes* to find its way back." (Hermann Keller on the Fugue in E-flat major, Book I)

Each of the preludes and fugues as a coupling, an expression of a new and specific way of being in love.

Unforeseen relationships.

The reentry of the fugue subject, like a trace memory bringing us back to ourselves (Fugue in F-sharp Minor, Book II).

Preludes let you be yourself; fugues let you become yourselves.

Inversions of the fugue subject as a form and sign of independence and autonomy.

"The augmentation of a subject is for Bach a symbol of inner greatness." (Hermann Keller)

437

"Small measures transmit the impression of agility, nimbleness . . . large measures convey the feeling of spaciousness, of inner peace." (Hermann Keller)

"What each and every aesthetic object imposes upon us, in appropriate rhythms, is a unique and singular formula for the flow of our energy. . . . Every work of art embodies a principle of proceeding, of stopping, of scanning; an image of energy or relaxation, the imprint of a caressing or destroying hand which is [the artist's] alone." (Raymond Bayer)

The almost Eastern European flavor of the subject of the Fugue in D-sharp Minor, book I provides the *story* of this piece.

The free-floating ambiguities of the rising and falling fifths and fourths in the subject—corresponding to the rising and falling half-arches which come together on the note D-sharp ("a vacillating balance")—provide the seeds for the thickening of the *plot*. (A similar structural ambiguity functions at the heart of the sarabande from the C minor Unaccompanied Cello Suite.)

By means of threefold stretti, segmentations of melodic cells, all kinds of inversions, and rhythmic condensations and foreshortenings, the story's conclusion is slowed down and even reversed in such a manner that plot deepens and thickens.

(I am thinking of the Russian formalist critics' notion that a *story* is the raw material of narrative, whose events occur in their chronological sequence . . . while the *plot* is the narrative as actually shaped, whose speed may be changed and its direction reversed at will.)

Thus in this fugue we find a chain of shorter and longer breathing and gestural patterns, a gentle but intense tossing back and forth of musical ideas.

About Webern's *Symphony*, Ernst Krenek once wrote: "The accuracy and elegance with which the reversibility of these models is worked out emanate a peculiar fascination, seeming to suggest a mysterious possibility for circumventing the one-way direction of time." And this idea applies to the D-sharp minor fugue, whose ineluctable final bars draw into themselves past, present, and future, consuming them and yet realizing—through the pressure of fulfillment—an inevitable consummation.

"In the other five-voiced fugue of *The Well-Tempered Clavier*, in C-sharp minor [Book I], the voices are introduced from the bass in rising order; in the B-flat minor fugue [Book I], the order is reversed: the soprano I begins, the bass enters as the last voice. This relationship can hardly be accidental, as both fugues are symmetrical to each other in *The Well-Tempered Clavier*: the C-sharp minor fugue a half step above C (the first tonality), the B-flat minor fugue a half step below B (the last tonality)." (Hermann Keller)

Nabokov writes: "Attainment and science, retainment and art— the two couples keep to themselves but when they do meet, nothing else in the world matters." So must structuralism and phenomenology— which, like science and art, seem to be antithetical means by which to approach and explore the preludes and fugues—form a harmonious relationship, one which can mirror and reflect upon the crystalline geometry of the interior life of music.

The Well-Tempered Clavier as the supreme embodiment of how things work.

The subject-response, statement-answer structure of the fugue embodies the idea of an action and its consequences.

(Just like the episodes that prepare the next entry of the subject while relaxing the form, I am sitting here waiting to discover where I am going.)

The individual lines of Bach's fugues make a true counterpoint because they are friends to and with one another.

In Bach, harmony is the transparent medium through which the contrapuntal lines wend and find their way.

"All of the effects of fugue (except that of the vertical gravitation of key and key-contrast) were effects formulated in the early years of the Renaissance—in the generations before the tonal grammar of tension and relaxation had been made articulate. And their participation in the poise and balance of centrifugal harmony, the web-like detentions of cadence structure, seem largely the result, at most, of a synchronicity that was voluntary on their part." (Glenn Gould)

Bach's fugues are like dolphins which propel themselves through water, listening to the reflections of the sounds which they emit.

The astonishing, rapid chromatic modulations in the Fugue in B Minor, Book I, remind you that in music from Vincentino and Gesualdo to late Beethoven and Wagner, modulations of this type are almost always a sign of your having entered a molecular realm of love in which every moment is becoming new.

Concentrate on the first two notes of the Fugue in B-flat minor, Book I: B-flat—F. One descends to the other, one descends to become the other, one is the other . . .is all alone . . . and ever more shall be so.

Notice the following eight notes of the choral-like fugue subject—an almost evenly falling and rising figure—standing in relation to the first two notes as the body to the soul.

Become aware of how the leader and companion voices begin to entrance and twist around each other until the tension, in rapture, rises to release itself in a third voice, which they now become (having each been it before).

(Prelude to fugue as "foreplay" to "embrace.")

The answer to the riddle of what is most rigid and yet most free is: the fugue.

"The likeness of God can be found in time, which is eternity in disguise." (Abraham Heschel)

Saint Augustine, it has been said, confessed to his betrayal of his own youth because of his love for eternity. Bach's music never betrays its love for the everlastingness and endlessness of the life he lived and felt in the present.

"Feeling and life are eternal." So too certain qualities and characteristics which reflect a life that refuses, in Paul Goodman's terms, to "prevent the continuum of the soul and the world (the flux) from growing in meaning, importance, and menace." Risk, agility, daring, inventiveness, persistence, ingenuity—all of these Odyssean qualities manifest themselves in certain daring and dashing fugues: A-flat major, Book I; E minor, Book II.

"Music is the mediator between the spiritual and the sensual life." (Beethoven)

From the Great Fugues to Beethoven's *Grosse Fuge*: There are moments in *The Well-Tempered Clavier* that anticipate Beethoven's late quartets and piano sonatas—the B-flat minor and B minor fugues, Book I, for example.

Beethoven said: "Music is the electric soil in which the spirit lives, thinks, and invents." Bach would have substituted the word "soul" for "soil," but it would have amounted to the same thing.

Beethoven's sense of longing (the German *Sehnsucht* expresses it more truly) was fiercer than Bach's, for his world had fallen away—even more than Bach's had—from those sources of creation which nourished and developed mathematical and cabalistic means of using the simplest musical proportions and fundamentals. Beethoven found himself in a world no longer filled with certainty; yet in the certainty of his desires—in the desires themselves—he found his way back to the divine process: "And I shall behold God out of my flesh."

Numbers disclose their secret: In the first prelude of *The Well-Tempered Clavier*, broken harmonies disguise a five-voiced movement that includes all of the twelve semitones; and we begin to observe a fugue subject of fourteen notes (the numerical-alphabetical translation of the letters B-A-C-H), which, through continual stretti, are repeated twenty-four times (an allusion to the twenty-four keys traversed in the work). In the cabala, the alphabet is an instrument of creation. But more than that, the creation of the cosmos—as of *The Well-Tempered Clavier* (this "work of all works," as Schumann called it)—is the result of the creation of letters and numbers.

Twelve signs of the Zodiac, twelve days of Christmas, twelve months of the year, twelve hours on the clock face, twelve patriarchs, twelve apostles, twelve lictors, twelve peers, twelve knights, twelve tones.

Regarding Schoenberg's use of the twelve-tone row, Charles Rosen has written about the order of twelve notes being not only a melody but also a "quarry for melodies."

Several of Bach's fugue subjects have the permutative force of cellular motifs (e.g., Fugue in C-sharp Minor, Book I), and one of these subjects in particular (Fugue in B Minor, Book I) suggests the contour and the sense of a twelve-tone row. (Its subject contains not only all twelve notes of the chromatic octave but also all twelve half-tone steps of the scale.)

Spitta might well be mistaken for an anti-Schoenbergian critic when he describes this fugue's subject as traveling "slowly, sighing, with bitter, even pain-distorted features on a seemingly endless path." This path—which travels from tonic to dominant via dominant, subdominant, and second dominant—is both a musical quarry and an exploration of itself, in whose midst blossoms radiant diatonic sequences (reminding me of "frost-flowers, tiny bright and dry like / inch high crystal trees of sparkling silver mold"—Lew Welch). And it is as if the details of rowlike chromaticism were being pulled back from (or entered into) to reveal—in distant or enlarged perspective—the realm of repetition.

With one musical law answering and joining another (the Greek *nomos* means both "law" and "melody"), Bach unites, as he prophesizes the development of, two antithetical but seminal twentieth-century musical ideas: the strength of the row, the bliss of periodicity.

In the preludes of *The Well-Tempered Clavier*—many of them reworked and refashioned pieces—we can see in microcosm, though not in the order in which the preludes occur, the formal evolution of Western music: from scale passages and broken chords to more individuated models (two- and three-part inventions, arioso movements and pastorales) to small concerto and two-part preclassical sonata movements.

A certain kind of style or form suggests a particular kind of feeling—so that the way you express something is already its expression: e.g., *arioso, badinerie, passepied*.

Everyone wishes to discover motivic relationships between every prelude and fugue, but often—in spite of Bach's sense of motivic experimentation—there are only simpler and deeper kinds of relationships, like the way gestures follow each other or the way things happen to be placed together.

"The destruction of Pompeii really began when they started to dig it up." (Freud)

In spite of his joy—as strong as is his joy—Bach cannot help expressing the notion that conclusions are destructive, that endings—no matter how deeply accepted—are filled with grief (this grief that is akin to and defines joy).

The "joy" motive (Fugue in F Minor, Book I)
The "sobbing" motive (Fugue in F-sharp Minor, Book I)
The "sigh" motive (Fugue in B Minor, Book I)

It's not that thoughts and feelings don't want to end—as at the conclusion of the Fugue in G-sharp Minor, Book II—but rather that they want you to realize how real they are.

Certain fugues, like Rilke's conception of fate, are nothing more than the condensations of childhood.

The Fugue in C-sharp Major, Book II, begins with tiptoeing children who grow into passionate but increasingly more persistent and less playful adults.

The Prelude in C-sharp Minor, Book II—like the even more extraordinary Three-Part Invention in E-flat Major, begins with a footfall—shy but stately steps (as of baby mice or deer) whose pauses, hesitations, and accidental coordinations result in momentary ordinations of gentle but unacknowledged embraces.

Walking down the same street again and noticing things for the first time—in this way we listen to Bach's music, with the attentiveness of falling in love.

In the coda of the Fugue in C Major, Book II, the subject takes on protective coloration and then discloses itself.

The subject for the Fugue in G-sharp Minor, Book II, "glides with lizard-like nimbleness in triplet eighth notes." (H. Riemann)

Bach delays the entry of the bass voice in the Fugue in C Minor, Book II. When it appears, it does so in augmentation such that the subject's spritely, puckish steps now become a series of self-conscious and self-dramatic mimelike gestures, suggesting wariness and disguise.

445

"The defiant shaking of its locks"—Spitta's description of the rising thirty seconds of the subject of the Fugue in D Major, Book I.

The Fugue in A Minor, Book II—quarter notes splitting into eighth notes, thirty-second notes and trills whirling in as countersubject—"represents an individual man, and he rages!" (J. N. David)

The Fugue in F Minor, Book II—with its skittish, "dark merrymaking" subject (J. N. David)—demonstrates, according to Tovey, "that life without stretti, inversions, and so on can also be beautiful."

The Prelude in E-flat Minor, Book I: "The first nocturne in clavier music, a nocturne with the clarity of a starry night." (Hermann Keller)

Prelude in E Major, Book I: "Like boughs clad with new foliage the light arpeggio triplets sway, with their motion at the tips of the branches, as though rippled by the wind with cheerful little trills of the feathered songsters sheltered within; below reigns peace (a resting bass and a slowly accompanying middle voice) . . . " (H. Riemann)

"All day long I shook with weeping; then I noticed how the evening sun threw its brilliant light on the scattering blooms of the cherry tree." (Lady Sarashina)

It is Frederika Henrietta, a princess of Anhalt-Bernberg, whom we have, in part, to thank for the creation of *The Well-Tempered Clavier*. Having married Prince Leopold of Saxe-Cöthen, Bach's enthusiastic patron, she became jealous of the composer, and, having no interest in music, decided to break up the musical activities at the palace. It was during Bach's enforced leisure in 1722 that he wrote the first twenty-four preludes and fugues, completing the second set in 1744, six years before his death.

"By a strange coincidence, the same oculist [Sir John Taylor] operated on Bach and Handel. Both operations failed, and both men ended their days in total darkness." (R. H. Miles)

Bach's last composition—which, in total blindness, he dictated to his son-in-law Johann Gottlob Harrer—was a chorale prelude on *Vor deinen Thron tret Ich* ("Before Thy Throne I Stand"), a message to let God know that the composer was ready. Its opening phrase contained fourteen notes; the entire melody, forty-one. Since fourteen and forty-one—the numerical translations of BACH and JS BACH respectively—are inversions of each other, Bach was attesting numerologically to his belief that, in more ways than one, his end was his beginning.

"Bach is the beginning and end of all music." (Max Reger)

If complexity and intensity were the criteria for determining a closing fugue to *The Well-Tempered Clavier*, then the Fugue in B-flat Minor, Book II, would have been the obvious choice. With the augmenting note values of its subject (suggesting the division of cells) that, indomitably, defines itself by first holding its breath, pushing ahead and expanding, then imitating itself with stretti at the time distance of a half note and at the intervallic distances of the seventh and the ninth—sometimes in inversion and contrary motion—this intricate and fissionable composition holds claim to being the contrapuntal apogee of the entire work.

The concluding Fugue in B Minor, Book II—almost coy, impatient, and skittish, serious in its sequences but unwilling to surrender to the direction they portend—is a charming *passepied* in 3/8 time. "There are styles of thinking that are styles of dancing," wrote Ortega y Gasset. And all of Bach's musical thought is a form of dance. It is therefore fitting that the final fugue of *The Well-Tempered Clavier* allows Shiva his last dance with the world. As it is written: "For one cycle of creation Shiva dances. For the next cycle he dreams. We think we are living in the real world and Shiva is dancing. We are not. He is dreaming."

"It was there for the first time, with complete peace of mind and without outside distraction, that I gained a conception of your Grand Master. I expressed it thus: it was as though eternal harmony conversed with itself, as it might have come to pass in the bosom of God, shortly before the creation of the world. So moved was I by it in my inmost consciousness that it seemed to me I neither possessed nor needed ears, least of all eyes, nor any other senses." (Goethe to Zelter, June 21, 1827, after the organist von Berka had played to him from *The Well-Tempered Clavier*)

(1983)

A SONG FOR DREAMING

Sometimes, in moments of bewilderment or happiness, you may catch yourself singing or whistling a song whose words, on reflection, explain how things really are with you—"Good Day Sunshine" when it's raining, "Rain" when it's sunny, "Hello Goodbye" when you don't know whether to stay or go. In all kinds of weather and situations, the song interprets you.

At other times, often late at night, there are different kinds of songs, more mysterious and self-reflective, whose phrases, images, or rhythms come back to fascinate and haunt you, as if from remembered dreams, both resisting and encouraging your attempts to explain them. Like dreams, these songs appear to understand themselves better than those who try to make sense of their radiant, fragmentary lives.

I am referring here not to a song like Bob Dylan's "I'll Be Your Baby Tonight," which, in the context of *John Wesley Harding*, seems incongruous; nor to trancelike songs such as the Beach Boys' "Don't Talk (Put Your Head on My Shoulder)" or the Supremes" "Remove This Doubt"—dreamy and impassioned as they are—but rather to something like George Harrison's "Long, Long, Long" from the Beatles' *White Album*. Such a song, seemingly tagged onto the end of the record as an afterthought, transmits the sense of an auditory hallucination. Almost an apparition, "Long, Long,

Long" evokes a sense of rapture in its suggestion that one becomes what one loves ("Now I can see you, be you") and its music of deep silence which, as the philosopher Max Picard once said, "in dreaming begins to sound."

To the sound of the slow-motion footfall of acoustic guitar and bass, Van Morrison's radiant, archetypal vision of a woman on her horse of snow has recently brought me back to perhaps the most haunting of these mysterious songs, "Slim Slow Slider," the three-minute blues reverie that concludes the timeless *Astral Weeks* album, recorded in 1968.

Coming as it does after "Madame George" and "Ballerina," "Slim Slow Slider" can be taken simply as the last of the album's three mythopoeic images: the transvestite, the dancer, the rider on her horse:

> *Slim Slow Slider*
> *Horse she ride is white as snow*
> *Slim Slow Slider*
> *Horse she ride is white as snow*
> *Tell that everywhere you go*

I used to think that Van Morrison should have ended "Slim Slow Slider" after this first stanza, whose image-making power, as Yeats knew, not only wakes analogies but also penetrates to the Great Memory. The horse as symbol is both a complex and a ubiquitous phenomenon in mythology and dreams, representing, at various times and places, the instincts, the unconscious, clairvoyant powers, and even the cosmos itself. Interestingly, in German and Celtic mythology, to dream of a white horse was once thought to be an omen of death. And in an astonishing if unconscious way, Van Morrison draws on this ancient symbolic meaning and, in three additional telegraphed stanzas, uses this wondrous hovering image—Yeats's "transparent lamp about a spiritual flame"—in order to convey two simultaneous ideas: the dissociation and alienation from Pure Being and the loss and death of Love:

Saw you walkin' down by Ladbroke Grove this morning
Saw you walkin' down by Ladbroke Grove this morning
Catching pebbles from some sandy beach
You're out of reach

Saw you early this morning
With your brand new boy and your Cadillac
Saw you early this morning
With your brand new boy and your Cadillac
You're going for something and I know you won't be back

I know you're dyin' baby
And I know you know it too
I know you're dyin'
And I know you know it too
Everytime I see you I just don't know what to do

From a horse white as snow to a Cadillac: the beloved rides away—out of reach, won't be back, dying—the world falls from grace, and the soprano saxophone wails in careening, homeless patterns as the song disintegrates.

It has been said: "For one cycle of creation Shiva dances. For the next cycle he dreams. We think we are living in the real world and Shiva is dancing. We are not. He is dreaming."

There are plenty of songs to dance to; there are so few songs for dreaming, inviting you to recompose and re-create them, extending the dream onward.

> Many say that life entered the human body
> by the help of music, but the truth is
> that life itself is music.
>   —Hafiz

(1984)

ACKNOWLEDGMENTS

INDEX